JOYBeing

Praise for *JOYBeing*

"*JOYBeing* offers a beautiful blend of wisdom and practical tools that empower readers to cultivate joy in their daily lives. This book is a must-read for anyone seeking to enhance their emotional well-being and live a more fulfilling life."

–DR. MARSHALL GOLDSMITH

Thinkers50 #1 Executive Coach and
New York Times bestselling author of *The Earned Life, Triggers, and What Got You Here Won't Get You There*

"I remember the day I realized that to deal with the pressures of work and stressors of a chaotic, divisive world, I had shut down my emotions. I didn't feel pain, but I also couldn't feel joy. I wish I had this book then, as it took me years to revive my sense of wonder and humor. Please read *JOYBeing*. Savor the beautiful blend of wisdom and use the tools to reignite your love and joy."

–DR. MARCIA REYNOLDS

Author of *Outsmart Your Brain: How to Master Your Mind When Emotions Take the Wheel* and *Breakthrough Coaching*

"Joy is the fundamental expression of flow, purpose, and creativity. Doing our inner transformational and reflective work with commitment is a pathway to change our inner state. Gila and Ann are drawing a conclusive and comprehensive map of self-exploration and self-reflection to develop an inner state of being and joy. As leaders, we have the response-ability to walk our talk and expand the radius of our awareness, state of being, and joy to be an inspirational force in the world. This book - *JOYBeing* - is a gateway to that authenticity."

–THOMAS HÜBL, PhD

Author of *Healing Collective Trauma* and *Attuned*

"During these times of uncertainty and bedlam, *JOYBeing* offers a necessary medicine for the Spirit. The personal reflections of the authors Ancel Seritcioglu and Van Eron, in addition to their offering of pragmatic practices and insights, make this a valuable doorway into the exploration of leading a grounded, joyous life."

–RICHARD STROZZI-HECKLER
Founder of Strozzi Somatics and author of
*Embodying the Mystery: Somatic Wisdom
for Emotional, Energetic, and Spiritual Awakening*

"Authors Ancel Seritcioglu and Van Eron do important work to offer research studies, differentiate joy from happiness, and identify practices to deepen this life-giving emotion. In our fast-moving world, learning the pathway to experience and hold joy is literally life-giving. For leaders, coaches, and anyone interested in resilience and vitality- this book is a must-read, a must-have, and a source of repeatable joy."

–DOROTHY E. SIMINOVITCH, PhD, MCC
Leadership Coach and author of
*A Gestalt Coaching Primer:
The Path Toward Awareness Intelligence*

"The newest offering from transformational coaches Gila and Ann, *JOYBeing*, is an invitation for leaders to turn their attention inward to their life purpose, sources of meaning, emotional experience, and embodiment. This inward examination is the core transformational pivot needed for leaders to inspire others, create followership, foster creativity, and drive adaptive change in an ever more complex context. I commend the book highly for unlocking new thresholds of aliveness and happiness, both flames for higher potential."

–AMY ELIZABETH FOX
CEO, Mobius Executive Leadership

"*JOYBeing* is a book that reminds us of the profound joy and aliveness hidden within, especially when life is challenging. This book offers practical tools and ways to nurture our inner vitality, embrace life's challenges, and cultivate resilience in our daily lives. I recommend reading a bit daily to grow your garden of joy!"

—JACKIE STAVROS, PhD
Professor, Lawrence Technological University
Co-author of *Conversations Worth Having* & *Learning to SOAR*

"In their uplifting book, Ann Van Eron and Gila Ancel Seritcioglu invite us to explore the profound impact that small moments of joy can have on our wellbeing. They show us how to enrich our inner selves using the fertile and transformative metaphor of gardening, through which we can cultivate our capacity to experience and exude the 'high-frequency emotion' of joy. They provide the reader with tools to 'tend to their inner landscape' by expanding inner awareness, unearthing obstacles to joy, and nurturing *JOYBeing*. Gila and Ann show us that *JOYBeing* is not a destination but a journey to be lived in the present moment. As I read the book, I found myself sowing my own seeds of *JOYBeing* through the ideas and exercises planted in my own inner garden, and I am grateful to each of them for taking me on such a heart-warming and inspiring journey."

—MICHAEL MERVOSH
Psychotherapist

"In these challenging times, *JOYBeing* is an essential guide that provides hope and inspiration, guiding you to reconnect with your inner joy and spread positivity to those around you. Ann and Gila provide practical tools and heartfelt stories to inspire you to cultivate a flourishing inner garden of joy. A must-read for anyone seeking to enhance their emotional wellbeing and live a more fulfilling life!"

—JACKIE STALLINGS EVANS
Leadership Coach and author of
Rise: Game-Changing Success Strategies for Women Leaders

"Given how amazing coaches Gila and Ann are, I am not surprised that this book is full of wisdom and a practical approach to bringing more joy into our lives as a way of being. I am sure the book will be a major contribution to anyone reading it. I highly recommend this book."

—DOST CAN DENIZ, MCC
Executive Coach and author of *Cesur Sorular*

"*JOYBeing* reminds us that joy is both within and all around us, waiting to be discovered with the right intention. In a time when negativity seems overwhelming, this book is a much-needed resource to support our well-being. The authors beautifully guide us to these sources of joy."

—REINER LOMB
Author of *Aspire: Seven Essential Emotions for Leading Positive Change, No Matter Where You Are*

"*JOYBeing* is a powerful reminder of how our vitality, life force, and overall sense of joy are not constructs of the mind but rather lived experiences that can be cultivated and nurtured in our everyday lives. It provides a clear pathway to embodying our aliveness and is a gentle invitation to remember what it's like to fully enjoy the experience of life."

—GIULIO BRUNINI
Master Somatic Coach and Facilitator

"*JOYBeing* is an inspiring and practical path for experiencing what we all want: more joy, aliveness, and wellbeing in our lives. Just the description of "wellbeing" is worth the book's price. This book is a MUST READ for anyone seeking to live a more fulfilling and joyful life."

—LAURIE ZUCKERMAN
Executive Coach and Consultant

"Ann and Gila are the living, breathing embodiment of *JOYBeing* – not because their life circumstances are inherently joyful, but because they have cultivated an Open Stance to all they encounter. A lifetime of self-discovery and practice has led to this book, which offers memorable exercises that can transform your experience of living. I have deeply benefitted from Ann and Gila's teaching and modeling."

—LINDA MILLER, PhD
Cultivating JOYBeing course participant

"Ann and Gila are the consummate professional coaches/teachers. They embody joy and share their lived experiences with grace and openness. Their guidance is grounded in multiple disciplines, enabling the learner to find applications for personal growth and use of self in work with others."

—NORA O'BRIEN-SURIC
President, Health Foundation for Western & Central New York,
Cultivating JOYBeing course participant

"Ann Van Eron and Gila Ancel Seritcioglu provide us with a lifeline to *JOYBeing*! Their most recent collaboration on the book *JOYBeing* is a masterful accomplishment! Their teachings are both pragmatic and encouraging, reality-tested by their extensive coaching and lived organization development experience. They challenge us to face down our embodiment of beliefs, assumptions, biases, behaviors, fears, and anxieties that, simply put, prevent us from knowing joy. They guide us on a self-awareness journey inward – demonstrating through experiential practices that joy ultimately comes from within, a precious gift waiting to be discovered and nurtured. I found this book both motivating and inspirational, impressive in its scope and attention to research. In our ever increasingly polarized world today, this work could not be more timely or profoundly needed."

—KATHLEEN FITZSIMONS, PhD
Executive Coach, Cultivating JOYBeing participant

JOYBeing
Connecting With Your Essence and the Rhythm of Life to Thrive and Inspire

Copyright © 2025 by Ann Van Eron and Gila Ancel Seritcioglu

Published by: Open View Press, Chicago, IL, USA

All Rights Reserved. No part of this book may be used or reproduced in any manner whatsoever without the expressed written permission of the authors.

Address all inquiries to:
Ann Van Eron
(312) 856-1155
Avaneron@Potentials.com
www.Potentials.com

ISBN: 978-0-9975136-1-5
E-book ISBN: 978-0-9975136-4-6

Library of Congress Control Number: 2024920162

Editor: Tyler Tichelaar, Superior Book Productions
Cover and Graphic Design: Salon Couture Books
Illustrations: Ann Van Eron
Cover photograph: Shutterstock.com / Asset ID: 1104958547
Photographs in book: Unsplash, Rawpixel, and iStock
Every attempt has been made to source properly all quotes.

Ann Van Eron, PhD &
Gila Ancel Seritcioglu, MA

JOYBeing

Connecting With Your Essence and
the Rhythm of Life to Thrive and Inspire

DEDICATION

For our families and leaders, parents, and others who inspire.

May you each connect with your essence
and spread joy and hope to make life better for others.

Acknowledgments

We are deeply grateful to our coaching and corporate clients as well as the enthusiastic participants in our Cultivating JOYBeing courses. Your willingness to explore joy alongside us has been a source of inspiration. We have learned from each of you and appreciate your openness and contributions. It has been wonderful to grow and learn with you.

We extend our sincere gratitude to all the authors cited in this book, as well as the many more who have influenced our thinking and work. Your ideas and writings have provided a rich foundation for our exploration of joy and connection. We are honored to be a part of the global coaching and leadership development community, and we are continually inspired by the collective wisdom and dedication to fostering personal and professional growth.

To our colleagues and friends, your support and encouragement have been invaluable throughout this journey. Your belief in our vision of inspiring joy, openness, and connection has been a source of motivation.

Deep gratitude goes to our families. Thank you for your unwavering support and the joy you bring to our lives.

We are filled with immense gratitude to all who have walked this path with us. This book is a testament to the collective effort, love, and wisdom of a community that believes in the power of joy and connection. May this book serve as an inspiration and a guide for those seeking to cultivate joy in their lives and the lives of others. Together, let us thrive and inspire.

CONTENTS

1	**Step into Joy**
7	• How It All Began
9	**CHAPTER 1 Cultivating the Garden Within: The Essence of JOYBeing**
19	• JOYBeing: A Holistic Approach to Wellbeing
31	• The Path for JOYBeing: Creating Your Garden
41	• Practices
45	**CHAPTER 2 Basking in Our Garden: Experiencing the Energy and Aliveness of the Present Moment**
51	• Noticing Our Inner Garden's Climate
55	• JOYBeing and Mindfulness of the Present Moment
57	• Nurturing the Art of Being Present
65	• Practices
73	**CHAPTER 3 Tilling the Soil: Connecting with Our Emotions**
77	• Tending Our Inner Landscape: Thoughts, Emotions, and Sensations
81	• Why Emotions Are Vital for a Thriving Inner Garden of JOYBeing
86	• How to Work with Emotions
87	• Growing Emotional Wellness: 4A Recipe for Working with Emotions
92	• Practicing the 4A Recipe
97	• Practices
103	**CHAPTER 4 Weeding: Unearthing Obstacles to Cultivating a JOYBeing Garden**
108	• Reacting vs. Responding to Differences and Uncertainty
110	• Adopting an Open Stance
113	• Unearthing and Quieting Our Critical Inner Voice
116	• Attending to Our Inner Voices
119	• Taking an Open Stance Toward Ourselves
121	• Clearing the Ground with Self-Compassion
126	• Practices

129	**CHAPTER 5** Sowing the Seeds: Planting Inner Awareness	
135	• How We Bury Our Emotions to Survive and How This Impacts JOYBeing	
137	• Recognizing Our Emotions and Working with Our Moods	
141	• Uncovering Depleting Emotions and Restoring Emotional Vitality for JOYBeing	
145	• Recognizing Our Traps	
153	• Emotion Mood Reflection Indicator (E-MRI)	
160	• Practices	
165	**CHAPTER 6** Sprouting and Growing Our Inner Garden: Nurturing JOYBeing	
170	• Reconnecting with Our Inner Child	
175	• Cultivating Play, Creativity, and Flow	
177	• Integrating Our Inner Voices	
179	• Connecting with Our Wise Self	
183	• Transforming Challenges into Opportunities for Growth and Enhanced JOYBeing	
187	• Practices	
193	**CHAPTER 7** Thriving and Flourishing in Our Garden: Expanding JOYBeing in Different Parts of Our Lives	
200	• Sowing JOYBeing Seeds in Relationships	
203	• Connecting to JOYBeing in the Workplace	
209	• Leading with JOYBeing	
213	• Creating a Culture of JOYBeing at Work	
224	• Nurturing Communities of JOYBeing	
228	• Practices	
229	**CHAPTER 8** Committing to Our Path of JOYBeing: Embracing Our Future Self	
236	• Hoeing Purpose and Commitment	
245	• Practices	
247	**CHAPTER 9** The Ripple Effect: Impacting the World Through JOYBeing	
252	• Reaping the Benefits of JOYBeing	
255	• Our Wish for You	
265	**Notes**	
269	**About the Authors**	

Step into Joy

"Joy is a return to the deep harmony of body, mind, and spirit that was yours at birth and that can be yours again. That openness to love, that capacity for wholeness with the world around you, is still within you."

John O'Donohue

JOYBeing

Imagine your inner self as a garden, a sanctuary where you can cultivate joy, aliveness, and wellbeing to blossom and flourish. What kind of a garden or landscape do you envision? What does your inner garden look and feel like? Which varieties of plants, flowers, or trees do you imagine? What kind of nourishment and beauty do you sense in this garden of your inner self?

Just as devoted gardeners tend to their plants with loving care and attention, cultivating joy and aliveness requires dedication, which includes setting an intention, ongoing awareness, meaningful choices, and continuous routines. Cultivating a life of aliveness and vibrancy is resolute, focused, and ever-rewarding purposeful work. It requires that you plan and prepare the ground and engage in daily practices that begin with a tiny seed. It calls for vigilant oversight of your garden. And we, the authors of this book, will show you the way. Our goal is to support you in expanding your perspective and creating a vitality space that allows you to thrive and bloom in every aspect of your life.

Planting seeds for JOYBeing opens us to an embodied state of mind. That mindful body determines how open and fertile your inner garden will be.

Just as gardeners prune, weed, and nurture their plants, you can release inner clutter and find clarity in the present moment. Embracing each moment's simplicity and beauty creates meaning, connection, and possibility.

Why is developing a sense of JOYBeing important now?

We are confronting unprecedented uncertainty and change at this pivotal moment in our world, where turmoil and polarization seem to overshadow tranquility. We are witnessing conflicts, climate change, inequalities, technological disruption, mental health issues, humanitarian crises, and shifts in numerous structures and systems. Even in such times,

> "When love meets happiness, it becomes joy."
>
> — *Jack Kornfield*

we can do something powerful: connect to our joy and aliveness by embracing both the challenges and opportunities of our lives—doing so is JOYBeing. Our emotions are contagious, and JOYBeing is the source that enables us to experience and spread possibility and hope to others. And here's the beauty of it—each of us can contribute to creating a better future.

Think of it like this: When we are joyful and vibrant, we inspire those around us. So, let's embrace JOYBeing and use it to make a difference in the world. Every small act of kindness or connection can create a ripple effect of positivity, making your community and the world a better place for everyone.

Managers, leaders, coaches, teachers, students, parents, and people of different walks of life, ages, and backgrounds who have participated in our Cultivating JOYBeing courses or been coached by one of us or collectively, have grown their inner gardens and experienced a flourishing sense of JOYBeing. They are people who choose to enhance their lives and thus trust that they are also making a difference for others. You will meet some of them and hear their stories as you travel through this book.

Gila

As the second child in a Jewish family with roots stemming from Persia and Spain, my familial narrative carried a complex tapestry of heritage and history. The stories of my grandparents' flight from the Spanish Inquisition on one side, and from the Bolshevik Revolution on the other, seeking refuge in Istanbul, echoed throughout our family stories. Unexpected, tragic losses among my father's extended family and stories of past generations' traumas on both sides influenced me with their unconscious, unspoken energy, which was in the background of our household.

Growing up within this context, the space for openly expressing challenging emotions was absent. Crying or revealing sadness felt like an unwelcome intrusion into the family's carefully guarded emotional boundaries. Despite my Hebrew name, which means joy, I was disconnected from joy and always felt like I wasn't good enough, even when I was trying to do my best. I felt inadequate and unseen as a child, and I longed to be recognized for who I truly was, even though my parents were doing their best for me in their own ways.

My pursuit of acceptance turned into a cycle of overachievement and selfless giving to others in order to get external validation. This vicious circle was a big trap for me in those days since I could not truly connect to the joy inside of me.

After I graduated from university, I founded a preschool with a trusted friend and colleague. Only then did I find myself in the nurturing realm of young children and their genuine, naive, beautiful energy. The unconditional love and acceptance radiating from those innocent souls healed my wounded spirit. In the children's pure, genuine presence, I unearthed my self-confidence, self-worth, and self-esteem, and I started, step-by-step, to blossom. During my experiences in those long years, I eventually realized that joy, which my name represents, wasn't just an idea; it was something real and reachable.

Thus began my journey of self-discovery. I began to peel off the layers of numbed emotions accumulated over the years in order to connect to my gifts. This journey became a turning point to reclaiming the lost parts of myself and fostering a profound connection with the dormant parts of my being. Through an ongoing process of self-work as an expressive arts therapist, and later as a Gestalt, somatic, and executive coach, I gradually made contact with joy and JOYBeing, setting the stage for an enriching transformation, which found new life in this book.

> ### Ann
>
> I was the oldest of six children in a family of modest means. I took on many responsibilities and learned to work hard. My parents, both good people, had very different perspectives and argued often. My family faced many challenges, and life seemed to be a struggle with little room for joy. A strong religious background reinforced my propensity for being selfless and giving to others. I didn't think I could or should experience joy when so many around me were suffering. Joy seemed elusive to me.
>
> I started working at a very early age to pay for college, and I continued the pattern of striving, overworking, and being hyper-focused on productivity and financial security. I deeply desired to make a difference. I built a business focused on supporting leaders and helping others as an executive coach and organization development consultant. While overworking and being responsible seemed effective, stress and worry were my companions. I remained disconnected from joy for many years. I became a learner and a seeker, and I explored many avenues for embodying wellbeing. Over the years, I learned and taught about the power of taking an Open Stance: noticing when we contract and are in judgment toward others, and then shifting to being curious and open with others. I support leaders across the globe in engaging in open-minded conversations. I see the undeniable need for joy in the workplace and within myself.
>
> I set a clear intention to discover joy for myself and my clients. When I began focusing on being open to myself and befriending my emotions, I experienced more joy. With intention, awareness, and practice, I have shifted old patterns of struggle and experienced the enlivening energy of JOYBeing. In this book, I am excited to share what Gila and I have learned and how it is indeed possible to experience joy and the exhilarating feeling of aliveness.

Throughout this journey, you will learn how to plant, tend, and grow your own inner garden, experience joy and aliveness, and spread your bounty and beauty to others. It's not enough to envision your inner garden—you must also take action to be aware and make intentional choices to nurture its growth. We will lead you through the process of creating your inner garden of JOYBeing and offer you simple practices and tools in each chapter. Experimenting with and using the most effective practices for you is the key to cultivating JOYBeing and inspiring others.

How It All Began

This book was co-created from a place of desiring more joy. Our story began when we, Ann and Gila, met twenty years ago, each from different ends of the world—Chicago and Istanbul.

We started this adventure because we wanted to explore and more readily access the joy inside us. We wanted to live with more joy and aliveness. When we met at a coach training program, we agreed that experiencing joy is essential for living a fulfilled and harmonious career and life. We knew this in our heads, but we were not experiencing enough joy in our lives. We had not embodied joy.

Step into Joy

We each recognized that amid addressing other issues, clients long for more ease, connection, and joy at work and home. They often search for ways to manage their stress, anxiety, and uncertainty. We join them in the desire for more joy and spaciousness. Inspired by our clients and our desire to make a difference, we committed ourselves to exploring the path of joy and began with ourselves. We joined together on this mission and have explored many avenues. This quest is how this book, *JOYBeing*, came to life. We want to share this meaningful journey with you.

Through our process of learning and discovery, we created the term "JOYBeing," which expands the definition and possibility of joy into a way of being, experiencing aliveness, and living life fully.

We all want more joy in our lives, and we have each been on our own journey to find more joy. The paradox is we have been looking for something that has actually been in us but covered up all along, waiting to be dis-covered. *Discovered*. The fog covers the beauty of the landscape and our inner garden. The beauty is always there. When the mist dissipates, we can see the seed or plant, growth, and natural beauty. Like the clouds covering the sun, we have discovered JOYBeing.

In this book, we aim to share the learning, experiences, and practices we have found valuable. In a simple, accessible, and creative format, we wish to give you a path to experience more joy and vitality. We have significantly benefited from this exploration and are excited to share what we have dis-covered and continue to practice with you. We will share examples from our individual coaching practices as well as from the Cultivating JOYBeing live virtual course that we facilitate together.

If we can experience JOYBeing, we know you can too, if you so choose.

May this book be a guide and a trusted companion to connect you with your inner power and true essence of JOYBeing. May it inspire you and the countless lives you touch with the possibilities it unveils.

CHAPTER 1

Cultivating the Garden Within: The Essence of JOYBeing

> "The beating heart of the universe is holy joy."
>
> — Martin Buber

JOYBeing

When you ask a parent what they desire for their child, you will almost always hear, "I want my child to be happy." Generally, we experience happiness as generated by external circumstances. We make happiness a goal and continue to search for it throughout our lives. We tell ourselves, "I will be happy when I get a good grade, finish school, find a partner, buy a house, get a promotion, take a vacation, etc." We base our happiness on external conditions. We continue to chase happiness into the future.

We adapt and experience a hedonic treadmill. We continue to set new goals to achieve happiness. People who make happiness their primary goal are often disappointed and rate themselves as less happy than others. Chasing happiness does not serve us. We tend to look for happiness outside of ourselves. Usually, our experience of happiness is short-lived since we easily habituate and then desire something else.

An explosion of books and research on happiness has occurred in the last few decades. Happiness has been characterized in different ways. For example, in *Happier*, Tal Ben-Shahar, a *New York Times* best-selling author, defines happiness as the overall experience of pleasure and meaning. Martin Seligman, the founder of positive psychology, identifies happiness as composed of meaning, pleasure, and engagement. The Greater Good Science Center describes happiness as capturing fleeting positive emotions along with a deeper sense of meaning and purpose in life.[1]

We differentiate happiness from joy. Joy is a short but powerful emotion. The *Merriam-Webster Dictionary* defines joy as "the emotion evoked by wellbeing, success, good fortune or the prospect of possessing what one desires." Usually, our understanding of joy is mixed with happiness. Even scientists use happiness, joy, wellbeing, and positivity interchangeably. We, however, have found it useful to differentiate between happiness and joy.

We define joy as a momentary internal positive experience that creates a sense of aliveness and excitement that enhances our energy for living

---
[1] https://greatergood.berkeley.edu/

CHAPTER 1 Cultivating the Garden Within: The Essence of JOYBeing

and connection. Even when external challenges exist, we can experience internal joy and a sense of wellbeing. We experience joy in our bodies, while happiness may live more in our minds. We see joy as encompassing happiness, and for us, it is something bigger. Our experience is that when we feel joy, we are also happy.

In *Atlas of the Heart*, Brené Brown observes, "Based on our research, I define joy as an intense feeling of deep spiritual connection, pleasure, and appreciation. While experiencing joy, we don't lose ourselves; we become more truly ourselves." Joy gives us an indication of what is important to us and awakens us through sensations.

Children naturally experience joy. That's because joy is instinctual, and we are born with the potential for a sense of aliveness. When external factors support our conditions in childhood, we are more likely to make contact with this potential and experience both joy and happiness. An ideal life includes an abundance of joy and happiness.

> *Joy arises when we are open to both the beauty and suffering inherent in living. Like a great sky that includes all different types of weather, joy is an expansive quality of presence. It says yes to life, no matter what!*
>
> — Tara Brach

Joy is a high-frequency emotion. Psychologists generally define joy as an intense, momentary experience of positive emotion. Gratitude, compassion, and awe are also high-frequency emotions. When we experience these positive or high-frequency emotions, we feel more alive. We feel a sense of spaciousness and openness. A different part of our brain is activated than when we are contracted or fearful.

Neuroscience supports the benefits of embracing joy. Four primary chemicals in the brain affect joy: dopamine, oxytocin, serotonin, and endorphins. We feel joy in our bodies because of the release of these neurotransmitters in the brain. So, when something we perceive as joyful happens, our brain receives the signal to release these chemicals into our central nervous system. We generally have positive thoughts and feelings when we feel happy and joyful. Studies suggest that happy and joyful responses originate partly in the limbic cortex.

Joy cannot and should not be ignored. It is a quality that makes life worth living. Joy is fundamental to human existence and wellbeing. Cited in the *Journal of Positive Psychology*, George Vaillant confirmed, "We cannot understand human beings unless we understand joy and how joy comes to be." In true joy, our souls open, giving our existence a certain fluidity and ease. We can choose how to engage with or respond to our surroundings every moment. Growing internal awareness about the body's wisdom, the sensing self, is essential for experiencing joy.

We are all searching for joy, flow, and aliveness. It is easy to feel that joy is out of reach, yet it is much more available to us than we believe. Just as we cannot see a seed growing until it emerges from the soil, our innate inner joy can be hidden. We can take small actions to experience joy and aliveness within. We can develop habitual patterns that connect us with joy.

Beliefs that inhibit joy constrain our capacity to experience life's richness. We place joy beyond our reach when we convince ourselves that it is a luxury we can't afford due to time constraints and too much to do, or because we must earn it to be deserving.

The notion that our joy is undeserved in the face of others' suffering is another self-imposed deprivation. Similarly, the belief that more pressing matters exist than cultivating joy leads us to overlook the profound effect small moments of joy can have on our wellbeing.

Sometimes, people fear to feel joy because they worry it might lead to disappointment. Some think they need to be super-successful or perfect before they're allowed to feel joy, thereby setting up an impossible standard that makes it hard to feel content. Our environment may also make us think showing joy is wrong or showing off, making people hesitate to express positive feelings.

Some people believe that focusing on joy is selfish; they don't realize it helps us feel better overall, be stronger in tough times, and positively influence others. If we can notice and let go of these limiting ideas and beliefs, we can discover how joy can make our lives better, and we can even spread positivity to the world.

CHAPTER 1 Cultivating the Garden Within: The Essence of JOYBeing

By acknowledging and challenging these varied resistances to joy, we can cultivate a more open and inclusive mindset and foster a deeper appreciation for the transformative power of joy in our lives.

For a moment, take a breath. Notice your resistance to feeling joy or your tendency to dismiss or postpone joy. Which of the habitual patterns mentioned above are familiar to you? Take another breath, send compassion to yourself, and remind yourself that joy is like an inner garden available to you no matter what. Even if your inner garden of joy feels parched and dry, it can emerge with vibrancy if you water it with intention and give it the right support and attention.

Joy is like a signal trying to tell us something important. When we feel joy, it's our body's way of saying, "Hey, pay attention! There's a message here." This message is easy to miss because joy comes and goes pretty quickly. But if we listen closely, joy is saying that we belong, we deserve good things, life has meaning, and we can connect with others and enjoy the special moments in life. This feeling happens when we are connected to a place, a person, a community, ourselves, and our values.

Now, think about how you notice joy in your body—those sensations or signs

Ann

I harbored a profound longing for joy for the longest time, but my belief it was unattainable lingered as a persistent shadow. How could I revel in joy with the echoing cries of suffering from the countless who are in need worldwide? Joy seemed like a luxury, something I didn't have time for or deserve.

I had the misconception that joy had to be grand, like an exuberant burst overflowing with dancing and singing, which seemed beyond my reach. This conviction did not deter me from studying joy and exploring numerous avenues to connect with it.

The revelation that joy could also be subtle and was in reach all around me marked a turning point. I became open to embracing moments of joy—a simple appreciation of a sunny day, extending help to someone, completing a task, engaging in a heartening conversation with a friend, hearing a cat's purr, coaching an executive, or learning something new. In these simple instances, I discovered a connection, a sense of hope, and an underlying joy. When I am aware of experiencing moments of joy, I feel a sense of aliveness and connection with myself and my surroundings.

The burden of overwork and worry dissipates when we are immersed in the recognition and experience of joy. A rewarding sense of connection, possibility, and meaning blossoms in its place. When acknowledged and embraced, these moments of joy evoke a profound gratitude for the gift of life—a sense of JOYBeing.

JOYBeing

> "Joy is an expression of the awakened heart, a quality of enlightenment. When we live in the present, joy often arises for no reason. This is the happiness of consciousness that is not dependent on particular conditions. Children know this."
>
> *Jack Kornfield*

that joy is present. It could be a smile, a warm feeling in your heart, a happy expression, or a lightness in your chest or around your face. People often express joy through smiling, laughter, or even tears of happiness.

Joy shows up in small moments, like when you're amazed or surprised. It can even mix with other feelings. It is like a quick burst when you feel a sense of meaning, belonging, and the possibility of good things. In those flashes of joy, we find reasons to be alive and appreciate life.

Get curious about what brings you joy. Notice the hidden details, such as a brief conversation with a person on an elevator, a sunny day, or a hug from a friend you have not seen in a long time. Joy is often felt in smaller things, more than you might expect. Noticing the ordinary allows us to create and experience the extraordinary.

In his book *Hardwiring Happiness: The New Brain Science of Contentment, Calm and Confidence*, Rick Hanson posits we are wired to focus on the negative, but we can learn to cultivate and enhance the positive. We are like Teflon for the positive and Velcro for the negative. Such attention may have served us to survive as a species. However, with awareness and choice, we can change our brains and experience more joy today.

CHAPTER 1 Cultivating the Garden Within: The Essence of JOYBeing

With intention and repetition, we can adopt new practices and habits to allow ourselves to experience greater joy and aliveness. It is possible to raise our capacity to feel more joy.

By connecting more deeply with our inner sense of joy, we gain greater access to our creative life force energy. We have more capacity to create meaningful connections, a fulfilling life, and flourish.

By reading this book, you are setting an intention to release and fully experience your joy and aliveness. Start noticing when you close, clamp down, or limit your joy. Also, observe when you allow joy and a sense of aliveness to become embodied. Envision yourself experiencing and radiating joy. Begin to notice where you go on autopilot and shut down joy. We will provide ways to work with our habitual patterns that limit joy as we explore new ways to experience what we call JOYBeing.

Gila

I used to believe my happiness relied on controlling external circumstances. Therefore, a huge part of my life was based on trying to manage outside situations in order to feel joyful.

During COVID-19, I was trying to take extra good care of myself. Then I caught the virus just a few days before an intimate small surprise party I was planning for my husband's sixtieth birthday. I felt great disappointment and sadness, like that of a child whose toy was taken from her, since I had put so much energy and excitement in preparations. However, this experience became a wonderful teacher for me. If I had been the old Gila, I would have created a drama out of this situation.

Instead, I had a lot of faith and reminded myself of my life motto "Trust the process and the surprise will come." With this faith and awareness, I chose to see this time as an opportunity to rest rather than a problem to worry about. Out of this space of contemplation came the creative design of this book and many other heartfelt ideas.

Connecting to JOYBeing allowed me to focus on what was happening in my interior, which shifted my perspective. I was able to experience a sense of aliveness inside me. Through the choices I made and with this new mindset, I was able to move toward experiencing and meeting my new self.

JOYBeing: A Holistic Approach to Wellbeing

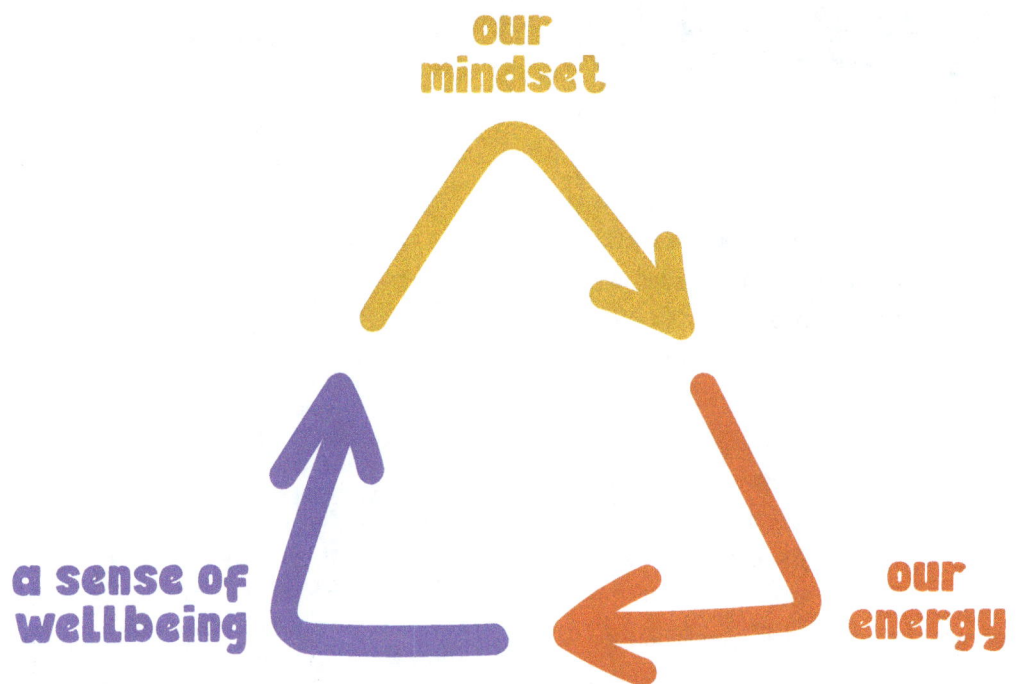

We believe a fulfilling and satisfied life requires attention to three fundamental interrelated areas: **our mindset**, how we use **our energy**, and a **sense of wellbeing**. These three areas create the context for a sense of aliveness and JOYBeing.

Our *Mindset* determines how we approach life. While it is natural to notice what is not going well, we can choose to be open and cultivate thoughts that empower and inspire us. A JOYBeing mindset is an open mindset that embodies the qualities of curiosity, compassion, courage, non-judgment, being grounded, being centered, and presence. This mindset is about being receptive to new ideas, eager to explore, empathetic toward others, brave in facing challenges, unbiased in perception, balanced in perspective, and fully engaged in the present moment. A JOYBeing mindset encompasses a growth mindset.

CHAPTER 1 Cultivating the Garden Within: The Essence of JOYBeing

According to Carol Dweck in her book *Mindset*, having a growth mindset means you believe people can continually develop and learn.

With a JOYBeing mindset, we take an Open Stance toward life, managing our judgment and contraction, and shifting to being open and curious about possibilities. We believe in our ability to embrace change and setbacks as an opportunity for learning and growth.

Having a JOYBeing mindset involves cultivating keen self-awareness and clarity regarding our inner sensations, emotions, thoughts, and beliefs. This heightened awareness empowers us to make informed decisions aligned with our core values and overarching world perspective. With a clear understanding of our inner landscape, we can navigate life's challenges with resilience and purpose, consistently choosing paths that lead to personal growth, fulfillment, and making a difference. We trust that through this kind of presence, we can positively influence those around us and throughout our world.

Energy, in the context of human experience, is the vital force that drives our physical, mental, and emotional activities. It is a vitality that fuels our actions, thoughts, and emotions, enabling us to engage with the world around us. The way we manage and direct our energy significantly influences our overall quality and experience of life.

Energy follows attention and intention. Wherever we put our attention affects how we use our energy and how we experience our day-to-day living. When we focus our attention on what is going well, such as learning new things, building relationships, and connecting with nature, we experience a greater sense of aliveness. However, when we focus on negative or unproductive thoughts, such as what is not going well, we drain our energy, leading to feelings of fatigue, stress, dissatisfaction, and disappointment. Where we choose to put our attention is crucial in determining how we use our energy.

Intention refers to the purpose behind our actions. When our

20

JOYBeing

intentions are clear and aligned with our values and goals, we use our energy more efficiently and meaningfully. When we set a positive intention to notice and experience joy, we prioritize our actions for positivity, creativity, and vitality. This purposeful use of our energy enhances our wellbeing. Being mindful of where we place our attention and ensuring our intentions are aligned with what we deeply care about can support us in consciously managing our energy more effectively for a more harmonious and fulfilling life.

Are you aware of how you are using your energy? Are you putting your energy into what is most important to you and what you are longing for, or are you depleting yourself by spending your energy in places that don't serve you?

With awareness, we can regulate our energy to attend to our internal and outer experiences. We allocate our energy through the choices we make such as how we enter a gathering or how we use our time. Are we aware of how we use ourselves in an interaction? How we resource and use our energy shapes our daily experience and impacts those around us. By harnessing our energy with purpose and alignment, we can cultivate a harmonious resonance between our inner being and the external world, allowing us to navigate challenges with clarity and grace.

In the dance of energy, awareness, and intention, we can discover the profound potential within ourselves to manifest our deepest longings and contribute meaningfully to the world around us. Mindfully managing our energy fosters a balanced and centered presence that nurtures our sense of wellness, enabling us to live a more fulfilling life.

By recognizing the interconnectedness of our energy with the world around us, we unlock the power to cultivate positive change on a broader scale. When we approach interactions, tasks, and endeavors with mindful energy, we not only enhance our personal wellbeing, but we ripple positive effects outward, influencing those we encounter and the environments we inhabit. This ripple effect amplifies the significance of our actions, emphasizing the responsibility we hold in co-creating the collective experience. Thus, by aligning our energy with intention and values, we contribute to a more harmonious and thriving interconnected world, creating a sense of meaning and purpose.

Wellbeing includes physical, emotional, intellectual, spiritual, and relational thriving. Wellbeing is created with a positive mindset and a conscious use of energy. For us, wellbeing is a skill to be cultivated. Achieving a state of health and joy is not just a passive outcome but an active process requiring intentional effort and practice. Wellbeing is a holistic state of thriving, where an individual experiences a high quality of life and is effectively able to cope with challenges. Achieving wellbeing involves cultivating positive self-care habits and practices, managing stress, and nurturing a sense of connection with oneself, others, and the greater environment.

By embracing the joy of being alive, we attune ourselves to life's richness and complexity. This perspective encourages us to seek moments of awe, wonder, and passion in our daily lives rather than living in our heads using our energy primarily focused on mental concepts. JOYBeing is about experiencing the beauty in the mundane and the significance in the fleeting moments. By cultivating a deep awareness of our experiences, we open ourselves to a more enriched and authentic existence.

JOYBeing is an embodied way of being. The relationship we have with our bodies plays a crucial role in our overall wellbeing and sense of aliveness. Listening and honoring our body's needs, responding to pain or discomfort with compassion, and avoiding self-destructive habits inspire vitality. Having a profound appreciation

> *I don't think [the meaning of life] is what we're seeking. I think [it's] an experience of being alive, so that our life experiences on the purely physical plane will have resonances within our own innermost being and reality, so that we actually feel the rapture of being alive.*
>
> *— Joseph Campbell*

JOYBeing

and respect for ourselves is integral for wellbeing.

Physical wellbeing includes exercise, healthy eating habits, enough sleep, and rest. Intellectual or mental wellbeing involves curiosity, learning, clarity, integration of thoughts, and the ability to focus on and realize goals. Emotional wellbeing requires being aware and centered with our emotions so we are able to cope with life challenges; it includes the ability to be empathetic and compassionate toward oneself and others. Spiritual wellbeing involves having a clear purpose, a sense of meaning, and a connection with oneself, others, nature, and the divine; it's experiencing a sense of essence. Contributing, experiencing a sense of satisfaction, being creative, and attending to our environment also contribute to our wellbeing.

Because we are an interconnected system, taking small actions in any of the wellbeing components can influence our sense of wholeness and JOYBeing. For example, exercising and moving our body, learning a new skill, attending to our emotions, or reflecting on our purpose and what is meaningful can influence our sense of joy and aliveness. When we engage in a creative endeavor (such as painting or making music), we are of service to another, or we build relationships, we take action supporting JOYBeing. Ultimately, wellbeing is achieved through a balanced and harmonious relationship with ourselves. When we have such a relationship, we create the foundation for a richer, more fulfilling life characterized by a deep sense of inner joy and vibrancy.

Each of these fundamental three components—mindset, energy, and wellbeing—is essential in itself, and collectively, they set up a solid basis for experiencing JOYBeing. We need to continue to pay attention to each area to create a sense of wholeness and fulfillment.

Take the JOYBeing Self-Assessment Quiz

CHAPTER 1 Cultivating the Garden Within: The Essence of JOYBeing

JOYBeing is the joy of being. We define JOYBeing as connecting with awareness to the internal energy of aliveness in us as we experience and manage the challenges and joys of life. We experience a sense of meaning and connection. JOYBeing is the joy of being alive. It is our ability to be awake to experience all facets of the rhythm of life. In this state, our presence can make a difference and be a source of inspiration.

JOYBeing isn't just a passing feeling; it's a powerful force that helps us stay strong or stay present amid life's ups and downs. It's like an inner garden and sanctuary that gives us the strength to face challenges gracefully and appreciate each moment as it comes. JOYBeing creates an upward spiral shift. It is transformative, and it can ideally become our primary way of being and living. When we are in this state, we engage with life with more emotional vitality, a sense of belonging, and purpose.

Joy, despite its transient nature, serves as a discerning indicator of what holds profound significance for us, illuminating the path toward fulfillment and purpose. It directs us toward experiences, relationships, and activities that align with our values and aspirations, guiding us to prioritize what truly matters. By noticing joy, embracing it, and acknowledging its significance, we can cultivate a deeper sense of integration in our lives, harmonizing various aspects of our being and fostering a greater sense of wholeness.

Moreover, joy encourages us to engage fully in the present moment, enriching our experiences and nurturing our connections with ourselves and others. Ultimately, by honoring joy as a guiding force, we embark on a journey toward greater authenticity, meaning, and fulfillment.

While joy is transient, JOYBeing is a state of experiencing a sense of aliveness and vibrance. JOYBeing is the process of becoming. Life is our medium for developing JOYBeing. The experiences we go through serve as our

JOYBeing

teachers; they create opportunities to achieve a level of maturity and growth. JOYBeing is our ability to trust the rhythm of life, choose aliveness, and feel the joy that life offers us through its natural flow. It is our ability to see and feel the beauty in things even when life is dark.

Through JOYBeing, we feel connected with ourselves and our resources and can take purposeful action. In this state, we are less needy, have more capacity to connect with others, and are more fulfilled. JOYBeing is experienced when we accept ourselves as we are and when we allow our authentic self to guide our actions. JOYBeing evolves with a positive mindset and conscious use of energy and practices to support our health and wellbeing.

Even when facing challenges, a hard assignment at work, a sick family member, an accident, or a disagreement with a friend or colleague, we can connect with our inner garden of vibrant energy and the flow of being alive. With this constructive JOYBeing mindset, we can approach life differently. JOYBeing is influenced by, but not dependent on, outside circumstances. JOYBeing is within us and is available to us at all times, even when we might not be feeling it. When we are connected with the radiance of JOYBeing, we are more likely to feel satisfied in our relationships, career, and life.

JOYBeing is embracing and living life fully. Embracing life includes opening and savoring all of it, both its joys and sorrows. The joy of meeting a loved one, eating a meal, making progress on a project, having a difficult conversation at work, or suffering disappointment are all moments when we can experience JOYBeing by connecting to our body and the vitality of our life energy. JOYBeing is more than a concept. It is the embodiment of inner aliveness, openness, and connection with our essence. It encompasses connection to the physical, mental, emotional, and spiritual parts of ourselves.

When we are experiencing JOYBeing, we are alive, in flow, creative, and connected to the life force inside us. The French call this *joie de vivre*, a way of being where we are at ease, open, in flow, and in full connection with

CHAPTER 1 Cultivating the Garden Within: The Essence of JOYBeing

ourselves—even during difficult times. JOYBeing allows us to experience the full range of emotions even during moments of loss or uncertainty.

Gila's client, Faye, experienced a tragedy during the height of the COVID-19 pandemic. In the span of a single week, she endured the devastating loss of not only her father but both of her grandparents. The stringent and heartbreaking COVID restrictions prevented her from attending their funerals to bid them a proper goodbye. The grief and isolation threatened to overwhelm her, yet Faye allowed herself to lean into and accept her emotions. Rather than closing up and denying her pain, she courageously worked through it with support to experience her emotions fully. At times, it seemed as though the darkness would never lift, and she feared the joy once present in her life would be forever extinguished. However, even during this difficult time, she noticed moments of joy in being with her children and friends. She experienced a new connection with herself by becoming aware of the life energy that sustained her by whispering that she had a choice to trust and continue to embrace life.

We all have had challenging experiences. We have experienced sadness, loss, disappointments, and worries many times. The pain from these different experiences ignited our search for JOYBeing and gave birth to this book. We believe JOYBeing is the medicine for our pain in difficult moments. When we started our search for joy, we were hoping to have more fun and positive experiences. However, we found something deeper and more meaningful that has changed our lives, which we are glad to be able to share with you. We have also had a lot more fun in the process.

JOYBeing allows us to find and experience the beauty in life, no matter what. JOYBeing, like the sky, is always present and available to us. Whatever the weather is—clouds, storms, rain, sunshine—the sky is always present and holds beauty and the energetic life force to stay awake and move forward.

Throughout this book, we will refer to joy as a positive emotion and JOYBeing as the state of connecting with our aliveness, even in the face of the rhythm of life's challenges.

> "When you do things from your soul, you feel a river moving in you, a joy."
>
> —Rumi

Check in with yourself:

- ✓ When was the last time you felt fully and deeply alive? Was it today, or at a gathering, or perhaps a special day like your wedding or a birthday? Perhaps it was when you fell in love. Perhaps it was an ordinary day when you picked a flower from your garden and took in its beauty.

- ✓ What were you doing?

- ✓ Who was with you?

- ✓ Let yourself really feel the joy and aliveness in your body. What are you seeing, hearing, smelling, tasting, or touching?

- ✓ What sensations are you experiencing in the moment as you connect to that experience? What do you notice in your body? Pay attention to where the sensation lives inside you.

- ✓ Notice your experience.

- ✓ Allow yourself to savor and strengthen the sense of aliveness.

- ✓ Plant this sense of aliveness in your heart, and know that you can revisit it often.

CHAPTER 1 Cultivating the Garden Within: The Essence of JOYBeing

We all have experiences of aliveness. We can learn to recognize, savor, and fully live these moments, plus connect to more of them. You can connect with JOYBeing anytime or anywhere.

We ask our coaching clients and participants in our Cultivating JOYBeing classes to look for moments of joy and record them in a journal or draw them, take a photo, or find another meaningful way to share them with a friend. Many small moments that often go unnoticed are examples of JOYBeing.

For example, Sara, a manager in a corporation, reported that attending a Zumba class with her friend awakened joy. Completing a project gave Joel, an IT manager, a sense of relief and joy.

> **Gila**
>
> When I take a morning walk by the Bosphorus, feeling the gentle touch of the breeze against my skin, inhaling deeply the salty scent of the sea, and hearing the symphony of seagulls flapping their wings, I am immersed in a sensory experience that awakens my soul. The sight of fishermen skillfully reeling in their catch, their movement synchronized with the ebb and flow of the tide, fills me with awe and admiration. As the birds chirp excitedly to see if they can get their share from the net, their melodies mingle with the lapping of the waves. At that moment, I feel grateful for life, which is a beautiful gift to me. An ordinary moment transforms into an extraordinary one. That is JOYBeing. As I walk, I see people talking on their phones and not being aware of the beauty and richness of the present moment. This is a moment of awakening for me, noticing that I want to walk and live life fully awake.

> **Ann**
>
> A moment of JOYBeing for me is when I take my ninety-three-year-old neighbor to the park. I can feel her childlike eagerness to go in her smile and quickened pace as we approach our favorite bench. We have the perfect view and enjoy being present as we watch young children playing soccer and others riding swings. I feel the cool breeze, hear birds chirping, see various dogs running and exploring, and soak in the aliveness of being in the moment. I am glad to share company with a dear friend among the beauty of trees and nature with a sense of community embracing all generations amid the city of Chicago. The pure but deep dialogue of connection and friendship warms my heart. I feel a sense of meaning and aliveness in this experience.

Cem, a father of two young children, shared the joy of playing with them at the local park. Melissa, a grandmother, found joy in taking a walk after her cup of coffee in the morning. Engaging in art, listening to music, learning from a podcast, and reading a book were shared by others. Deniz, a college student, feels a sense of joy after exercising. Another student noticed that her moments of joy are when she is engaged in meaningful conversations with friends, professors, and peers. Jeremy, a leader, experiences joy after a team meeting where decisions are made.

Many moments of joy are simple everyday experiences. When we pay attention and expect to notice moments of JOYBeing and the sense of aliveness, we seem to experience more instances of pleasure, meaning, belonging, and thriving.

JOYBeing lives in us as we feel our inner garden and landscape and are aware of what is happening outside of us. Where we choose to attend and how we choose to be present in the moment influences our vitality and creativity. We are continually at choice. We can build the habit of making choices that serve us, to connect with aliveness and our life force. Even in difficult times, the choice for JOYBeing can connect us to our resilience and our desire to thrive.

JOYBeing is aligned with taking an Open Stance. Taking an Open Stance is about noticing when we are contracted, in judgment, controlling, or closed and, with awareness, shifting to being curious, compassionate, courageous, kind, and noticing possibilities. From this Open Stance, we are able to attend to the world with greater resilience, embrace the present moment, and realize potential.[2]

When we are closed, we have a narrow vision and are focused on our security and safety. When we are open to ourselves and others and we trust life, we experience JOYBeing and are open to possibilities. We walk with a sense of curiosity, compassion, courage, vitality, and spontaneity.

> **Gila**
>
> When my younger daughter left for college in the US, the emptiness at home with no children was overwhelming, especially when I walked near her untouched room. The pain of missing her was palpable. To heal, I turned to creativity. Engaging with my guitar, I composed a song and penned its lyrics. This artistic act transformed my pain into a revitalizing energy, unknowingly connecting me to a deeper sense of aliveness. Back then, I wasn't familiar with the concept of JOYBeing, yet that was precisely what I was experiencing.
>
> During my lowest point, staying in the emotion and choosing life became my beacon through the darkness. Art, music, and nature have always been pillars of support, opening new doorways for me in navigating life's challenges and illuminating the path forward.
>
> The path to JOYBeing is like cultivating an inner garden. It requires planting seeds or setting our intention for JOYBeing and increasing our awareness that leads to choices and possibilities. By tending the garden with patience, perseverance, and trust, we can build the practices and habitual patterns to create a new self.

Like many, we both have had the experience of our daughters going away to college in different cities and countries. We experienced sadness, loneliness, and pain as a result. It was not easy to connect with JOYBeing. However, in this journey with you, we will share how we opened to the possibility of creativity, flow, and aliveness.

---

[2] For more on Open Stance, see Chapter 4 of this book and Ann Van Eron's *Open Stance: Thriving Amid Differences and Uncertainty*.

The Path for JOYBeing: Creating Your Garden

> ❝
> **You have to know
> yourself to go beyond yourself.**
>
> *Sri Nisargadatta Maharaj*

CHAPTER 1 Cultivating the Garden Within: The Essence of JOYBeing

Once upon a time, there was a boy who longed to become a surfer. But he was only ten, lived too far from the sea, and had no money to buy a board. He still dreamed about it though. Night and day, with his eyes closed, he could see himself surfing the waves. He could even feel it. He could smell the sea and feel the tension in his muscles. Concentrating really hard and continually shifting his balance, he imagined himself riding the waves. It was really exciting. He managed to pull it off more and more often. Now. This wave is mine. This very wave. Wow! This is it. This is great. But would he ever be able to surf for real?

One day, he and his parents set off on vacation. They were going to the Cote Sauvage, in Brittany, France. He had no idea where that was, but after a ten-hour drive, they arrived at their destination, feeling hot and tired. As soon as he got out of the car, he smelled the sea. Thrilled, he ran to the beach, and what he saw there in the evening light was amazing. Several boys were lying in a group in the water. Like young walruses, they were waiting for the right wave. As soon as a beautiful wave rose up, they quickly paddled over and leaped on the boards to catch the wave. One of the boys surfed toward the beach and yelled: "You want to try? It's very cool. Have you done it before?"

The boy said timidly: "No never, but I'd love to try."

The surfer handed over his board. It was a nice white one with a small blue dolphin on the bottom. The boy grabbed the board, determined to give it a go. He paddled through the powerful surf with some difficulty, as he had done so often in his imagination. At the sight of the first high wave, he stood up, planting his feet firmly on the board. He held his breath. Would he be okay? Yes, he was okay. He was doing great. This is what he had dreamed of. This is what he used to see when he closed his eyes and thought of surfing. And now his dreams were coming true. Of course, he still had a lot to learn. It did not always come as easily as that first time, but because he really wanted to surf, he got better and better at it.

This boy is now a well-known surfing instructor in Scheveningen, on the Dutch coast, where he teaches hundreds of children. He teaches them trust and letting go as well as surfing. Trust that the right moment will come along. This moment. Trust that the next wave will always come along, and to let go of the idea that the waves ought to be moving exactly the way we want them to. Surfing the waves of life gives you insight not only into your own nature but also into the ever-changing natural world of which you are a part.

— Eline Snel, *Sitting Still Like a Frog*[3]

---

[3] From *Sitting Still Like a Frog: Mindfulness Exercises for Kids (and Their Parents)* by Eline Snel with the foreword by Jon Kabat-Zinn © 2013. Reprinted by arrangement with Shambhala Publications, Inc., Boulder, CO. www.shambhala.com.

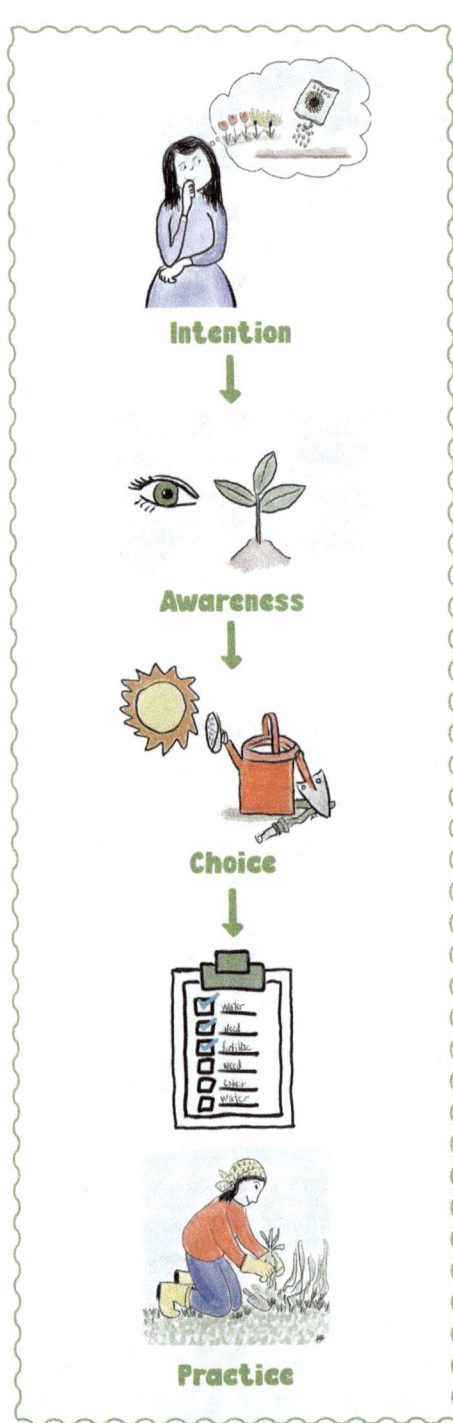

This inspiring story demonstrates the path to JOYBeing, which can be cultivated through the following four steps: setting an intention, being aware, making a choice, and engaging in practice. Let's now look at each of these steps in more detail.

1. Setting an Intention

Just like a garden, every creation starts with an intention. An intention reflects our longing. It is the creative power that activates the energy of possibility. When we set a clear and compelling intention of experiencing JOYBeing, we have begun our journey.

An intention is about setting our attention toward what excites us. When we know what is meaningful to us and we set our intention, we begin to move toward it. An intention is about staying focused on what compels us and keeping it in our conscious awareness. When our focus and attention is aligned with our intention, we activate energy to move forward.

It's easy to lose contact with our goals. Setting our intention and reviewing it regularly inspires us to recall what is most important to us. It requires us to take a step back to envision what is

CHAPTER 1 Cultivating the Garden Within: The Essence of JOYBeing

compelling and inspiring us. When we set an intention, we are taking responsibility for how we want to live our lives, and this supports us in being proactive in our choices.

How would your life be different if you experienced more JOYBeing and aliveness every day? What would you be seeing, hearing, feeling, and noticing differently?

Your intention can be as simple as:

- ✓ I intend to live a life of JOYBeing.
- ✓ I intend to experience the fullness of life.
- ✓ I intend to bring positivity to my day.
- ✓ I intend to notice and savor moments of joy.
- ✓ I intend to connect with my inner resources.
- ✓ I intend to fully open space to embrace all my emotions.
- ✓ I intend to bring more laughter and play into my life.
- ✓ I intend to connect with more openness and meaning.

2. Being Aware

We cannot experience JOYBeing without awareness. There is a vast, new life inside of us—a world full of possibility and potential.

Awareness involves noticing our internal life as well as the world outside of us. Awareness is like a flashlight or torch. Wherever we point the light becomes our focus. By paying attention, we direct our energy with intention, and what we focus on expands.

Awareness is essential for desired change. We must allow our essence to be visible. How we track our observations or data and interpret them influences our ability to make choices. Only then can we meet our true essence and empower ourselves to live in awakeness.

Being aware incorporates all of our senses and intuition. It's a full-body process that allows us to experience our full range of emotions.

Noticing moments of JOYBeing allows us to make purposeful choices aligned with our intentions.

An overwhelmed client of Ann's felt like she was stuck on a nonstop roller coaster. When it was pointed out that she was telling her story as if she were still on that ride—holding her breath, tense, and reactive—she became aware of how this affected her focus and energy. When asked to slow her breath, she discovered she could choose where to direct her attention. This awareness helped her see that she had been focusing too much on others and external events, neglecting her own needs. With this insight, she began to prioritize herself and address her own wellbeing.

3. Making a Choice

When we are aware and clear about our intentions, we can be more at choice in our actions. When we are unaware, our habitual patterns drive our actions.

It is easy to focus our awareness and choices on attaining extrinsic things we believe will bring us joy. We can get focused on chasing things such as belongings, money, and career success. We can easily convince ourselves that the grass is always greener on the other side of the fence and spend a lot of time and energy pursuing extrinsic goals rather than being open to experiencing joy in the moment.

Once we attain an extrinsic goal, we acclimate and the happiness fades. We tend to set another goal, and the cycle continues. Our attention is on an extrinsic motivator rather than joy. The journey is what actually gives us more joy, not the destination.

We are continually at choice. Choice lives in the moment and is invaluable because it opens us to new possibilities and perspectives. Joy isn't something we wait for, but something we can choose. When we set our intention on experiencing JOYBeing, we need to be aware and make choices that support us. With continual awareness and choices, we build the habitual patterns that strengthen JOYBeing.

When we assess the status of our internal garden, we can make better choices about what is needed. Just as we note that plants and trees need water, sunlight, fertilizer, weeding, and care, we can assess what we need to connect with JOYBeing. For example, we may need more connection with others or ourselves, more rest, more nourishment, or some fun. Being aware of what we need allows us to make the choices that serve us in the moment.

4. Engaging in Practice

Just as we continuously tend a garden, we can build new muscles with practice. New behaviors form when we move with awareness and repetition. We can learn and integrate new patterns due to neuroplasticity. In recent years, we've come to understand we can consciously train our brains and embody behaviors that become part of a new self and way of being. By allocating our energy with intention into new practices, over time we develop new qualities of being and habitual patterns that serve us.

An embodied life of JOYBeing requires internal practices that build a new self. Imagine developing the habit of noticing what is going well and realizing moments of joy. As checking in on our mood and emotions becomes a habit, we will easily be able to center ourselves. The more we practice and keep our intentions in awareness, the more readily our choices support us.

Lynn, a participant who joined our virtual Cultivating JOYBeing program, shared that after years of experiencing anxiety and stress and after trying multiple ineffective solutions, she began to experience more JOYBeing. She adopted the mindset and practices we will be sharing with you throughout this book. Through committed practice, she opened to the possibility of creativity, flow, and aliveness, which enabled her to reframe her interpretation of the meaning of life. As a result, she reported experiencing vitality, vibrancy, and enhanced relationships.

Jean, Ann's coaching client, felt demoralized and unhappy with her job. She felt she was not appreciated and wanted to look for another job. Her intention

> *We are what we repeatedly do. Excellence, then, is not an act, but a habit.*
>
> *Aristotle*

was to experience more joy and satisfaction at work and in her home life. As we reflected on what supported her energy and what depleted it, she became aware that she felt and acted like a victim. She was blaming others for her dissatisfaction. She did not believe she could experience joy. She was not taking action to support her joy and sense of aliveness. With this awareness, she started making choices to support herself. For example, she started going to the gym, she met with a friend, and she reached out to colleagues at work to strengthen relationships. She created some regular practices, such as exercising, communicating with colleagues, choosing projects that inspired her, and engaging in art. She reported that she was experiencing JOYBeing, and she noticed that these changes and practices helped her appreciate her current role at work and her personal life. In addition, she received positive feedback about her job performance.

Richard Strozzi-Heckler, founder of Strozzi Institute and a pioneer in somatic leadership, states, "We are what we practice." He suggests we are always in some sort of practice from the moment we wake until we go to bed. Observing our practices enables us to see who we are. Conscious and deliberate practice enables us to embody JOYBeing. The question is: Are we aware of what we are practicing? We also need to be aware that our practices are aligned with what we want to experience and who we want to be in the world.

This book's creation is a specific example of the four steps of the JOYBeing path. We had the joint intention of experiencing more joy in our lives since we felt we were missing joy. We were overworked with busy schedules and many demands in different areas of our lives.

After heartfelt sharing about our experiences, we decided to be a support to each other. We practiced paying more attention to moments

CHAPTER 1 Cultivating the Garden Within: The Essence of JOYBeing

when we were, in fact, experiencing joy. We set an intention to discover how to be more joyful. To support our awareness, we reflected and identified moments of joy and noticed our patterns and how we limited joy in our lives. As we paid more attention, we were surprised to become aware of many more experiences of joy than we had realized.

We then chose to allow ourselves to focus on and enjoy even more moments of joy. With practice, we created a new habitual pattern, a way of being that, over time, allowed us to experience inner joy and aliveness, which we named JOYBeing.

We continued to face and process the challenges of life without forgetting our commitment to joy. We have found this experience so valuable that we continue to enrich ourselves in this journey, and it is truly our joy to share this process with you.

Throughout this book, we will introduce a range of practices that will support you in cultivating more aliveness and JOYBeing, building a centered presence that allows you to live a more fulfilled life.

In summary, happiness is external and lives in our thoughts. Joy is an internal emotion experienced in the moment that gives us a message of connection, meaning, and possibility. JOYBeing is an enlivening state that keeps us vibrant with the joy of being alive. It's a habit that we want to cultivate and radiate to live positively and influence others.

The path to JOYBeing includes setting our intention, becoming aware, making choices, and engaging in practices that will be the foundation of creating a new self and connecting with our inner garden of joy and aliveness. The following chapters offer a collection of practices and tools that will enrich and support your journey of cultivating JOYBeing. You can experiment and assess which practices are most effective for you. We have chosen practices that have been valuable for us and our clients.

> The sun does not shine for a few trees and flowers, but for the wide world's joy.
>
> *Henry Ward Beecher*

For us, the metaphor of JOYBeing as an inner garden has come alive, helping us to frame and sustain our focus. We each routinely check in on our inner garden at various times throughout the day to connect with aliveness. We envision energy flowing from the ground where seeds of joy are planted and sit with the vibrance and energy of growing flowers, plants, and trees. Some days, our inner gardens are rich and abundant with a wide range of wildflowers and fruit, and we bask in the joy of life and all that is possible. We are grateful to be alive.

Other times, we notice the soil is dry with a barren garden. At these times, we know we need to reconnect with our purpose, connect with others, take care of ourselves, and engage in activities we enjoy. Like tending to a garden, we try to incorporate regular practices like walking, being in nature, drawing, and conversing with friends to sustain and nurture our inner gardens. We hope our flourishing inner gardens will be of benefit to those with whom we interact, given that emotions are contagious. We encourage you to visualize and make it a practice to tend and enjoy your inner garden of vitality and aliveness. Take a breath and notice what kind of an inner garden you are nurturing.

Practices

As you embark on this journey of JOYBeing with us, we recommend you use a journal to reflect on your awareness, experiences, and learnings.

1. BECOMING CLEAR ABOUT OUR INTENTIONS

Reflect on your mindset related to JOYBeing.
- ✓ Do you believe joy is your birthright and available to you?
- ✓ How does experiencing joy support you in living and achieving your goals?
- ✓ How is it possible for you to allow more joy into your life?
- ✓ How can you create space to notice moments of joy?
- ✓ What actions and activities can you choose that inspire joy?
- ✓ How can you incorporate the mindset of JOYBeing? What will support you in remembering this choice?

Reflect on how connecting with the goal of experiencing JOYBeing supports your values and what is most meaningful to you.

Take a moment to write down your intentions for your JOYBeing journey.
- ✓ What is it that excites you in life?
- ✓ Why is this important to you?
- ✓ What will support you in recalling your intention for JOYBeing?
- ✓ What are some steps you will take?
- ✓ What will you practice differently that will serve you?

2. ASSESS YOUR ENERGY

In your journal:

- ✓ Take note of what increases your energy.
- ✓ What depletes your energy?
- ✓ What patterns do you notice?
- ✓ What will support you in increasing your energy and emotional vitality?
- ✓ What's the cost of not enhancing your energy?

3. AWARENESS OF MOMENTS OF JOY

Take a few deep breaths, and relax your body. Notice your feet touching the ground and feel grounded. Check in with yourself where you are tense and send your breath to those parts. Let yourself float back in time just briefly.

- ✓ Identify a moment of joy and aliveness that you have experienced in the past.
- ✓ What were you doing?
- ✓ Notice your sensations. What is happening in your body now?
- ✓ What was the occasion? Is there anything specific about your activity or place? What value is awakened in you?
- ✓ Is anyone next to you?
- ✓ What do you notice about your energy when you connect with joyful moments? Notice your sensations and savor these experiences.
- ✓ Are you aware of a common pattern?

Continue to identify moments of joy during your day and where you feel them in your body. Where are you, what are you doing, and what supports you in noticing joy?

Build your list of what brings you joy. Create a daily practice of noticing patterns and moments of joy that you experienced that day and recording them in your journal. You may also make it a practice of sharing joyful moments with a friend or partner.

Practices

4. SAVORING MOMENTS OF JOY

Notice when you experience a moment of joy in real-time or reflect on a memory of joy and go beyond noticing it to savoring the moment as if it were a rich piece of chocolate or a good meal.

- ✓ Notice where you experience joy in your body.
- ✓ What message is it evoking in you—a sense of care, belonging, connecting, hope, pleasure, thriving, fun, aliveness, or something else?
- ✓ Practice reconnecting with those moments so they can be available to you whenever you choose.
- ✓ Notice the effect of choosing to savor joy on you and those around you.
- ✓ Plan for and anticipate moments of joy, such as seeing a friend, being in nature, and engaging in a fun activity.
- ✓ Identify songs that inspire joy and listen to them often. Consider developing a JOYBeing playlist.

Ann

I've discovered immense value in experiencing and revisiting joy-filled memories. Among those instances are the opportunities I have enjoyed conducting OASIS Conversations Courses across Europe and various corners of the globe. The visceral reconnection with the joy of crafting and sharing a leadership program with a diverse global audience, including engagements with the United Nations and other mission-focused organizations, is truly invigorating. The thrill of witnessing the positive reception of the conversation process I developed and the satisfaction of sharing it with people from every corner of the world brings me joy.

I also enjoy traveling, experiencing different cultures, and making a difference for leaders and their teams. I am grateful to have found a fulfilling profession in coaching, writing, and teaching, and being able to make personal contributions to the quality of life in organizations and for individuals. When I appreciate this experience, a delightful tingling permeates my body, and a buoyant lightness settles in my chest. In these moments, I feel joy and am grateful to be alive. Reconnecting with such enlivening memories reconnects me with what matters most to me—experiencing community and belonging, making a difference, encouraging potential, and creating. When I experience or recall these joyful memories, I feel better able to face challenges and experience joy in the moment. What joy-filled memories can you draw on to connect you with JOYBeing?

CHAPTER 1 Cultivating the Garden Within: The Essence of JOYBeing

5. NOTICING WHAT DISTRACTS YOU FROM JOY

We each have our conditioned patterns that distract us from joy. Here are some we see. Which are familiar to you? What patterns limit your experience of joy?

- ✓ Not engaging in things that invite joy
- ✓ Thinking small moments of joy don't matter
- ✓ Taking on too much, being too busy and overcommitted to various tasks and responsibilities
- ✓ Focusing on the negative, staying in a state of dissatisfaction, not experiencing gratitude
- ✓ Comparing ourselves negatively to others
- ✓ Being distracted from the present by focusing on the future and worrying
- ✓ Focusing on the past and not being present
- ✓ Being disappointed in people and life situations
- ✓ Trying to change a situation or a person
- ✓ Feeling you don't deserve or expect joy
- ✓ Being unaccustomed to experiencing joy
- ✓ Excessive use of digital devices

Gila

I connect to exquisite moments of joy when I reflect on my childhood days of celebrating birthdays, special days, and Jewish holidays with family and friends gathered around large tables. These gatherings, filled with laughter and love, are the heartbeats of my most cherished memories. Yet my deepest moments of joy also arise from the enduring friendships I've cultivated over the years. The journeys we've embarked upon, whether exploring new places through traveling or delving into the depths of our inner selves, are treasures that enrich my soul.

Spending time in nature, creating and appreciating art and music, meeting new and diverse people, and spending quality time with children and loved ones have all been profound sources of rejuvenation for me. Each experience is a thread in the tapestry of my life, weaving together moments of connection, inspiration, and growth.

Today, I feel truly blessed to have chosen a path that not only supports but also amplifies the things I love. My passions have seamlessly become both my work and my lifestyle, allowing me to live a life that is as fulfilling as it is purposeful. This journey of walking toward integrating JOYBeing into every aspect of my life is a testament to the beauty of following one's heart and embracing the fullness of life.

CHAPTER 2

Basking in Our Garden: Experiencing the Energy and Aliveness of the Present Moment

> "*If you want to be happy, be.*"
>
> — *Leo Tolstoy*

JOYBeing

Can you recall being outside on a beautiful sunny day, seeing the blue sky, and noticing you are glad to be alive? You let yourself experience the moment of basking in the sunshine, feeling the breeze, and hearing the joyful sound of birds. You are present. You are not worrying about the future or fretting about the past. Notice what happens in your body as you experience this moment. We experience joy and aliveness when we are in the present moment.

We spend a lifetime paying attention to what is missing in our lives. When we ask people what they want in life, they invariably say they want to be happy, joyful, healthy, and successful—even if they already possess these attributes. We have not learned to be in the moment and appreciate our current experience. We are often chasing time without awareness. When we are twelve, we can't wait to be fifteen. When we are fifteen, we can't wait to reach our twenties. When we get our degree, the project completed, the right job, or the right partner, only then do we think we will be okay or happy. We chase time without noticing how the years pass. And… when we are fifty or older, we wish we were younger.

This is called the hedonic treadmill. Hedonic adaptation is where the effects on happiness fade over time. We are always chasing the next carrot or reward. And shortly after achieving success, we set another goal. We think we will experience joy—someday. Sadly, we are missing our present moments—where we can only experience real joy.

Observe children at a playground or zoo. They naturally know how to bask in the present moment. They don't have a lot of past to regret, and they have not yet learned to worry about the future. As we grow older and life becomes more complex, it is easy to lose our sense of wonder and excitement about life and the world. The good news is we can regain this energy and excitement by building the habit of being grounded in the present moment and open to what is possible. When we live in the present moment, we can experience life at a deeper, more meaningful, and joyful level.

The idea of being present in the moment is a challenge since life has so many things to attend to. We are bombarded with distractions, overloaded with more information than we can take in, burdened with others' expectations of us, and challenged by accelerated technological and global changes. Today, the uncertainties of global climate change, systemic inequities, and worldwide conflicts distract us.

We experience reality and authentic connection in the present moment. A participant in one of our leadership classes shared that he often would think about an email he needed to write or reflect on an interaction with a colleague when eating a home-cooked meal. Only when his wife asked him if he liked the meal did he realize he was eating and what the food tasted like. He missed experiencing the delicious food and a real connection with his family. When he made a conscious effort to be present in the moment, taste his food, and experience his family connections, he felt a genuine sense of aliveness and connectedness. It was a new and joyful experience for him. He is not alone. Too often, we miss experiencing the joy of our present moments.

So, how do we keep ourselves present? Choice lives in the moment. When we are unaware, we often make decisions that don't serve us and we experience regrets. Our lives take place in the present moment. When we don't choose to be in the present, we miss the joy of our relationships and experiences.

Of course, being present is difficult when we are faced with uncertainty and challenges all around us. While we may want to hide or lash out, when we are present with our sensations, thoughts, emotions, and what is happening, we can also be present with others. Our emotions influence others, and our attention and presence is a gift. It may seem like a small gesture, but connecting with our aliveness enables us to connect more fully with others. When someone is present with us, we experience a sense of connection, aliveness, and joy—something we all need these days.

Our definition of being present is *"attending to the moment with acceptance of what is, with choice."* Attending is being aware and observing the moment in the here and now. It is accepting that some things are beyond our control. Multiple realities exist so the choice of where we focus affects our experience. Are we focusing on what is missing, or are we open to exploring what is possible in the moment?

Pause for a moment. Take a breath. Are you aware of what you are choosing to pay attention to at this moment?

Noticing Our Inner Garden's Climate

> If your mind is expansive and unfettered, you will find yourself in a more accommodating world, a place that's endlessly interesting and alive. That quality isn't inherent in the place but in your state of mind.
>
> *Pema Chödrön*

In *The Power of NOW: A Guide to Spiritual Enlightenment*, Eckhart Tolle shares his message that living in the now is the truest path to happiness and enlightenment. He states that when we are intensely present in the now, we respond from deep consciousness and flow with ease and joy. Tolle says the only important time is the one we think about the least—the present. The reason only the present matters is that everything *happens* here. Everything you feel and sense takes place in the present. When you think about it, the past is nothing more than all present moments that have gone by, and the future is just the collection of present moments waiting to arrive.

Being present is a skill that can be cultivated. It is simply noticing what is and what we are experiencing in the moment; it is shifting our attention from the past or future to what is occurring in the here and now.

When we are present, we can be attentive and focus on a person, conversation, project, or task without distraction or the sense that we should be

CHAPTER 2 Basking in Our Garden: Experiencing the Energy and Aliveness of the Present Moment

somewhere else. So often, our energy and focus are scattered, and we miss the aliveness, beauty, and possibility at hand. Being present is a gift to ourselves and others that allows us to be engaged with living, connected with others and the world, open-minded, and open to possibilities.

Research suggests focusing on the present moment enhances our sense of wellbeing and health, and it reduces our sense of depression and anxiety. When we are in the present, we have a greater sense of being fulfilled and are more positive about our lives. This relaxed state supports physical, emotional, and social health. When we are attuned to ourselves, we are more capable of building strong, supportive, and meaningful relationships. When we are in the present moment, we are more likely to see opportunities and possibilities. We experience a greater quality of life at work, at home, and in our communities.

When we are present, we experience the joy and fullness of life, and we are more likely to spread this sense of aliveness to others.

We actually are better positioned to achieve our goals when we cultivate the skill of being present. We can be more attentive to what is required and more centered and relaxed in the process. We see more avenues and opportunities to succeed.

> *Happiness is not something readymade. It comes from your own actions.*
>
> —Dalai Lama

A lot of the time, we are operating on autopilot. We are focused on making plans, checking things off our to-do lists, and rushing toward an imagined future. How many times have you driven to a destination and not recalled the journey? Perhaps you got your chores and work completed or spent time with your family and realized you were not really present. You may have been focusing on what you needed to do next or reviewing the past. Can we actually enjoy some of these simple moments of our lives?

We all have many distractions these days. We are overwhelmed by the news, social media, and other people's demands for our time and energy. Often, we feel we have little space for ourselves.

Each of us tends to develop habits that once served a purpose but may no longer be beneficial. Take, for instance, the habit of worrying about the future; as students, it might have supported our success by encouraging diligent study and preparation, resulting in good grades. However, today, this habitual anxiety can rob us of the joy of being present and reduce our ability to discern and explore various options.

Similarly, the tendency to dwell on and relive the past may have originated as a strategy to learn from mistakes and avoid poor choices. Yet the persistent focus on the past consumes energy that could otherwise be directed toward fully embracing the current moment and new possibilities.

In the face of loneliness and life challenges, many of us adopt coping patterns that we believe provide safety and shield us from life's difficulties. However, it's crucial to recognize that evading unresolved issues is not a sustainable solution. In doing so, we inadvertently constrain our ability to fully experience the richness of the present moment.

We all have experienced small and big traumas in our lives. Part of our growth process is to explore what may be hindering our life energy and work through our challenges. This requires befriending our emotions and learning from them. We benefit from slowing down and connecting with spaciousness, allowing more silence and stillness. When we attend to the ordinary with a sense of openness and curiosity, we make room for the extraordinary in the present. When we pay attention, we extract the juice and experience the essence and aliveness of our moments.

While life will always offer challenges and there will be many difficult moments, JOYBeing resides within each of us, waiting to be nourished and awakened. Finding JOYBeing can be elusive because our inner garden isn't always in perpetual bloom. There are seasons of growth and decay and times of vibrant flowering and quiet dormancy. Just as nature has its cycles, so, too, does our life. Times of challenge exist when our resilience and patience are tested; we may feel we are walking through a storm. These moments can leave us feeling depleted and uncertain, but they also offer opportunities for growth and transformation. By facing them with courage and an open heart, we can uncover hidden strengths and deepen our understanding of ourselves. By navigating these difficult times, we cultivate the wisdom and fortitude needed to flourish, enriching the garden of our inner life.

> *When you connect to the silence within you, that is when you can make sense of the disturbance going on around you.*
>
> — Stephen Richards

Ann

I once believed my tendency to worry was a constructive and protective tool for anticipating challenges and supporting me in planning and achieving goals. While, by external measures, I did get a lot accomplished, I failed to enjoy life's journey fully. I overcommitted, overfilled my overflowing to-do list, and strived to get too much done. My focus on meeting others' needs eclipsed the importance of slowing down and cultivating a genuine connection with my inner landscape and the current moment.

It's been an evolution for me to choose to move from a focus on the future to connecting with my sensations and embracing the current moment. Ironically, since embodying the practice of being present and fostering focused attentiveness, I have forged deeper connections and experienced more success in my professional endeavors. Most significantly, this shift has brought about the joy of being—JOYBeing.

Recognizing the contagious nature of emotions, I aspire to inspiring others to savor the power of being present and open. A palpable distinction exists between interacting with individuals consumed by stress and urgency and those authentically attentive and immersed in the moment.

The effect of someone offering their undivided attention is profound. We sense the difference and are influenced by the emotions and energy of those around us. Discovering that our presence holds the potential to make a positive difference and create new possibilities for others has been truly uplifting and life-enhancing. I now recognize my more open energy toward myself and others actually supports others.

JOYBeing and Mindfulness of the Present Moment

JOYBeing is experienced when we are aware and embrace the present moment as it is. We are not looking for perfection and wishing things were different. We appreciate what is, surrender to our reality of the moment, and know we can be choiceful about our next steps. This way of being is the path to JOYBeing. By paying attention to the mud, stones, and holes as well as the sunset, trees, and flowers, we can embrace the full experience of life and JOYBeing.

The present moment is a time to become aware of what is happening

within us. Through this meaning-making and acceptance, we are positioned to experience JOYBeing. For example, we may process and respond to a sad or stressful event as well as a happy celebration or a touching moment of connection. Even by entering the beauty of our pain, we can experience a sense of aliveness. The crucial step for JOYBeing is not to ignore, resist, control, or escape current suffering, which is a normal part of life, but to be fully open, allowing vulnerability and trusting the process of life.

JOYBeing is related to mindfulness in the sense that we are open, without judgment about what is happening in the moment. This awareness enables us to make choices in how we respond rather than react unconsciously. In addition, we are noticing and savoring moments and recognizing life's enriching aspects. This counteracts our propensity for a negativity bias. We are wired to protect ourselves and seek safety, and we naturally notice what may not be going well or could be dangerous. We are also free to choose how we welcome the moment. We notice and connect with our emotions and moods. Here we have choices in our responses.

Being present offers many benefits, such as the reduction of stress and anxiety, greater health and connection with others and our environment, and experiencing the aliveness of JOYBeing.

> **No mud, no lotus.**
> *Thich Nhat Hanh*

Gila

When I established my preschool in 1991, my focus on achievement led me to constantly rush ahead. I was always immersed in to-do lists and striving for the next goal. This doer drive served me well in handling the workload, but I failed to realize the price I paid, which took away my ability to savor the present moment. Balancing multiple roles, I took pride in my efficiency, yet I missed out on the simple joys with my children and loved ones.

Over time, I began to recognize the hidden cost of this relentless pace. As I cultivated the practice and gift of slowing down, I discovered the benefit of paying attention to the richness of my inner world. Through this introspection, I unearthed the value of embracing the present moment and decoding the messages of my emotions, which had been kept silent and unseen for many years. Only then did I truly begin to enjoy the aliveness and vibrancy of life, excited by the journey I was on, rather than merely focusing on the destination. I felt liberated and a sense of lightness, which connected me to JOYBeing.

Nurturing the Art of Being Present

When our mind, body, and soul are aligned, we are truly alive and connected with our essence. With this alignment, we experience our sensations and a sense of flow or oneness with life. Bathing in this moment creates the experience of JOYBeing, which is the sense of being alive.

Great power is found in being aware of the moment. JOYBeing is being aware of our thoughts and feelings, as well as the world around us. It means being aware of our reactions to our environment and how we interact with others. It means being present in our lives and not letting our minds incessantly wander off into the past or future, experiencing depression or anxiety.

When we are present in the moment, we can appreciate the joy that comes from living in the here and now. We can appreciate the beauty of nature, the joy of spending time with friends and family, or the simple pleasure of a good book or a great meal. We can feel the warmth of the sun on our faces, the coolness of a rain shower, and the energy of a good conversation.

JOYBeing allows us to be more aware of our emotional states and needs and to take time to appreciate the small moments of joy and contentment. We can use our awareness to choose moments of kindness, gratitude, and understanding toward ourselves and others.

> *Past and future are in the mind only— I am now.*
>
> Sri Nisargadatta Maharaj

Just as we have learned to distance and distract ourselves from the present moment, we can build the habit of being present and living in the here and now. Building this skill takes intention, awareness, choice, and practice. Our goal is to enhance our awareness of what is happening within us and around us at the moment. Internally, we become aware of our body, mind,

CHAPTER 2 Basking in Our Garden: Experiencing the Energy and Aliveness of the Present Moment

and emotions. Externally, we expand our awareness of what is happening in our immediate and larger environment.

Ellen Langer, a renowned research psychologist, suggests that simply paying attention to what is new and different is a natural way of being present. For example, if you visited one of our homes for the first time, you would naturally be attentive and notice the art, the books, the photos on the wall, and even the plants. It would be natural for you to be present with us as we shared stories related to the photos. You can practice waking up by noticing new details around you.

> *When you are fully present, you are capable of perceiving what is occurring in yourself as well as in the person you are with.*
>
> *Marcia Reynolds*

Let's practice paying attention to your senses. Pause for a moment and take a conscious breath.

- ✓ What do you see, hear, smell, touch, and taste in your environment?

- ✓ Notice the objects around you—what colors do you see, what shapes do you notice, and what textures are around you?

- ✓ Notice any tension in your body.

- ✓ Allow yourself to pay attention to each sensation and notice what you experience in the moment.

CHAPTER 2 Basking in Our Garden: Experiencing the Energy and Aliveness of the Present Moment

Being present and aware is a simple and profound experience that can easily be missed. While taking a walk outside, are you noticing the sound of birds, the feeling of the ground beneath your feet, or the sight of leaves flowing in the breeze? Or are you getting lost in your thoughts? Are you experiencing the joy of being alive?

Life has many routine activities, such as brushing our teeth, driving, folding laundry, doing dishes, and eating. We can use these activities to practice being present. We can pay attention to doing the activity and experience our sensations. For example, you can notice the warmth of the clothes as they come out of the dryer. We can practice coming back to and experiencing this moment and choose to connect with a sense of aliveness and experience a sense of joy.

Appreciating that life is messy and embracing imperfection is also helpful. We can accept that we are always learning and growing and that we will experience uncertainty and not see the whole picture. We can trust that we can be resilient.

Building the muscle of being present and choosing aliveness requires us to be awake. It takes dedication and practice.

> *Your presence is a being intervention.*
>
> *Dorothy Siminovitch*

60

Meet Alex—A Coach

Alex, a dedicated professional coach, is on a mission to infuse more vibrancy into his client sessions. His work with a diverse range of clients has revealed a common thread—many individuals are not fully savoring the joys of life. Alex's passion to spread more joy and aliveness is not just a personal goal, but a commitment to enriching his clients' lives. Reflecting on his journey, Alex shares, "I believe that by honing my coaching abilities and embracing a more vibrant approach, I can unlock the potential for profound transformations in both my clients' lives and my own."

Alex realized he had the belief, "I must have all the answers and solutions to be a successful coach." This mindset created a sense of pressure to know the right way forward with clients. In the face of uncertainty and challenges in coaching sessions, he felt a sense of inadequacy and stress. This stress limited his ability to connect with his clients, be present, enjoy his work, and grow with them. He was missing out on the richness of collaborative exploration, and he lost his sense of playfulness. Recognizing the impact of this mindset, he embraced being more present with a sense of curiosity, openness, and cocreation to experience greater joy, aliveness, and wellbeing in his coaching practice and life.

In addition to shifting to a JOYBeing mindset to be more present and playful and allow more joy, Alex paid attention to his energy and allowed himself to be grounded and notice moments of joy. He set the intention to notice and experience joy. He practiced being mindfully aware of his energy and focused on being open, curious, and non-judgmental. He embraced being more authentic and connecting with his clients to share insights and enjoy the richness of collaborative exploration. Acknowledging that growth and transformation are iterative processes that involve learning from successes and setbacks allowed him to relax his self-criticism and foster more genuine connections and creativity with himself and his clients.

Alex referred to his inner garden as a lush green transformation garden of flowers with bright colors. He planted seeds of being present, being open, and self-discovery as foundational plants. But he didn't stop there. Just as a garden requires careful tending, pruning, and attention, Alex's inner garden needed consistent nurturing and reflection to facilitate growth and evolution. By engaging in practices like centering, mindfulness, active embodiment, continuous learning,

CHAPTER 2 Basking in Our Garden: Experiencing the Energy and Aliveness of the Present Moment

and embracing new perspectives, he cultivated a fertile ground for transformation to take root. Alex planted the seeds of experimentation, flexibility, and continuous learning.

After attending the Cultivating JOYBeing course, Alex reported, "I am grateful that I am enjoying myself more and experiencing more authentic, fun, and creative relationships with my clients. When I am more present and relaxed, I notice my clients also become more present and experience more JOYBeing."

In *Open Stance*, Ann shares the process of noticing when we are contracted or in judgment, then stopping, stepping

Gila

When I was growing up, expressing emotions, especially crying, was not encouraged in my family. Instead, I learned to hold back my tears whenever sadness struck. This suppression had a cost on my health, often resulting in throat and stomach issues, a physical manifestation of the emotions I kept bottled up inside.

To cope, I developed an invisible mask—a smile that masked my genuine emotions during challenging times. I didn't want to burden my loved ones or fall short of their expectations. I wore this mask of happiness and strength, concealing the storm of emotions raging within me. As a little child, the mulberry tree in our garden became my sanctuary, a place where I could hide to release the tears and hidden emotions I had been holding back. This hiding and armoring became a habitual pattern that defined a large portion of my early years.

As I grew older, this pattern persisted. I would sit through emotional movies, fighting back tears, suppressing my life energy and my urge to cry. The strain of holding back my tears left me physically tense, my throat clenched as I pushed back the tears that begged for freedom.

In moments of sadness or upon hearing distressing news, I'd instinctively put on that learned smile, creating a strange sense of detachment within myself. It was as though I was distancing myself from my genuine, authentic emotions. And even today, in rare instances, I find it challenging to confront that part of me, the part accustomed to masking emotions under the guise of "Everything is fine. I'm okay" when actually it isn't.

Recognizing this pattern of numbing difficult emotions—as well as my longing for joy and vitality—became the catalyst for change. I embarked on a journey of self-work, reframing beliefs and granting myself permission to feel free. This inner transformation gave birth to Cultivating JOYBeing workshops, a journey supported by somatic work and multiple trainings.

Through these processes, my energy, posture, and presence underwent a significant shift. Instead of closing myself, I became more open and upright, fundamentally altering my entire being.

This is the inquiry state we want to be in—not fixing, but awakening to our feelings, attending to them in the present moment as they are happening, allowing them space so a new course of action can emerge.

Becoming aware of, attending to, and attuning to the wisdom of my body, and listening keenly to the voice of my emotions, allowed me to rediscover a sense of freedom. I breathed new life into a part of myself I had long neglected. This newfound awareness enabled me to reconnect with the authenticity and life energy I had forgotten, a place where true liberation resides. A place of JOYBeing!

> *Time isn't precious at all, because it is an illusion. What you perceive as precious is not time, but the one point that is out of time: the Now. That is precious indeed. The more you are focused on time—past and future— the more you miss the Now, the most precious thing there is.*
>
> *Eckhart Tolle*

back and cooling down, and shifting to being open. The focus is on being open-minded, curious, and compassionate to others and what transpires. We can use this same process internally. When we are mindful or aware that we are focusing on what is missing, what is not going well, and the difficulties of life, and we let our emotions deplete us, we can recall our propensity for a negativity bias and choose to stop, step back, and shift to savoring the natural joy and aliveness within us. We are always surrounded by beauty, possibilities, and opportunities for joy.

We can always make the choice to become aware of our inner garden and our sense of ease and contentment. With practice, we notice our interconnection with the world and others. We connect with JOYBeing—the joy of being alive. This moves us toward a creative and sustainable life.

Yes, it takes awareness and practice to develop the muscle of noticing and shifting to savoring moments of joy and connecting with our natural aliveness. Of course, we continue to face hardships and challenges. We experience pain and sorrow. However, we can focus on this present moment and appreciate that we are here experiencing this aliveness and inner flow of energy. This simple moment

CHAPTER 2 Basking in Our Garden: Experiencing the Energy and Aliveness of the Present Moment

allows us to connect with our natural innate aliveness and sense JOYBeing.

We can develop many practices to support our connection with JOYBeing. We are each unique, and we need to experiment to find what best enhances our sense of aliveness and joy. In this book, we offer a number of useful practices.

We need to start by slowing down, taking a few deep breaths, becoming aware, and placing our attention on what is happening now. This requires letting go of distractions such as scrolling through social media, watching the news, or thinking about the past or future—whatever might get in the way of what is most compelling or important to us at the moment.

When we practice being present, we can appreciate the beauty around us and experience an appreciation and gratitude for life. Even during difficult times, when we are present, we can appreciate being alive. Amid difficult experiences, when we are present to our emotions and allow them to move through us, we support our resilience and future wellbeing. With awareness, we can make better choices, make deeper connections, and support our health.

Taking a few moments to find stillness and come back to our breath can help us reduce stress and give us a sense of peace, calm, and joy. Taking the time to practice JOYBeing and be in the moment is a powerful tool for cultivating inner harmony and peace.

We want to practice JOYBeing, center ourselves more effectively, and face all aspects of life, including stress, pressures, and disappointments so that we embody this new way of life. When we are aware of the moment, we are mindful, centered, and experiencing JOYBeing.

Having a clear purpose to live a life of JOYBeing gives us a sense of direction, motivates us, and allows us to focus on what's most important. With this purpose, we are able to set goals, work toward them, and experience a sense of meaning and fulfillment. Being aware of our intention for JOYBeing supports us during challenging and difficult times. Moving with this intention provides us with a sense of identity and awareness of who we are and how we can make a difference. It can also inspire us to take action to make positive changes in our lives and those of others.

Practices

According to Thich Nhat Hanh, a popular Buddhist teacher, "We know how to sacrifice ten years for a diploma, and we are willing to work very hard to get a job, a car, a house, and so on. But we have difficulty remembering that we are alive in the present moment; the only moment there is for us to be alive. Every breath we take and every step we make can be filled with peace, joy, and serenity. We need only to be awake, alive in the present moment."

1. MINDFULNESS MEDITATION PRACTICE

Mindfulness is the state of mind where we intentionally practice coming back to the present moment. It is an ancient practice that invites awareness and builds the muscle of attention. Research supports that the practice can enhance positivity and wellbeing. You can start with five minutes and devote more time as you experience the benefits. We find it useful to start our day with this practice. It helps to ground and center us and prepare for what is to come.

- ✓ Choose a quiet place.
- ✓ Set your phone or a timer for five minutes or your desired time.
- ✓ Close your eyes.
- ✓ Bring your attention to your breath.
- ✓ Send breath to your body, starting from your feet and moving upward to your head, giving breath to each part to invite more vitality and JOYBeing.
- ✓ Allow yourself to go deeper with each breath.
- ✓ When your mind wanders, and it will, gently bring your attention back to your breath.

CHAPTER 2 Basking in Our Garden: Experiencing the Energy and Aliveness of the Present Moment

An extension of the above practice is to focus on thoughts, emotions, and sensations.

- ✓ Notice your breath, your thoughts, or your emotions. Try to stay with it. When you notice you are distracted, simply go back to observing. This builds the skill of paying attention.
- ✓ Allow a sense of wonder as you observe.
- ✓ Relax your body and notice your thoughts; appreciate that you are more than your thoughts, and over time, allow your thoughts to settle.
- ✓ Notice a sense of peace as things slow down, your thoughts subside, and you dwell in the present moment.
- ✓ Become aware of and name the emotion you are experiencing, such as worry, sadness, ease, or joy.

You are now building the skill of noticing and naming without reacting.

You can also practice with an app that guides you. Martin Boroson's One-Moment Meditation app leads you through one minute of focused attention. Notice the difference even a minute of mindful attention can make.

> " *The present moment is filled with joy and happiness. If you are attentive, you will see it.*
>
> — Thich Nhat Hanh

Practices

2. ACTIVE EMBODIMENT PRACTICE

Present-moment awareness can be achieved through mindful attention during daily activities, which supports JOYBeing. By paying attention, we can identify what is needed and move toward it. Our intention with JOYBeing is to experience the somatics and emotions of joy and aliveness in our bodies.

Make it a practice to bring your attention to the present moment. With open eyes, notice the sensations in your body rather than simply thinking about your experience. This can be done while walking in nature and noticing the sensations of the sounds, smells, and sights of the surroundings. Make it a practice to open up to your senses and be fully present with whatever you see or do, such as cutting vegetables, driving a car, taking a shower, brushing your teeth, exercising, or listening to music.

The key is not to judge yourself when you recognize you have not been present but to gently bring yourself back to the awareness of the present moment, just as we come back to noticing our breath when meditating. This practice builds the muscle of attention and sensing. Allow yourself to savor your somatic experiences.

Also valuable is engaging in activities that heighten your energy and sense of aliveness, such as reading a good book, taking a walk in nature, listening to music, engaging in art, and being with friends. Allow yourself to experience the moment and let go of worry about the future or concerns about the past. Move your attention to your body, noticing sensations, emotions, and internal dialogue. Continue to enjoy your experience.

CHAPTER 2 Basking in Our Garden: Experiencing the Energy and Aliveness of the Present Moment

The real meditation practice is how we live our lives from moment, to moment, to moment.

Jon Kabat-Zinn

Gila

For me, embodying the present moment has always come initially through music, followed by the arts and being in nature. These activities have always been pillars of support, guiding me to a deeper connection with myself. Even in the most challenging moments, these art forms have been my place of refuge, allowing me to sit with difficult emotions, unraveling their depths to uncover new meanings.

Trusting the innate wisdom of my soul has been pivotal—I have opened pathways to explore depths without any predetermined agenda. As an expressive arts facilitator, I've marveled at how, through art and music, I've opened new gateways of possibility, for my clients and myself, expanding my awareness beyond measure.

Nature, in its serene embrace, has consistently offered me a reset button, a way to recalibrate my perspective and embrace gratitude. Moments of silent time with nature, be it a brief walk or a short meditation, have been very transformative. They've supported me in reestablishing my connection with my body and infused me with renewed energy and vitality. Through these experiences, my senses sharpen, leading me toward greater clarity.

In our "Coming Back to Center" workshops,[4] a journey I've been delivering with a colleague for over a decade now, we find our sanctuary in nature. These workshop series are purposefully designed to facilitate a deep connection with the present moment, fostering a sense of aliveness. They serve as a pathway for participants to experience the profound beauty of life, to revel in the magnificence of nature, and to embrace a centered leadership presence in full connection with themselves in the present moment.

In essence, these elements—painting, music, and nature—have been instrumental in shaping my journey, providing anchors that ground me in moments of turmoil, bringing me back to my center and elevating me toward living a life of JOYBeing. They've become not just avenues of expression but gateways to a richer, more profound understanding of myself and the world around me.

---

[4] www.comingbacktocenter.com

Practices

3. CENTERING

Centering is useful for practicing being present so you can experience the moment and be at choice. Life continuously moves us out of our center. We can practice coming back to center and returning to the present moment.

When we do so, we can be in a state of flow and welcome the unknown.

Many different centering practices exist. We offer one based on Richard Strozzi-Heckler's work. He defines centering as being present, open, and connected with purpose. The practice focuses on the organizing principles of length, width, depth, and on purpose.

Move your attention to your body, noticing sensations, emotions, and internal dialogue. Move from the thinking self to the sensing self—from your head to your feelings.

Center by bringing your attention to your breath and to two inches below your belly button, which is often called the hara, our physical and spiritual center of gravity. Stay connected with your sensations and feelings rather than your thoughts.

Gila

Centering has become the guiding principle and focal point of my life's work. Each morning as I begin my day, I embark on a centering practice that aligns me with my core being. Throughout the day, I return to this practice, using breath and mindful centering to remain anchored in a state of JOYBeing.

Maintaining this centered state constantly isn't possible since life's challenges always pull us away from our center. During such moments, the practice of coming back to center becomes invaluable. Realigning ourselves in the moment allows us to live in harmony with our values, tapping into our inner resources and life energy.

Our "Coming Back to Center" workshop series is designed as immersive experiences. They have served me as a beacon, illuminating my path back to center whenever life's turbulence threatens to disrupt my balance. I have often witnessed participants say how they have transformed through the experiential processes, practical tools, and different centering practices we provide. I have also witnessed how this new way of being has opened a new path for them.

CHAPTER 2 Basking in Our Garden: Experiencing the Energy and Aliveness of the Present Moment

Center into your body's length. Imagine a line running through you and connecting to that center line. Settle down by feeling the ground beneath you. Lengthen by straightening up and connecting with the sky above your head. Allow more space between your vertebrae. Feel your spine and sense of dignity.

Center into your body's width. Bring your attention to your horizontal line. Breathe and allow balance of your left and right sides. Take a few breaths and allow your ribcage to expand horizontally. Notice your personal space, your connection to people and the world.

Center into your depth. Become aware of the balance between your back and front. As you focus on your back, become aware of your history and everything that has led you to being who you are today. Next, bring your attention to what is in front of you and the possibilities available to you from this place.

Now, move back to your center line. Appreciate and feel the lightness of the present moment. Allow yourself to experience a sense of being centered.

Place your hand at the center of your body's gravity, two inches below your belly button, and connect to your purpose and sense of meaning as you take a breath.

Ann

My journey of connecting with JOYBeing, a state of being where joy is not just an emotion but a way of life, has been a long and winding road. I have experimented with many forms of meditation and processes. I've consistently participated in many self-development programs and been an avid learner, focusing on growth and working through inner challenges.

As an executive, team, and somatic coach, I have worked with many leaders to connect with joy. The key lies in uncovering what resonates within us and bridging the gap between our internal and external worlds. My joy unfolds in the present moment within nature's embrace, through the strokes of drawing and writing, in the dance with art and beauty, and in the symphony of conversations and connections. But it's most vivid, and brings a warmth and connection, when I am fully engaging with others.

I start my day by grounding myself and centering. I connect with my sensations and presence. Uniting with my inner garden landscape, I envision connecting with the energy from the ground and the sky, and I appreciate the interconnectedness of life on the planet. Connecting with this aliveness and experiencing openness lays the foundation for a day of ease and receptivity to life's joys and challenges. I sense the vibrancy of colorful flowers and nourishing vegetables in my inner garden, a sight that brings an inner smile. I envision sharing the abundant bounty from the garden to enrich others. From this centered place, I can be at ease and am open to my potential. Throughout the day, noticing my breath and state of being allows me to recognize emotions and reactions, empowering me to gently shift into a centered and Open Stance with myself and others.

Throughout the day, I often ask myself, "Are you open and connecting with JOYBeing?" Checking within through this simple question allows me to connect with my sensations and sense of aliveness. I feel my feet on the ground, pay attention to sensations, and am present with the person I am with, or even the process of cutting vegetables or brushing my teeth. By being in the moment, I connect to what is most important, making me ready to engage with others and the joy of life.

Practices

4. GRATITUDE PRACTICE

Gratitude is a powerful way to become more present in the moment and experience JOYBeing. It helps us recognize life's gifts and appreciate what we have rather than focus on what is missing.

Our days rarely go according to plan or are free of unexpected challenges. Some of us can naturally appreciate the sweet moments as they happen throughout the day, but most of us need to cultivate this sense of gratefulness.

Gratitude is our emotion that relates to our ability to feel and express thankfulness and appreciation of the moment.

Gratitude is one of the quickest and most effective ways to experience joy and aliveness. Research shows that when we focus on what we are grateful for and feel it in our bodies, we experience joy and aliveness. Gratitude lives in the heart, and its effects are proven to be long-lasting.

A simple practice is to recall and share:
- ✓ What are you grateful for about yourself?
- ✓ What are you grateful for about others?
- ✓ What are you grateful for in the world?

Another practice for cultivating gratitude is keeping a gratitude journal and recording grateful experiences. We suggest you write about three or more experiences you are grateful for on a daily basis. Examples include noticing something in nature, an object of beauty, a pleasant conversation with a friend, a good cup of coffee, or helping someone with a problem.

Ann

One night, in the usual rhythm of waking up, I was taken aback to find myself immersed in gratitude reflections: "I am thankful to be in a warm home, grateful for the presence of family nearby, and cherish the moments spent with friends." In that quiet space, a natural sense of gratitude welled within me, not just for specific aspects of my life but for the gift of being alive. It was a stark departure from the past, when waking up often brought forth thoughts of worry for others and preoccupations with looming tasks.

I have cultivated a daily practice of reflecting on what I am grateful for. More than words on paper, I intentionally delve into the emotional and somatic experience of gratitude. I savor the sensations of being healthy, connecting with friends, appreciating nature, and finding joy in art. The practice goes beyond verbal expression; it is about experiencing gratitude viscerally, allowing the sensations and emotions to permeate my being. This practice forges neural pathways that enable us to embody joy and gratefulness. Through conscious awareness and continued practice, I am confident we can all cultivate the enduring trait of being grateful and joyful.

5. BEING PRESENT WITH YOUR INNER GARDEN

Bring your attention to your inner garden and take a few deep breaths.

Notice the details of your garden and surroundings. What is your ground like? Sense and feel the texture and stability beneath you. Is it grass, rich soil, or perhaps sand?

Pay attention to the energy present in your garden. Is it calm and serene, vibrant and lively, or a mix of both?

What kinds of plants does it sustain? What does your garden need? Does it need watering, weeding, new plants, or harvesting?

Imagine the sun shining down on your garden; feel the gentle rays nourishing the plants and soil. Be present with the weather, whether it's a gentle or strong breeze, a light or heavy rain, or a sunny or cloudy day.

As you spend time in your inner garden, notice how it makes you feel. What emotions arise? How does your body respond to inner aliveness?

Spend a few moments contemplating and understanding the care and attention your inner garden requires.

As you bring your awareness back to the present moment, stay connected with your inner sense of aliveness and JOYBeing.

Visit your inner garden often to cultivate a deeper connection to your inner aliveness.

> *The only way to find happiness is to understand that happiness is not out there. It's in here. And happiness is not next week. It's now.*
>
> *Marshall Goldsmith*

CHAPTER 3

Tilling the Soil: Connecting with Our Emotions

> **The only way out is through.**
> — *Robert Frost*

Tending Our Inner Landscape: Thoughts, Emotions, and Sensations

Imagine standing on a plank of wood on the floor. Just notice how you feel. Now imagine that the same plank of wood is placed between two tall buildings, and you are asked to stand on it. What do you notice? What are your sensations and emotions? Perhaps you experience contraction, tension, anxiety, or perhaps curiosity and excitement. What emotions would you be experiencing if you were supported by a safety belt? Notice how your sensations and emotions change depending on your background experiences, situations, and thoughts.

Emotions are central to our wellbeing and human nature. They are the driving force behind all human behavior. Our emotions and emotional lives determine who we are and how we interact with the world. Emotions provide us with data of what is happening in us as we relate to the world. Being aware of our sensations and emotions in the present moment and being able to name our feelings allows us to be more at choice regarding our actions.

> *I was given a box of darkness. Only later did I discover this was a gift.*
>
> — *Mary Oliver*

We can think of the word emotion as E + motion. The E is for energy in motion. Emotions support us in moving toward what we perceive is important and moving away from what is not. Emotions are like waves of energy that pass through us and mobilize or immobilize us from taking action. For example, if you are excited about exploring a new place, you are more likely to plan a holiday to visit. If you become aware that you are tired, you will likely take a break or a breath to reenergize yourself. Our sensations and emotions are messengers that give us data about what's happening in us so we can respond and make choices that serve us.

Emotions alert us when to say yes or no to something. We interpret our emotions and sensations by naming our feelings. Sensations are the raw data from which emotions emerge, and we name them feelings. For example, if we are on a high plank between buildings, we may sense our heart beating and experience the emotion of fear or excitement. One person will say, "I feel excited," and another will say, "I feel afraid." Feelings provide us with clues about where to pay attention, where to focus our energy, and what actions to take. What differentiates successful leaders, professionals, teachers, parents, and all humans is not just their IQs but also their ability to be aware of their and others' emotions and then know how to work with this awareness. This is emotional intelligence (EQ).

Many of us become so busy or distracted that we do not notice our emotions or name our feelings. If we listen to and actually feel them in our bodies, emotions serve us by calling our attention to things that help us be more effective. Naming our emotions and accepting them without judgment supports us in shifting to having access to more of our brain, the neocortex, and being more at choice. It is useful to have an open mindset and welcome our sensations and emotions as bringing us messages. Research supports that when we attend to our emotions, we enhance our health and wellbeing.[5]

Emotions arise from the chemicals released in the brain. These can be dopamine, oxytocin, or serotonin, for enlivening or high-frequency emotions such as joy, gratitude, and excitement, and adrenaline and cortisol for depleting or low-frequency emotions such as anger, worry, and sadness. Emotions are a natural part of our being and serve to protect us. When we are in potential danger, our survival mechanisms are activated in the amygdala part of the brain, which allows us to react immediately. At times, our behavior may seem irrational when we feel threatened. However, when we are aware our prefrontal cortex is activated, we can slow down, reflect on our behavior, and make choices that serve us.

---

[5] Frederickson, Barbara. *Love 2.0: Creating Happiness and Health in Moments of Connection.*

JOYBeing

Being emotionally aware of what is happening inside us provides us with information about what's important to us and what we want or don't want. With this awareness, we can express ourselves more clearly, resolve differences, and engage in more effective relationships. When we are unaware of our emotions, we are more likely to act out automatically and engage in habitual patterns that may no longer serve us.

Numerous studies show that awareness of our emotions or emotional agility can help people alleviate stress, reduce errors, become more innovative, and improve job performance.[6]

To manage our energy, we need to pay attention to our inner landscape and our emotions. Sometimes, our attention can become so focused on our external environment that we become disconnected from ourselves and our emotions, including our joy and passion. This can easily result in stress and dissatisfaction. However, it is never too late to reconnect with our emotions and our inner richness, which is always available to us.

Without the skill of noticing and addressing our emotions, we tend to suppress or numb ourselves, blame others, move away from what is present, and experience less satisfaction and joy. When we live disconnected from our emotions, we are disconnected from nature and life. Emotional awareness is the first step toward building emotional intelligence, a critical skill that requires continual practice.

Children naturally experience emotions and express feelings like curiosity, anger, and joy. As we grow up, based on our upbringing, we learn how to manage and express our emotions. Some of us are taught to ignore and numb emotions, while others are encouraged to express them. We are influenced by many factors, including our families, institutions, communities, and cultures, which affect our view of the role of emotions and giving voice to feelings. With awareness and practice, we can become skilled at enhancing our emotional awareness.

---

[6] David, Susan. *Emotional Agility: Get Unstuck, Embrace Change, and Thrive in Work and Life.*

Why Emotions Are Vital for a Thriving Inner Garden of JOYBeing

Joy happens in the moment, and it is a positive experience. JOYBeing is our ability to be with all emotions, including what many of us label as difficult or negative emotions. We believe our emotions carry messages for us. Of course, some emotions are uncomfortable, and we prefer to act out or disconnect from them. However, if we are able to be curious and compassionate to see the wisdom in the messages emotions carry, then we can take a different perspective, learn, and be more at choice. With this JOYBeing mindset, we actually experience more joy, openness, and aliveness. JOYBeing embodies and enables us to experience the moving energy inside of us.

The emotions we try to push aside or hide don't vanish; they linger in our subconscious, craving attention and affecting our relationships and wellbeing. These depleting emotions limit our ability to manage our life energy. They act as directors, influencing and shaping how we interact with others, how our bodies feel, and how we show up in the world, blocking our joy. These emotions demand to be heard, draining our energy and affecting our mental and physical health until we acknowledge them.

But one day, we realize every emotion, even the messy and painful ones, deserves a place within us. We learn to face them head-on, embracing them instead of avoiding or numbing them. By showering these neglected feelings with love, attention, and understanding, we provide them with a home in our hearts, freeing ourselves from their control. This shift allows us to break free from the cycle of suppressing emotions and explore a new path of self-acceptance and emotional closeness, leading to a sense of relief and unleashing our creative energy.

Rather than refer to emotions as positive or negative, we refer to them as enlivening or depleting our energy. In his book *Power vs. Force*, David Hawkins calculated the energetic frequencies of different emotional states. Even though his research methodology is not universally accepted, his thinking is useful for us to identify high-frequency and low-frequency emotions rather than labeling emotions as positive or negative. When we experience a high frequency or enlivening emotion such as gratitude, joy, or peace, we feel lighter, at ease, and have more energy to take action; therefore, we may experience more abundance. When we experience low-frequency or depleting emotions such as fear, worry, or apathy, we are likely to feel heavier and sluggish, requiring more energy to move. We sometimes say we feel drained and refrain from taking action.

JOYBeing is our ability to hold and be with all of our emotions, no matter their frequency. It is a muscle and way of being that needs to be cultivated. It doesn't happen by itself; we need to do the work required to live a life of JOYBeing and come back to our center with a sense of openness to what is happening inside and around us.

All emotions are interconnected and present in us as a system. When we numb ourselves, trying to control or protect ourselves from disturbing emotions that are perceived as negative, we also close ourselves to the full range of emotions, including joy. The way to have access to high-frequency or enlivening emotions is by attending to and accepting even those emotions that create discomfort in us.

Emotions live in our bodies, and we benefit by noticing our sensations and where we experience them in our bodies. There is always wisdom to learn when we pay attention to our somatic experiences. Perhaps you feel a tightness in your stomach. By understanding emotions

Ann

In the OASIS Conversations course I teach to leaders, a participant shared that he had experimented with the process of being open, present, and giving empathy to his sixth-grade son. He excitedly said it was the closest he had ever felt to his son. After the weekend, his son hugged him and said, "I loved being with you, Dad. I love who you are. You've changed. I am so happy." The father reported that previously he had focused on telling his son what to do rather than how to be present and connect with him. The change was transformative for both of them.

After hearing this story, I felt a tingling in my core, a sense of vitality and joy, and an inner smile. I felt grounded and delighted to be doing this kind of work. Genuine connection matters to me. I felt I belonged with this leader and the class participants. I experience joy when I feel I am contributing to the others' quality of life and making a difference. I am hopeful about what is possible.

JOYBeing manifests when I feel a deep connection and belonging with friends and family. I treasure moments of heartfelt conversations. I feel more myself and joyful when I am moving and have a sense of vitality and thriving, am physically healthy, and am psychologically sound. The joy of a creative flow, whether writing, drawing, learning, or designing workshops, is another source of fulfillment for me. I also enjoy being in nature and feeling the fullness of life when near water and trees, as well as when listening to music.

Recognizing the importance of these sources of joy, I've consciously worked to incorporate them into my life. I've learned that to experience joy in these and other areas, I need to let go of old patterns of being overly responsible for others and worrying about others. I need to allow myself to be in the moment and trust the process of life. By paying attention, you, too, can listen to the messages of joy and discover what fills you with the essence of being alive—JOYBeing. We each will find unique ways of connecting with our joy and aliveness.

Gila

My life has been a search toward finding and experiencing joy, an endeavor to make my existence shine with a radiant glow. My journey toward joy became clearer when I confronted my sadness, granting expression to the long-repressed parts of myself that yearned for acknowledgment. This pivotal shift happened after a tragic event—my father's sudden passing when I was twenty-six. My body spoke harshly to me when I suppressed my emotions, expressing its distress in a severe lower spine problem.

For years, I resisted the recommended operation, choosing to carry the burden of pain. Only much later, after extensive self-work and therapy, did I gain awareness of my ingrained patterns and how I had neglected my body for so long. The turning point came when I allowed space for tears and unearthed suppressed emotions, listening to their messages and giving permission for my reality to surface.

This newfound channel opened the door to a transformative process where I began to befriend my body, offering it the attention it had long deserved. Only in recent years did I find the courage to breathe new life into those worn-out parts that seemed beyond healing without surgery. By granting permission and liberating my body to finally receive the longing it desired, I was able to open space to a profound connection of JOYBeing and started working toward cultivating a powerful, centered leadership presence. My journey underscores the transformative power of embracing vulnerability and honoring the profound dialogue between my emotions and physical wellbeing.

---

intend to serve us, we can explore the sensation and its message. For example, you may feel worried, and that pushes you to take action to work hard, ask for a raise, or seek a new job. Our worry acts as a catalyst for understanding what is happening within us and taking actions aligned with our values and needs. With awareness, we can become aware of how our emotions may be serving us.

A financially secure person may still continue to worry about money because of old beliefs and habitual patterns. Becoming aware of our emotions and related life stories helps us be more at choice in creating our reality. So, rather than avoid or look away from low-frequency emotions, we can work with them by acknowledging them, giving them empathy, and making choices that serve us to experience a life of JOYBeing.

We can all learn to pay attention to what is happening in our bodies, our sensations, and our emotions. When we experience JOYBeing, we are more connected and attuned to ourselves, others, and our environment, and we are open to exploring our emotions. From this nonjudgmental space, we are open and more aware of our choices and possibilities.

Emotions represent different parts of ourselves. We want to embrace all of our emotions with kindness and respect to experience JOYBeing. With awareness, we can appreciate an emotion's reason for existence, and we are better able to make choices aligned with our values, who we are, and who we are becoming.

When we are not aware of what we are feeling, we can have the sense that our emotions control us, and we can fall into a trap where we allow them to dominate our lives through the stories we create. For example, if we experience anxiety about speaking up in groups, we may create a story that we are not good enough and act accordingly, thinking we need to be fearful and refrain from sharing our views. With this continued emotion and thought pattern, we may refrain from speaking, which could result in being invisible, dimming our presence, and failing to share our message.

We have a natural negativity bias built in to protect us. Our first instinct is to be aware of possible threats where we are disposed to experience lower-frequency emotions or what researcher Barbara Frederickson calls negative emotions. Her research suggests that in order to stay healthy and vital, we need to experience a 3:1 ratio of positive to negative emotions.[7]

We believe that with awareness and purposeful and intentional choice, we can take the responsibility of experiencing more high-frequency emotions and a wider perspective. If our natural response is to move toward anxiety and worry as a way of protection, we can be conscious and, with awareness of our bias, choose to be compassionate and curious. In this way, we can intentionally choose how to use our energy. For example, we can choose to reach out to a friend or spend time in activities that rejuvenate us and create a life of JOYBeing. If we notice we are negatively comparing ourselves to others, we can give ourselves empathy and self-compassion, allowing us to connect to the treasures of our inner garden and appreciate who we are.

Becoming aware of what we are experiencing inside our bodies is valuable. We must notice our sensations, emotions, and thoughts. Otherwise, they can control us, and we can feel like victims. A positive perspective or an Open Stance leads us to possibilities that support us in learning, growing, and enhancing our health and relationships. We will now explore how to work with our emotions.

> *Comparison is the thief of joy.*
>
> *Theodore Roosevelt*

---

[7] Frederickson, Barbara. *Positivity: Top-Notch Research Reveals the 3 to 1 Ratio That Will Change Your Life.*

How to Work with Emotions

We have been trained to focus our attention on the external world. This training is reinforced by our surroundings, including our family, schools, and workplaces. In addition, some of us fear focusing on our inner world, which includes our thoughts, feelings, and emotions, since we don't know what we might discover or what to do with what we have discovered. Most of us have not been taught or learned how to work and process our inner landscape. Only in recent years have emotional and social intelligence skills been introduced in schools.

To avoid painful or difficult emotions, many of us keep ourselves busy and distracted. For example, we may work a lot or overdo things such as exercising, shopping, eating, spending time on social media, and playing video games. These can be unconscious ways of avoiding emotions.

We also have an inner voice, often known as the inner critic, that constantly chatters, giving us directions on how to live. (We will explore how to work with our inner critic in the next chapter.) Because we can become overwhelmed by this voice and the related emotions, we may tend to distract and numb ourselves rather than be open and curious to explore their actual messages for us. When we numb ourselves to avoid uncomfortable emotions, we cut ourselves off from the energy of life and our aliveness and joy. All emotions are inseparable and exist in a bundle. Like a faucet, when we close ourselves to what we perceive as negative, we limit the full range of emotions, including what we perceive as positive.

Emotions are central to a meaningful life. When we learn to be, work with them, and process them, we take responsibility for our lives. We become the driver rather than the victim and manage emotions with respect.

Growing Emotional Wellness: 4A Recipe for Working with Emotions

Understanding and managing our emotions brings clarity, energy, wellbeing, and possibilities. We offer the following recipe for processing emotions, which are ingredients for creating emotional stability and JOYBeing. These steps are: *Awaken, Attend, Acknowledge, and Act.*

This process applies not only to emotions that may be disturbing to us, but also to strengthening and creating embodiment for high-frequency emotions.

Awaken (Notice Sensations and Become Aware of Emotions)

An emotion lasts ninety seconds in our body. Yet we can keep repeating and revisiting an emotion. It's the story that we create around an emotion that lasts longer and sometimes for a lifetime. Like the music and the words of a song, our emotions and the related narrative around it are two separate entities that need exploration. We need awareness and the ability to separate the story and our assumptions from the emotions as a way of being in contact with ourselves in order to be more at choice.

When we awaken to an emotion, we are able to notice our sensations and become aware of where that emotion lives in our body. When a baby cries, it's a sign for a parent to awaken and pay attention to what's happening. When you are cooking and you put your hand on a hot pot, you immediately awaken to the sensation and pull your hand back.

When you receive criticism, it is useful to notice your sensations and emotions before you react without awareness or deny their impact. For example, you may feel a tightness in your chest or stomach, a shallow breath, or a contraction in your body.

Noticing our high-frequency emotions is also important since it builds positive energy and strengthens our motivation to live fully and with meaning. It's valuable to notice a joyful moment in an interaction with a friend when you feel connected. For example, awaken to a moment of laughing or vulnerable sharing where you feel a sense of ease and comfort. Awaken to this moment by noticing your sensations, such as warmth in your chest and a smile on your face.

Awakening is noticing and being open to experiencing our sensations.
- ✓ What are you aware of inside yourself or in your environment that is catching your attention?
- ✓ Notice your sensation and where it lives in your body.

> Sometimes when you are in a dark place, you think you have been buried, but you have actually been planted.
>
> *Christine Caine*

Attend (Be With, Give Space to, Make Contact)

Attending is about paying attention and being with an emotion. It's about making space to be present and in contact with our experience. It is not avoiding or exaggerating but facing what is. Part of attending is paying attention to the conditions or past experiences that influence our experience. This is a reality check to see how the emotion is related to our background and related assumptions and whether it holds true for this moment.

When a parent naturally goes to check on a crying child to feel and understand what the child is experiencing, they are attending to the child and the child's needs. When your hand is burnt, you examine the injury and pay attention to your experience to assess what is needed.

After you notice the sensation of a critical statement in your body, such as a contraction in your throat or a tightness in your chest, rather than deny, numb, or exaggerate, you can be with the experience to understand and make meaning. Being with an emotion requires curiosity and openness rather than judgment.

As we attend, we create the ground for exploring and naming the emotion. For example, a critical comment could create the emotions of hurt, anger, or disappointment.

When you genuinely connect with a friend and attend to your positive experience of what gets evoked in you, you allow space for the flow of new energy. By being with the experience of contentment, joy, or gratitude, one is able to strengthen the muscle of creating cellular awareness of this positive emotion.

Attending is staying with an emotion and trusting that it will create new awareness. It is saying, "I see you" to the emotions. Here are ways to attend to your emotions:

Stay with your sensations and your emotions without judgment.
- ✓ What is the narrative you are creating?
  - ✓ Is this emotion familiar to you? How?
    - ✓ What is its message for you?

Acknowledge (Empathize and Accept with Compassion; Embody and Embrace Emotions)

Acknowledging is naming, embracing, and accepting our emotions—whatever they may be, without

CHAPTER 3 Tilling the Soil: Connecting with Our Emotions

judgment or bias. It is also about being compassionate and giving yourself empathy.

The parent will cuddle the child and say, "I feel your sadness. You are sad, cold, hungry, afraid, etc. I am here with you. You are safe with me."

With a burned hand, you may say to yourself, "I feel the pain. It hurts. I am and will be okay. I can handle this." This response is an alternative to belittling and criticizing yourself for this incident, and you may rush to call it a stupid mistake.

You can accept a critical statement and become curious to learn more. You can give yourself permission to feel the emotion and give yourself some space before you respond. You may say to yourself, "I am hurt, upset, or disappointed. I need to take a breath. I am okay and learning. I am noticing what I need." For example, you may recognize that based on your past, you might be overreacting or notice your tendency to deny your emotions.

Acknowledging emotions such as anger, hurt, or disappointment enables us to shift from our automatic reaction and choose how we will respond. We may notice a natural reaction to say yes to a request rather than decline when we have too much on our plate. By embracing our emotions, we appreciate their message and free up energy for action. We move from reactivity to responsiveness. Rather than fume about a request or a demand, we can become more aware and accepting of what we need.

A lot of us fail to attend to and acknowledge our high-frequency emotions, such as when we experience a connection with a friend or receive a compliment. We need to give ourselves permission to marinate and savor positive emotions rather than deflecting and moving away from them. Acknowledging high-frequency emotions like joy and gratitude creates expansion and embodiment, which enhances JOYBeing.

Acknowledgment is accepting and embracing all of our emotions and giving them permission to be and live in our bodies. We can acknowledge by asking ourselves:
✓ What do I need to be with and embrace this emotion? How can I be empathetic and compassionate?
✓ How is this emotion serving me?
✓ Can I appreciate its purpose and value in my life?

Act (Make a Choice, Affirm, Take Mindful Action)

With acknowledgment and compassion, we are positioned to take action with more intention, awareness, choice, and openness. Actions will depend on the situation and can include affirmations.

Ideally, a child will stop crying when comforted by a parent because she feels safe and supported. She can then go back to sleep or back to playing with ease. We want to be this kind of parent to ourselves, one who acknowledges emotions and takes the responsibility of providing support.

Once we feel soothed after a burned hand, we can put creme or a cold compress on it and continue cooking rather than deserting our cooking project or culinary aspirations. You may give yourself the affirmation, "I am a good cook."

When we experience a critical statement or a demanding request from someone, we can choose to share our experience, offer feedback, and express our needs.

We can thank a person who shares their perspective. We can say, "I heard you and appreciate your input. Tell me more." We can say to ourselves, "I am open to learning and growing."

High-frequency or positive emotions naturally move us toward action. For example, we may naturally thank our friend as we experience gratitude and connection and plan our next interaction.

As we experience joy or openness, we inspire this emotion in others. Both high-frequency and low-frequency (enlivening and depleting) emotions are contagious. Being aware of our emotions is important so we can better choose what to cherish in ourselves and in our interactions with others. Ask yourself:

- ✓ What is an action I can take based on my awareness?
- ✓ What is a new meaning I can give to this experience after having explored the emotion?
- ✓ What is an affirmation that will support me?

Practicing the 4A Recipe

Using the 4A recipe supports us in processing emotions and creates a sense of confidence and fulfillment.

When we make contact with our emotions, we liberate and connect with the music of our true selves. Like a seed blossoming into a beautiful flower, we connect with our infinite source. Just as our bodies know how to naturally heal injuries and illnesses, we all have the ability to connect with our emotions and experience healing through the wisdom of our inner life.

We believe that JOYBeing is our essence. We are born with it, but through our life experiences, it gets covered over. What if it were possible to be in the open, joyful JOYBeing state more often rather than just for brief moments? It is possible, and we can make it our way of being and living in the world. This way of being requires intention, awareness, choice, and practice, which is the path for JOYBeing.

We are always responding to external circumstances that affect our internal emotional ground. JOYBeing is less about what is actually happening outside of us and more about how we interpret what is happening and manage our energy.

Given our backgrounds and experiences, we have developed patterns for making sense of the world around us. For example, if your child gets a low grade in school, you may be upset and create a story that they will not be successful in life. Most likely, you learned that being successful requires good grades. As another example, you may experience anxiety when you don't get a raise at work because you then believe you will never have the home and life you desire.

We often create stories that feed our anxiety and worry. This tendency has served us by putting us on alert to protect ourselves. However, it also has its costs. It is natural to fall into our habitual patterns and experience low-frequency emotions. When we become aware of feeling like a victim and allow circumstances to overpower our emotions, we can remember our intention to experience JOYBeing and notice we have a choice in our response. We can appreciate the rhythm of life and that there are always challenges.

Meet Victor—A Professional

Victor is a career-driven professional who embodies ambition. He strives tirelessly for success and recognition in his demanding career. Despite his dedication and hard work, he has a lingering sense of emptiness, a void where joy and satisfaction should reside. Eager to unlock the secrets to infusing his professional journey with genuine happiness and fulfillment, Victor is on a quest to discover strategies to propel him toward tremendous success and nurture his inner sense of aliveness.

"I've climbed the corporate ladder, achieved milestones, and earned accolades, but amid all the hustle," says Victor. "I can't shake off this feeling of emptiness. There has to be more to success than just ticking off goals. I crave a sense of joy and aliveness that transcends professional achievements. I am not sure where to begin."

Victor's heartfelt words echo the sentiments of many career-driven individuals who, like him, are chained to the relentless pursuit of success. They, too, yearn for a deeper, more meaningful experience in both their professional and personal lives. Victor's realization about his lack of joy, that his worth is primarily defined by his career achievements and external success, strikes a chord with many.

Victor neglected his inner sense of joy and wellbeing while continuously pursuing external validation and career accomplishments. It is easy to chase

success without finding true satisfaction or fulfillment. Victor needed to learn to enjoy and be present in the journey. He could not expect to sustain the joy of reaching a mountain's peak, but he could learn to savor the trek. He needed to discover how to authentically connect with his inner garden and find joy and satisfaction.

Using the 4A Recipe, Victor learned to become aware of and feel his emotions. He attended to his sense of emptiness and noticed the narrative he was creating, which was familiar to him. He recognized that he felt he was only of value when he was striving. He noticed that this way of being was not serving him, and he was able to be empathetic and self-compassionate toward himself. He could also appreciate his efforts.

Ann

Since I grew up around anger, trauma, and disagreement, an overarching question has consistently captivated me: How can people with diverse perspectives coexist and collaborate harmoniously? I have worked to become aware of and manage my reactions and beliefs about how things "should" be.

For years, my exploration and teaching have centered around empowering leaders with the ability to offer empathy and cultivate emotional intelligence through a process I term OASIS Conversations. Within this framework, I underscore the significance of keenly observing our reactions and transitioning to an open mindset. Noticing our judgments and reactions and taking an Open Stance are critical skills for effective interactions. We can be more responsive and create meaningful connections when we know how to work with our emotions.

When I began applying the skill of treating my internal sensations and emotions as a caring parent would attend to a young child, I gave myself space to be with my emotions with curiosity and without judgment. I refrained from denying or reacting to painful emotions.

For example, when I sense a tightness in my chest and feel misunderstood by a family member, I now consciously resist my habitual patterns of reacting, retreating, or ignoring my feelings. Instead, as a parent would offer to a child, I allow space to attend and listen within. I then acknowledge and give myself empathy: "You feel hurt and disappointed." I recognize that my emotions are giving me the message that this relationship is important to me, and I am aware of my need to be respected and understood.

This mindful approach lets me relax and shift away from defensiveness and hurt, fostering a newfound curiosity about the other person's intentions. With increased capacity, I articulate my needs, share my experience, and engage in constructive conversation. I remind myself that we are all conditioned to react and often lack effective feedback skills.

The 4A process, encompassing Awakening, Attending, Acknowledging, and Acting, deepens my sense of inner awareness and JOYBeing. The more I embrace this practice of working with my emotions as a compassionate parent would with a child, the greater my acceptance of myself and others becomes and the more enhanced the sense of JOYBeing I experience.

Based on this awareness, he adopted the affirmation, "I am worthy simply as I am. I am enough without the striving." He reminded himself of this regularly.

With the adoption of the JOYBeing mindset and support of the 4A Recipe, Victor's perspective on self-worth expanded beyond career achievements and financial gains. This shift in thinking led him to explore other sources of fulfillment, such as relationships, self-care, and hobbies. The profound change in his outlook opened up new avenues of joy and aliveness, demonstrating the transformative power of a shifted mindset and new practices.

Victor envisioned a "balanced inner garden" where he could nurture his wellbeing and inner sense of joy. He planted seeds of self-discovery, self-care, personal reflection, and growth as foundational plants. He reconnected with old friends with whom he had lost touch. Victor focused on cultivating the plant of self-awareness, allowing him to understand his values, desires, and needs beyond his career ambitions. By tending his garden, he nurtured deeper connections with himself and others, fostering a sense of authenticity and fulfillment beyond professional success.

Gila

On February 6, 2023, when an earthquake struck eastern Turkey, the entire country, including myself, struggled with trauma, feeling a spectrum of emotions—fear, uncertainty, anxiety, helplessness, and pain. My immediate concern was the safety of those in the affected area, particularly my friends and extended family. Sadly, we discovered losses among our close circles.

Being far away intensified my feelings of helplessness and pain, leading to moments of guilt for having safety, shelter, and my children with me. But as I allowed myself time to embrace and understand these emotions, I found space to explore how I could be a support from a distance. By giving myself empathy, I was eventually able to mobilize myself. I initiated a project with a colleague for an NGO. Our goal was to carry out group sessions with a group of coaches from our Gestalt coaching school to help those affected by the earthquake navigate their pain. I aimed to guide them to understand their feelings of helplessness, sorrow, loss, and any emotion that was present so they could embrace themselves, voice out their pain, and eventually make contact with their inner resources.

Amid such intense trauma, permitting myself to attend and acknowledge my pain allowed me to transition to a state of JOYBeing. Staying in all these emotions, I was able to accept and transform my victimhood mentality, choosing instead to act from a place of empowerment and agency. In moments of trauma, grief is inevitable, and we all process our emotions in our unique time and manner in our sacred space. This giving space, time, and permission to accept the "what is" opens the connection to JOYBeing.

JOYBeing is our ability to be with our full range of emotions, giving them the space they need. We can use this energy for choices that serve the moment. With practice, we can build the muscle to move from the sense of being a victim to our resilient self.

Practices

1. EXPLORING EMOTIONS

Using the prompts below, explore an emotion that is most present for you at this moment.

✓ Name your present emotion.

✓ Where does it live in your body?

✓ Notice how familiar and frequently it is present in your life.

✓ Under what circumstances does it appear?

✓ What is the story you have created around this emotion?

Explore other emotions that you frequently experience.
Work with them using the questions above to gain more understanding.

CHAPTER 3 Tilling the Soil: Connecting with Our Emotions

2. OBSERVING AND NAMING OUR EMOTIONS

Naming our emotions and being aware of them and our thoughts is a key part of being emotionally intelligent. Try a little experiment. Notice how you feel when you say:

✓ I am angry.

✓ I feel angry.

✓ Something in me is angry.

Which one feels more comfortable to you?

Notice your experience with each of these statements. Creating some distance allows us to look at our emotions with more objectivity. In working with low-frequency emotions, when we change our internal language, we can be more available to be present with more resources to stay and process the emotion. In this way, we are allowing the observer part of ourselves to pay attention without judgment.

> **We cannot cure the world of sorrows, but we can choose to live in joy.**
>
>

Practices

3. USING THE 4A RECIPE

Using the 4A recipe will allow you to dive deeper and enhance or reframe your experience to formulate a narrative that will serve you to create new possibilities and a new way of being.

Identify an emotion you are experiencing and experiment with the 4A recipe using the questions below. This involves slowing down to connect with your sensations and emotions before immediately reacting.

Awake
- What am I aware of inside myself or in my environment that is catching my attention?
- What bodily sensations am I aware of? Where am I experiencing them in my body?

Attend
- Stay with your sensations and experience your emotions without judgment.
- What is the narrative I am creating around it?
- Is this emotion familiar? How?
- What is its message to me?

Acknowledge
- Name your emotion.
- What do I need to be with to embrace this emotion?
- How can I be empathetic and compassionate?
- How is this emotion serving me?
- Can I appreciate its purpose and value?

Act
- What is an action I can take based on my awareness?
- What is a new meaning I can give to this experience after having explored the emotion?
- What is an affirmation that will support me?

4. BREATHING TO TRANSFORM EMOTIONS

When we move the energy in our body, we feel energized and are able to regulate our emotions.

The first thing we do when we are born is breathe. As adults, we take between twelve to twenty breaths per minute, thus supplying oxygen to our cells and eliminating toxins from the body. Yet most of us don't give much attention to our breath.

Many useful forms of breathing exist. Here is one option we have been practicing and find valuable.

1. Take a steady breath in through both nostrils.
2. Inhale for four counts.
3. Hold your breath for two counts.
4. Exhale through your mouth for six counts.
5. Hold again for two.
6. Repeat the process.

The exhale should be longer than the inhale. The longer exhale activates our parasympathetic system, which creates more calmness and relaxation. Repeat five to six times.

Notice how this exercise affects you.

Pranayama is the control of breath. *Prana* stands for life force, while *yama* means control. Pranayama (life energy) is the practice of breath regulation. It's a main component of yoga. According to classical yogic texts, *prana* is the energy of the universe. Through breathing, we can control its intake. Daily Pranayama positively affects the autonomic nervous system. By breaking our unconscious breathing patterns, we are able to embark on a journey toward a higher state of awareness, aliveness, and joy.

Practices

BREATHING WITH INTENTION

Paying attention regulates our breath. By bringing more attention and intention to our breath as we inhale and exhale, we can create more life energy. With our inhale, we plant new seeds, and with our exhale, we let go of what doesn't serve us. For example, breathe in joy and release stress.

The list below can serve as a guide for choosing what you desire and what you want to release.

Inhale/Breathe In	Exhale/Breathe Out—Release
Serenity	Stress
Flexibility	Rigidity
Courage	Doubt
Positivity	Negativity
Abundance	Resentment
Health	Fear
Prosperity	Anger
Vitality	Something of the Past
More Joy	Frustration
Confidence	Sadness
Self-Love	Any Judgments
Self-Compassion	Negative Inner Chatter
Inner Peace	Impatience
Self-Worth	Limiting Beliefs
Gratitude	Discontent

CHAPTER 3 Tilling the Soil: Connecting with Our Emotions

Ann

I have delved into various mindfulness practices, recognizing my inclination to set ambitious goals and keep a busy pace. Transforming this tendency has been profound. I've intentionally carved out space for simply being and elevating awareness. Conscious breathing has emerged as a stalwart companion in calming my body and energizing my spirit. Each day, I take a few minutes to connect with gratitude and JOYBeing by journaling moments of positivity and joy, followed by about ten minutes dedicated to deliberate, mindful breathing.

Many forms of breathing can be explored. Focusing on the in-breath through my nostrils and allowing the out-breath to be twice as long with my mouth open has become a conduit to connect with the essence of JOYBeing. Additionally, directing my attention to my heart and visualizing its expansion as I breathe has proven a powerful practice. I review my commitment to taking an Open Stance and experiencing JOYBeing.

Cultivating this simple routine requires commitment amid the demands vying for our attention and the allure of busyness. However, allowing a few minutes to breathe consciously serves us and extends to our community. I encourage you to embark on your own experiment and observe the potential effect on your life and the lives of those in your sphere of influence.

> " *You are the sky. Everything else— it's just the weather.*
>
> — *Pema Chödrön*

CHAPTER 4

Weeding: Unearthing Obstacles to Cultivating a JOYBeing Garden

"If the first two decades of the twenty-first century have taught us anything, it is that uncertainty is chronic, instability is permanent, disruption is common and we can neither predict nor govern events. There will be no new normal. There will only be a continuous series of not normal episodes defying prediction and unforeseen by most of us until they happen."

Jim Collins

JOYBeing

Like a skilled gardener who meticulously tends to their garden, removing rocks and weeds to create fertile ground for flourishing plants, we can dedicate ourselves to nurturing our inner garden, clearing obstacles to allow our true potential to thrive. In the rhythm of life, we face many challenges and meet people and circumstances that may not always align with our expectations, aspirations, and desires. It's essential to look deep within ourselves, recognize our sensations, and remove the barriers that disrupt our balance, as well as address the invasive weeds that threaten to choke our vitality.

Imagine the rocks in our inner garden as the barriers that impede growth. These may manifest as judgment, fear, limiting beliefs, or self-doubt that stand in the way of our full potential. Just as a gardener removes these hindrances to allow the roots of plants to anchor deeply in nourishing soil, we can unearth and manage the mental and emotional blocks that hinder our evolution.

Similarly, the weeds in our inner garden symbolize the negative influences, beliefs, and unproductive patterns that limit our energy and suffocate our ability to experience joy and aliveness. Just as weeds compete with plants for nutrients and sunlight, these obstacles can suppress our sense of aliveness and drain our energy. When we uproot these limiting weeds, we cultivate a space where positivity, joy, growth, and resilience can thrive.

By conscientiously tending our inner garden and clearing away the obstacles that hinder our joy and aliveness, we create a fertile environment for personal growth, self-discovery, and transformation. We create the conditions for a well-tended garden to blossom with vibrant life, beauty, and the experience of JOYBeing.

Reacting vs. Responding to Differences and Uncertainty

We live in a pivotal time when we face polarization, globalization, technical changes, climate disruptions, political and economic uncertainty, inequities, systemic changes, and conflict. It is easy to feel perplexed and ungrounded and miss our connection to joy. We close down, contract, and engage in judgment as we focus on surviving amid our many challenges. Some wonder how we can experience joy and aliveness amid this uncertainty.

It is natural to close down and become self-protective when a situation causes us to make judgments of others or of situations. For example, it is easy to react when we feel someone is disrespectful by being late, has a different view, doesn't respond to our email, or simply is rude in how they speak to us. We also react when we worry about local and global conflicts or the likely impact of war and artificial intelligence. Our patterns of reacting become so habitual and automatic that we don't search for other possibilities. We react when people and situations do not meet our expectations and when we sense people are being mistreated. We are continually making judgments and believe we are "right." We are often unaware that being judgmental and reacting rather than responding with intention and choice detracts from our sense of joy and aliveness.

> **Attunement means that we are willing to be present with each other and to meet each other exactly where we are.**
>
> *Thomas Hübl*

When we become aware that we are judgmental and closed, we can learn to manage our reactions and energy and instead be a positive force for change. When we take an Open Stance to the rhythm of life, we can experience greater aliveness and positively influence those in our spheres.

We cannot escape the challenges of life that inevitably arise. These challenges come in various forms, from personal struggles to external obstacles, and they are an inescapable part of the human experience. However, each situation we encounter can be viewed from multiple perspectives. How we choose to handle these challenges truly makes a difference. By adopting a positive and proactive mindset, we can transform difficulties into opportunities for growth, learning, and self-improvement.

Responding to situations, rather than reacting impulsively, is crucial for maintaining emotional balance and making thoughtful decisions. When we respond, we take a moment to assess the situation, consider the possible outcomes, and choose a course of action that aligns with our values and long-term goals. This measured approach involves checking in with our sensations and recognizing what's happening within us, allowing us to understand our emotional triggers and manage them effectively. This self-awareness helps to avoid misunderstandings, reduces conflict, and fosters more constructive and positive interactions with others. In contrast, reacting often leads to hasty, emotion-driven actions that can escalate tensions and create unintended consequences. In these times, we lose the power of attunement and connection with ourselves and others.

This shift to being open not only helps us navigate through tough times, but it generates more life, energy, and growth on our journey. These challenges shape us and build our resilience. Instead of viewing difficulties as obstacles in our way, we can approach them with a mindset of curiosity and openness to create our ability to live life more fully. This acceptance opens new space for moments of peace and joy as we appreciate the ups and downs, the richness and the rhythm of life.

Take a breath and reflect for a moment:

- ✓ Can you imagine how your interactions would be different if you could weed out your automatic and habitual reactions and judgmental posture?

- ✓ When faced with a difficult situation, where is your focus? Is it on the problem, the potential solution, or what's happening in you?

- ✓ How do your thoughts and attitudes shape your experience of challenges?

- ✓ Can you recall a time when changing your perspective turned a challenging situation into an opportunity?

- ✓ What did you do differently?

- ✓ How does your response to challenges influence your overall energy and motivation?

Adopting an Open Stance

Adopting an Open Stance and responsive approach to the rhythm of life involves adopting flexibility and adaptability in our daily experiences. Instead of resisting unexpected changes, we can cultivate a mindset that welcomes spontaneity and sees value in life's unpredictability. This mindset supports us to remain present and attuned to the subtle cues and shifts in our environment, allowing us to respond thoughtfully to whatever arises. By doing so, we foster resilience, aliveness, and JOYBeing; then we are no longer struggling against life's current but flowing harmoniously with it.

Taking an Open Stance is about noticing when we are contracted, in judgment, controlling, or closed and, with awareness, shifting to being curious, compassionate, courageous, kind, and open to possibilities. From an Open Stance, we can more resiliently attend to our environment, embrace the present moment, and realize potential. When we remove the weeds and rocks, the plants grow and thrive easily.

Amid this tumultuous time of significant changes and events in the world, we continually interact with people with different perspectives and ways of doing

> *We cannot sow seeds with clenched fists. To sow we must open our hands.*
>
> *Adolfo Pérez Esquivel*

things. One of the most critical skills needed, especially for leaders, parents, coaches, and people who want to make a difference, is the ability to be open and calm amid differences and uncertainty to thrive. When we are closed or contracted, we see fewer options. Our amygdala is activated, and we have less access to our prefrontal cortex. When we know how to regulate our nervous system, we can support others in coregulating and seeing possibilities. When we are open, we naturally support others in being open. As we become aware, we can better deal with the intensity of our emotions and reactions and those of others. We benefit from noticing when we are closed and judgmental toward others, situations, and ourselves.

Taking an Open Stance starts by noticing our internal sensations or signals of when we are contracted or in judgment. We recognize that emotions are messengers. Rather than reacting impulsively or negatively, we stop, step back, and cool down. Then, with awareness and intention, we can shift to being curious and compassionate. We can engage in practices to build this mental muscle to be more skilled at stopping, stepping back, and ultimately, shifting to being open.

The more we practice checking in and noticing when we are somatically open or closed, the more we build the ability to catch ourselves from reacting and be the calm presence that can make a difference and experience joy. It is simple but challenging. Just like building our physical muscles, it takes consistent practice, and soon, we can lift a heavier weight. Given neuroplasticity and our ability to learn and grow, we know we can build this capacity.

It is valuable to identify your predominant somatic signal that indicates you are in judgment or reacting. For example, you may feel tight in your stomach or throat and have a loud inner voice saying what needs attention. You may feel your heart racing, your ears burning, or your face turning red or pale, or you may be fidgeting or feeling nervous. With awareness of our judgment, we can learn to stop, even when we genuinely sense we are correct

CHAPTER 4 Weeding: Unearthing Obstacles to Cultivating a JOYBeing Garden

(and don't want to pause). Then, we can identify what supports us in cooling down and shifting. Often, simply breathing more fully and recalling experiences of being open support us in knowing what it feels like to be somatically open. You may remember moments of being in nature or with friends that help you recall the expansive Open Stance experience of aliveness. We each have our own signals and can learn strategies that support us in shifting to being open.

A closed mindset rather than an open mindset, as mentioned earlier, floods our bodies with cortisol, triggering our amygdala and the fight-flight-freeze and appease response. On the other hand, when we're open and curious, we experience what scientists term a "tend and befriend" state. In this state, we're more likely to collaborate, attune to one another, and find a resonance of understanding. We experience a sense of aliveness and JOYBeing.

Suppose we can train ourselves to be open and embrace the unknown. In that case, we are better positioned to discover new possibilities.

Creativity and innovation can flourish when we are open.

It is valuable to recognize those moments when we are open to learning, open to others, and even open to ourselves. Pause and feel the sensation of openness in your body. One of our JOYBeing course participants, Nisha, has a favorite technique for fostering an open and curious mindset. She likes to recollect times when she was exploring a foreign land, curious, observing the differences, and relishing the mysteries to be uncovered. This Open Stance allows Nisha to see the world through various lenses. She finds this experience joyful and enlivening.

We can pivot more effectively from this open space and recognize common ground and possibilities. Emotions are contagious, and openness is contagious. When we adopt an Open Stance, we influence others with our curious, compassionate, courageous, and kind presence.

Stop

Step back & Cool down

Shift to being open

112

Unearthing and Quieting Our Critical Inner Voice

Just as we are judgmental and reactive toward others and situations in our environment, we can also react toward our inner self. Our thoughts and emotions are the manifestations of the different parts in us that talk to us internally. We benefit from being aware of the interaction of what's happening within us as well as what's happening externally. Giving space, listening, and engaging with our inner voices allows us to connect with ourselves and our world to make new meaning.

To fit into society and our community, we develop a critical inner voice—a voice of guidance that gives us direction about how we "should" behave. This internal critic emerges as a response to the societal norms, values, and expectations surrounding us. Its purpose is to serve us by helping us conform to social standards, meet expectations, and strive for success.

We all have childhood needs that were not satisfied, such as love, safety, trust, belonging, respect, and acceptance. This is part of the human condition. These unsatisfied parts may lead to various emotions such as fear, shame, anger, guilt, anxiety, and despair. When our needs are not met, our inner critic emerges to protect us. It often tells us who we "should" be or what we "should" be doing. The inner critic's voice offers messages that we usually translate into feelings of being rejected, fear of failure, being not good enough, trying to over-control, being a perfectionist, being restless, giving up, and many more.

Each of us adopted strategies and beliefs that we thought helped us to survive emotionally. Many of these may no longer be serving us. However, when faced with challenges, stress, and uncomfortable situations, these old patterns are often activated. We work and hope to eliminate them as we experience them as a negative force.

We personify these messages by naming them our inner critic. Our inner critic is seeking what it perceives may be best for us. It is working on our behalf, even

> *Don't be pushed around by the fears in your mind. Be led by the dreams in your heart.*
>
> *Roy T. Bennett*

if we might not be aware. Our inner critic shows us what needs attention. Often unconsciously, we strengthen this voice and give it more power. We fire neurons that create depleting emotions. We generally fight and resist the inner critic instead of working with it to understand its intent to serve us. Here, awareness is the key for change.

Making contact with our inner critic is a familiar discomfort. We each have this inner voice that is unique to us and integral to our identity. When we let this part dominate us, we disconnect from the liveliness, joy, and authenticity of our inner child.

We each feed parts of us that support us to be successful. These parts remind us how to behave and what is expected from us. Initially, they were formed to help us survive real or imagined threats. We all faced challenges and took action to be physically and emotionally safe. For example, we may have been taught that good people put others' needs ahead of their own. Such a belief shapes our actions and how we interact with others, though it may be to our detriment.

For example, even if you didn't have a difficult childhood, life still offered challenges, and you formed beliefs and strategies to be safe. Often, those beliefs were formed unconsciously. When someone praised your kind action, you sensed you would be valued or liked in the future by continuing to be kind. Maybe you started to be vigilant when a family member went into the hospital, and you were unsure when they would come back. Perhaps neighborhood children excluded you from play, so you developed a pattern of avoiding social interactions. Maybe your sibling got more attention, so you adopted efforts to control situations or people to become more visible. You may have received praise when you supported someone, so you learned to become a pleaser. Perhaps you received recognition when you did well in school, so you adopted an inner voice that said you must achieve or be perfect to be valued. Maybe you learned to avoid conflict when you saw the negative impact of your parents quarreling. Often, our inner critic leaves us with the sense that we are not good enough as we are.

For a moment, pause and take a breath. Are any of these patterns familiar to you?

By cultivating self-awareness and understanding the role of our critical inner voice, we can consciously choose when to listen to its guidance and when to challenge its limiting beliefs. Embracing self-acceptance, nurturing our desires and longings, and honoring our unique qualities allow us to find a harmonious integration between societal expectations and our own personal fulfillment.

While our critical inner voice may have good intentions, its influence can sometimes be limiting or overly harsh. It can create self-imposed pressures, instill self-doubt, and limit our ability to express our authentic self. Balancing the guidance of our inner critic with self-compassion and authenticity becomes crucial in fostering JOYBeing, growth, and fulfillment.

In an environment of high standards, comparison, and perfectionism, a core challenge for most people is feeling "not enough." This feeling of inadequacy and insufficiency disconnects us from our authentic joy, our life energy, and our potential. It can cause us to look for more external validation and engage in behaviors that negatively impact our sense of self. We often adopt limiting or destructive external habits to distract ourselves, such as overeating, excessive shopping, overworking, overexercising, social media consumption, drinking, smoking, and more. We also adopt destructive internal habits. For example, we negatively compare ourselves to others, thereby fostering feelings of envy and inadequacy. We can easily find ourselves focusing on what we don't have rather than celebrating what we have and who we are and making life-affirming choices. We experience self-doubt, questioning our abilities and decisions, which hinder confidence. We move into patterns of overthinking by ruminating on past mistakes or future worries that lead to anxiety and stress. We may procrastinate by avoiding tasks due to fear of failure. We can become perfectionists who set unattainable standards and feel inadequate or guilty when they are not met. We can also engage in constant negative self-talk and belittle and criticize ourselves. We can easily miss the joy of life.

Rather than expending our energy by comparing ourselves to others and feeling not good enough, we can focus on embracing our individual uniqueness and celebrating our differences to experience a greater sense of wellbeing.

Each of us possesses inherent worth and unique qualities that make us worthy and deserving of love, joy, and acceptance. Embracing our sense of enoughness involves cultivating self-compassion, and gratitude, becoming aware of and working with our narratives, and reframing our life experiences as opportunities for growth. By honoring our enoughness and loving ourselves, we nourish our inner seeds and empower ourselves to experience the joy of our inner garden.

CHAPTER 4 Weeding: Unearthing Obstacles to Cultivating a JOYBeing Garden

Attending to Our Inner Voices

We believe it is crucial to take responsibility for our own joy. No one else can or will. If we don't take responsibility for our own state of joy, suffering will have won, and we limit our possibilities. Now, let's explore how to connect and work with our critical inner voice.

Start by reflecting on the below questions:

- ✓ How does your inner critic stop you from experiencing joy?
- ✓ What does it say?
- ✓ Is it familiar?
- ✓ In what circumstances does it show up?
- ✓ How do you choose to address this voice?

Our inner critic says something about our identity that is followed by a should. To compensate for the depleting emotions that are evoked in us, we might overdo it by working hard, or give up and resign. It costs us. We pay a high price.

Ann

I grappled with a persistent feeling of inadequacy, and my inner critic responded with over-achievement, worry about finances, concerns for other people, and an overwhelming sense of responsibility. My focus was fixed on others' needs, often to my own detriment. My inner critic insisted on being selfless, maintaining a giving nature, and being a reliable and responsible person on whom others could depend. Despite external success, the relentless pursuit of overdoing and excessive responsibility drained time and energy away from personal goals and satisfaction. I didn't have time for joy.

However, the habitual patterns became more of a burden as I grew. My transformation began when I understood the origins of this inner drive and how it was trying to serve me. My inner critic tried to ensure I was responsible and a "good" person. This part thought it was my role to take charge and take care of others in need, a role that was useful in childhood.

I befriended this part with acceptance, recognizing its attempts to support me. With this understanding and connection, I cultivated an appreciation for my inner critic, reducing the need to engage in battles with its persistent shoulds. In an act of gratitude, I invited it to take a break, acknowledging I could make a difference without the accompanying striving, stress, and over-giving. I consciously made different choices, embracing self-acceptance and recognizing my needs as well as those of others. I began focusing on making a difference with my presence rather than trying to fix things. This enabled me to maintain my desire to make a difference and be of service.

Collaborating with my wise self, I embarked on a journey to reunite with the inner child I had once abandoned. My wise self is a steadfast supporter, enabling me to adopt a broader perspective and perceive possibilities beyond the limitations of my inner critic's narratives.

When our inner critic leads our life, we can become disconnected from our life energy and, at times, feel inadequate and not enough. What if we knew we were enough?

Knowing where and how our inner critic emerges is useful. This part once served us. However, when exaggerated and overly used in different contexts, it becomes a disadvantage to us and takes our energy by shadowing our JOYBeing. We need to become aware of our inner critic, or we simply react rather than consciously respond. For example, Cem, a coaching client, was an excellent student and a high achiever in school. He was overusing his focus on achieving, setting overly high business targets, and creating difficulty in collaborating with his peers and leading his work team. When he was unable to meet his business targets, he criticized himself and felt inadequate. To compensate, he was overly controlling and micromanaged his team. When he projected these feelings and expressed his anger to his team, he demotivated them instead of inspiring them. Overachieving had served Cem earlier in his life. However, doing it in the same perfectionist way was not helpful for him or his team. Only when he noticed his "shoulds" and made contact with his habitual pattern was he able to soften and be more appreciative in his interaction with himself and others. Once he became aware of his pattern and internal contraction, he could choose to take an Open Stance.

Our inner critic can be demoralizing, yet some find it to be an effective motivator. They believe that being hard on themselves supports them in pushing through challenges and achieving their goals. It's important to create awareness and manage excessive self-criticism since it can lead to stress and self-doubt. Distinguishing constructive criticism from destructive self-judgment is crucial for JOYBeing.

A good way of working with our inner critic is using the 4A recipe mentioned in Chapter 2 and the E-MRI process that will be shared in the next chapter.

Awake → Attend → Acknowledge → Act

The first step to addressing this part is to awaken to the emotion we are experiencing and notice its presence and purpose of being. We can notice our sensations connected to judgment and where it lives in our bodies. Rather than reject or fight this part of us, we can attend, notice, and have a conversation with it to understand its needs and what it is trying to convey to us. When we acknowledge and give empathy to this part, we can appreciate what this part is yearning for. Only then can we be more at choice to connect with JOYBeing and determine how we want to act.

When Cem received feedback on the impact of his interactions with others, he awoke to his emotion of frustration and sense of not being good enough. He attended to his feelings and acknowledged a pattern of trying to control others for the sake of success. With this awareness and empathy, he chose to take a different path. He chose to listen and be open to himself and his team's needs rather than insist he knew better and was right.

We can be very harsh when we react from our inner critic. However, when we can treat it as if it were a guide or a friend, we can actually move forward in life with more ease and JOYBeing.

Even when we are caught in the energy of our inner critic, we can appreciate its purpose and decrease its negative impact on us by naming it and befriending ourselves. Take time to consider your inner conversations. Would you talk in the same tone or words to a friend?

Gila

We come into this world immersed in various systems—our family, community (school, religion, neighborhood), and broader societal structures—each loaded with its own set of expectations. Due to the historical exile of past generations of Jews and antisemitism around the world, in my family the constant concern revolved around the question "Where is a safe place to live? Where is home?" This background led me to internalize the belief that academic success was my key to survival, regardless of where life took me. As a child, I always worked hard to be a great student and please my parents. These ingrained "shoulds" served me and pushed me forward but also came at a personal cost.

I've come to understand that while we don't necessarily have to discard these "shoulds," there's a transformative potential in how we pursue our objectives. It's about finding a path where we can chase our goals not just dutifully, but with a sense of joy and fulfillment. It's not about abandoning our aspirations but reshaping our approach to pursuing them, infusing our journey with a sense of purpose and JOYBeing.

Taking an Open Stance Toward Ourselves

We can apply the Open Stance process of stopping, stepping back, and shifting to experience a deeper connection with ourselves, to manage our inner critic, and to ensure a sense of JOYBeing.

When you assess your inner landscape, notice the quality of your inner soil. Do you see rocks and weeds? For instance, when you notice your inner voice berating you, "You are terrible; you will never succeed," and your stomach and chest are tight with stress, you can stop, step back, and shift your focus to your breath or a calming image. This process can help you reconnect with your inner curiosity, compassion, calm, and joy, and enhance your self-connection.

Begin by setting your intention to connect with your inner sense of joy and aliveness—JOYBeing. Step back and appreciate the power of noticing what is going well and try being open and nonjudgmental toward yourself. Trust that being open creates a broader perspective and more possibilities. An Open Stance allows you to approach challenges with curiosity and learn from them, fostering personal growth and enhancing your leadership influence.

Cultivate the habit of turning your attention inward and observing your emotional state. This practice involves noticing how you feel, what thoughts are running through your mind, and how your body reacts. Ask, "Am I open or closed?" Recognize the tendency to be self-critical and work to develop an understanding of your internal dialogue. Our internal voice can be harsh and unforgiving.

By noting your judgment signal, sensations, emotions, and thoughts, you can discern between a closed state marked by contraction, control, and judgment and an open state characterized by energy, expansiveness, spaciousness, and seeing potential. For example, a closed state might involve feeling tense, trying

> *The real voyage of discovery consists not in seeking new landscapes, but in having new eyes.*
>
> *Marcel Proust*

to control the situation, and judging yourself harshly. In contrast, an open state might include feeling relaxed, being open to different perspectives, and envisioning growth opportunities.

Practice curiosity, shift-free from judgment, and choose to be open and explore your feelings and thoughts. Embrace the crucial role of self-compassion, acknowledging that challenges are integral to growth.

Consider taking a few minutes for conscious breathing. We hold our breath when we are being judgmental. Allow your outbreaths to be twice as long as your in-breaths. Taking kind actions and prioritizing self-care pave the way for personal resilience and wellbeing.

You can challenge unhelpful thoughts with empathy and compassion and treat yourself with kindness and understanding.

Ann

For many years, I was on a relentless quest to become a better version of myself. I devoured training programs, books, and resources that promised growth and self-improvement. Each new piece of knowledge illuminated yet another area where I could improve. It felt like I was on a never-ending journey, and while I'm grateful for the knowledge I accumulated, something was always missing.

A fundamental transformation came when I embraced a different paradigm. I have since been using it with executive coaching clients and leaders in my programs. Recognizing that people are whole, resourceful, and capable, I apply the Open Stance mindset and process to myself. Instead of being judgmental toward myself and constantly striving for improvement, I focus on being open to my inner experience and trusting my inherent wisdom and potential.

I practice noticing my inner contraction and when I am judgmental or closed to myself and others. For example, if I feel I should achieve more, I may notice a tightness in my stomach and hear an inner voice saying, "You should get more done." I try to catch myself when I notice the contraction and somatic message. I envision a stop sign and stop my narrative. I step back and take a breath to cool down. I may get empathy from a friend or even take a walk outside. I invite myself to shift into being open. One strategy I have is to recall being at the beach in Santorini; then I notice my shoulders drop and relax. I have the space to explore my emotions using the 4A recipe, and I let go of my old narrative and move from being in my head to connecting with my inner aliveness and appreciating myself and life. Self-compassion is a crucial part of the Open Stance process.

Taking an Open Stance toward myself has become a habit. It's as if I am checking in on my inner garden and ensuring space for JOYBeing. I notice many more moments of joy these days, even amid challenges.

We are naturally whole, and the journey is about uncovering what stands in our way—like clouds obscuring the sun. This shift of adopting an Open Stance toward myself and others makes all the difference. Rather than feeling caught in a perpetual state of "not enough," I joyfully embrace the present moment, trusting that life will unfold in valuable ways.

Adopting an Open Stance alleviates the draining sense of comparison and fear that plagues many of us today and enhances our experience of JOYBeing. When we are open, curious, compassionate, courageous, optimistic, grateful, kind, and believe that we—and those around us—are whole and capable, we can fully engage with the present moment and with awareness respond as needed rather than react.

Clearing the Ground with Self-Compassion

Imagine feeling contracted and overwhelmed by negative self-talk. You may be saying, "I will never complete this project. I am a loser. I am an idiot. I can't compete with my colleague. I am a failure." How do such statements make you feel? Probably not so great. Such harsh criticism depletes and de-energizes us. We are reacting to self-destructive patterns.

Too many of us feel we are not good enough. We have a negativity bias and focus on what is not going well, which can lead to a toxic relationship with ourselves. However, we can create an energizing and self-supportive relationship with ourselves. And when we do so, we experience more JOYBeing.

While self-criticism is often depleting and condemns us, self-awareness involves becoming aware of what is needed and what can be worked on to support our growth without judgment.

When we see newborns or young children, we intuitively know they are intrinsically enough. Why should it be different for you? You were born good enough. You, like others, are trying to survive in a complex society.

You can give yourself empathy: "I know I am tired since I didn't get enough sleep. I am feeling overwhelmed with this project. I am frustrated with my colleague." Allow a wise part of yourself to give nonjudgmental empathy and compassion. You can ask what is needed. Perhaps you need a break, you need to call someone to discuss the project, or you need to ask for help. You can recall your strengths and assure yourself you are not a "loser." Self-compassion and empathy are essential tools for fostering self-growth and JOYBeing.

Through the above process, you can become aware of patterns that may have been useful in the past but are ineffective. For example, Ann's coaching client, Jill, realized she was overly responsible in childhood, and this pattern currently took a lot of energy because she felt responsible for too many people. By stopping and interrupting her pattern of jumping in to solve issues and stepping back instead, Jill created moments to reflect and shift to being open. Curious, compassionate, and courageous, she let go of her urge to jump in when it no longer served her adult children or staff members. By giving herself empathy and treating herself like a friend with self-compassion, she experienced more joy and aliveness. She ultimately had more energy to be of service.

Imagine your internal voice as a bird perched on your shoulder, constantly chirping its opinions about your worth and abilities. Have you ever paused to listen to your conversations with yourself? The words we speak internally hold immense power over our emotions and actions. Even the most accomplished individuals can find themselves locked in a cycle of self-criticism and doubt, such as a highly successful leader who confesses, "I hate myself. I never get things right. I'm a loser."

Studies by Kristin Neff, a leader in studying self-compassion, reveal a profound link between self-compassion and physical health. Our internal dialogue directly influences factors like blood pressure and overall health outcomes. Critiquing ourselves limits our potential and stifles our JOYBeing, creating a barrier to growth and fulfillment.

> Quiet the mind, and the soul will speak.
>
> *Ma Jaya Sati Bhagavati*

We must respect ourselves, practice self-compassion, and remove the weeds overpowering our inner gardens.

Self-compassion is a skill, a way of being kind to ourselves and treating ourselves like a friend who supports JOYBeing. Most of us learned how to be harsh to ourselves, which may have served a purpose at one time. It kept us in line with our family and community expectations, and it helped us to survive and succeed. Some of these old voices have lingered and not grown up. But as we evolve, it's crucial to let go of those outdated voices and nurture a compassionate inner dialogue. Self-compassion is a skill that can be learned and cultivated, and we have the power to change our internal narrative.

Suppose your child or a friend is going through a challenging experience, such as making a mistake or being embarrassed. Are you likely to be harsh or punishing? What are you likely to say to them? Probably, you would be kind and empathetic. You would say things like, "Everyone makes mistakes; you will be all right; you are upset and disappointed; things will work out." Notice how empathy and these supportive comments would make you feel.

We know how to be kind and friendly to others, so we must remember to be so to ourselves. Using our name when giving ourselves empathy, kindness, and encouragement is helpful. "Jeff, you are tired and could use a break. You are doing your best, and you are enough." Chris Germer, Kristin Neff's colleague, suggests asking yourself, "What do I need right now?" instead of beating yourself up when you feel ashamed or not enough. You may need a walk, a break, a friend, or a hug. Some have found it helpful to write a note to themselves to identify positive qualities and revisit them to reinforce self-compassion and care.

People who embrace self-compassion are more inclined to prioritize their wellbeing. By consciously cultivating a kinder, more supportive inner voice, we not only pave the way for a fulfilling and harmonious life, but we open ourselves up to a world of possibilities by using our energy to grow our inner garden. Research supports that self-compassion is linked to increased productivity, decreased stress, a sense of inner strength, and greater resilience. Self-compassion is a practice that requires commitment and effort. Still, the rewards of self-compassion and the potential for a more joyful and healthier life are immeasurable.

CHAPTER 4 Weeding: Unearthing Obstacles to Cultivating a JOYBeing Garden

> **Take a moment to reflect:**
>
> ✓ How is your relationship with yourself in both the good and dark times?
>
> ✓ What are you doing to remove the rocks and weeds that prohibit your growth and joy?
>
> ✓ How are you refraining from negatively judging yourself and instead choosing to support yourself?
>
> ✓ What are your strategies for nurturing self-compassion?

We encourage you to set your intention to pay attention to the cues your body is giving you. Allow yourself to be curious, compassionate, and kind toward yourself to create more awareness to make the choices that support your JOYBeing and resilience. By practicing self-compassion, you are building new neural pathways and habits that enliven you. We trust you will experience more joy and a greater sense of aliveness—JOYBeing. Your joy will be contagious. You will be better able to manage your energy and be more equipped to create connections and thrive in your current environment.

Meet Arun—A Leader

As a senior leader of a major organization, Arun had a full schedule. While most agreed that his insights and business acumen were top-notch, he was considered to be too abrupt and often cut people off. In fact, Human Resources had received many complaints about his style and bias. When his boss and HR told him to participate in coaching, Arun was quite angry and felt his coworkers were just too slow and not very bright. He believed he didn't have time for such foolishness.

Ann, his coach, talked with many stakeholders and shared the confirmation that Arun could have been

more effective in his interactions and that it was limiting his success. Arun felt tight in his chest; he still believed he was right and those around him were wrong. However, he chose to adopt an Open Stance. He learned to notice his chest tightening when he closed and was in judgment of others around him, including clients, colleagues, staff, and family. He practiced stepping back and taking a breath before responding. He then shifted into being open and curious. He recalled how he felt when engaging in a woodworking hobby where he felt the flow was open to what evolved. From this stance, he shifted how he interacted with those around him. Rather than assuming he was right and telling people they were wrong, he started asking questions to be able to understand the full perspective of issues. He practiced giving empathy and creating understanding and a sense of openness. His relationships dramatically improved.

Arun also noticed his inner critic, who told him he needed to have all the answers or he was not good enough. He realized he adopted this belief in childhood, and it had helped him manage some difficult circumstances and protect his siblings. He embraced a sense of self-compassion, recognizing that this inner need to control and be right had served him earlier in life, but it was limiting his emotional intelligence now. He recognized he could not have all the answers in such a complex time in his organization after several mergers and shifts in the marketplace and considering the uncertainty in the world.

As Arun practiced taking an Open Stance in his interactions and within himself, he reported that his relationships were much more meaningful, and he felt a sense of profound joy, perhaps for the first time. Reports from stakeholders and family members confirmed that they experienced Arun in a much more positive way. In fact, they reported he was now enjoyable to be with. His business results were more positive too.

Arun is now an advocate for taking an Open Stance and experiencing JOYBeing. Since he shared the process with leaders in his organization, they have become collectively more open and less reactive, and they report a greater sense of collaboration, joy, and aliveness.

Arun envisions his inner garden as a wide-open space that increasingly blooms with plants, fruits, and vegetation. He envisions spreading openness and JOYBeing to his organization and the wider community.

Practices

The following exercises will help you expand your openness to enhance your JOYBeing.

1. PRACTICE TAKING AN OPEN STANCE.

Ask yourself often, "Am I open or closed?" Notice your reactions to external conditions and internal thoughts.

When you notice your judgment and somatic signal that you are closed or contracted toward yourself, others, or situations:

✓ Stop—refrain from reacting.
✓ Step back and cool down—breathe, take a break, engage in a relaxing activity, get empathy from a friend, take a walk, etc.
✓ Shift to being open—be curious, compassionate, courageous, and kind. Be grounded, optimistic, grateful, and connecting. Recall the sensation of being in a calm state or a time when you are open.

Practices

2. WORK WITH THE "SHOULDS" OF YOUR INNER CRITIC TO HAVE MORE CHOICES.

Write a statement that you hear from your inner critic beginning with "You should...."

For example:

✓ This report is not good enough. You should work harder.

✓ You should be available to everyone and be responsible.

The should statement is an introjection that was swallowed without chewing that comes from our past. We don't check if the "should" serves us or the price we pay for the "should." Often, these beliefs are not valid in the present moment but might or might not have served us in the past. It is important to check them out in the present moment to validate whether they still hold true.

Read this sentence to yourself once more, replacing the *"You should"* with *"I should"* so that you are more aware and can take more ownership of the choices you are making. For example, "I should work harder" or "I should be more responsible."

When repeating these sentences to yourself, reflect on the below questions:

✓ How does this make me feel? Where do I feel it in my body?

✓ How does believing that this sentence is true serve me today?

✓ What's the cost I am paying?

✓ What might it be protecting me from?

Create a positive affirmation starting with "I" so you can practice building a belief that serves you now and is more aligned with who you are and supportive of JOYBeing.

For example:

✓ I can work with ease and be effective.

✓ I choose to be more generous to myself in supporting others.

3. PRACTICE SELF-COMPASSION.

Recognize that compassion is a skill that can be developed. Make time for yourself. Check in on your sensations and emotions.

Be kind, treat yourself as you would a friend, and talk to yourself in a respectful and supportive way. Care for yourself as much as you do for others.

Recognize that it is human nature to face challenges and hardships. Everyone makes mistakes. Forgive yourself and be kind and understanding.

Be aware of your thoughts and feelings and allow spaciousness to observe and note your experience. Give yourself empathy, and don't over-identify with your emotions. Recognize your strengths and know you are more than your emotions.

Build a strong relationship with yourself. Treat yourself well in good times and also more difficult times. Ask yourself, "What do I need right now?" Give yourself a hug or write a letter to yourself as a compassionate friend who would offer you positive support. Consider posting positive reminders of who you are where you will see them. When you provide yourself with validation and support, you will have less of a need to seek validation from outside of yourself.

Consider asking people in various aspects of your life what they experience as your strengths. Remind yourself of these.

Practice a Loving-Kindness meditation.

Extend it to yourself, those close to you, acquaintances, the world, and even foes. You may wish for ease, joy, connection, and creativity.

As you wish, allow yourself to experience each.

Find a time to practice. Make it a habit.

CHAPTER 5

Sowing the Seeds: Planting Inner Awareness

> *If you love what is in your way, you will transform.*
>
> — Richard Schwartz

JOYBeing

Richard Schwartz shares a touching story in his book Introduction to *Internal Family Systems*. According to an ancient legend, the gods suggested hiding peace and joy from humans until they were ready to find and value it. One god suggested hiding it on the highest mountain. However, another god thought it would be too easy to find there. The gods considered other options, including hiding it in a forest or the deep sea. Again, these ideas were rejected for the same reason. Finally, the wisest god suggested hiding it in the human heart—the last place people would look. The gods all agreed, and that is where they put it.

The gods were wise indeed. We look for joy outside of ourselves in relationships, work, entertainment, material wealth, and more. We fail to look inside ourselves to connect with our inner sense of joy and aliveness—the treasure of JOYBeing. This human tendency is one of our biggest traps, prohibiting us from experiencing JOYBeing.

Olivia, a participant in a Cultivating JOYBeing course, once remarked, "I don't think it's possible for me to have joy! I spend my life working and taking care of others. I don't know how to access joy." She's not alone. For many of us, joy seems elusive amid the hustle and bustle of daily life. We focus on our endless to-do lists or dwell on what is not going well. Our habitual patterns of striving and working hard limit our ability to notice and experience the available joy.

A block, shared by another participant, is the expectation that joy should be grand, like fireworks lighting up the sky. "I don't encounter joy in my day-to-day life. Life feels rather mundane with work and chores dominating my weekends." But what if joy doesn't always come in flashy displays? What if it quietly resides in the small, meaningful moments of everyday life?

Some look at us blankly when we ask people what they are doing to invite joy. Yet inviting joy into our lives requires openness and intentionality. We must actively create space for joy, expecting to encounter it in the simplest moments. Olivia's journey illustrates this beautifully. By taking small actions—being open to joy and engaging in interactions and activities that are meaningful to her, such as volunteering with children in an afterschool program—she gradually began to experience and radiate more joy.

But why does this matter? When we connect with ourselves and embrace joy, not only do we feel better about ourselves, but we also become kinder and more generous toward others. We are more satisfied and can be less demanding. Joy has a ripple effect and spreads. It is contagious and highlights what is meaningful, and life is better for us and those around us. Olivia reported that when she experienced more moments of joy, her spouse and children also began to invite moments of joy. Olivia felt more at ease within herself and grateful for her work and family life.

How can we cultivate more JOYBeing in our lives—experiencing the joy of being alive? It takes a commitment, like it did for Olivia. It starts with simple, intentional practices such as being aware and mindful and noticing what is meaningful. Paying attention to the beauty around us allows us to savor small moments, such as a connection with someone or nature. Clients often report that cultivating a mindset of gratitude by reflecting on what we are thankful for in day-to-day life are practices that expand joy. It's evident that when we focus on connecting with ourselves, others, and what is important to us, we experience JOYBeing. Engaging in meaningful conversations with others, nurturing relationships, allowing playfulness and variety, and not taking life too seriously expands joy. Making space to be in nature, experiencing beauty and creativity, and engaging in hobbies are sources that feed our energy. Furthermore, focusing on actions of kindness and service and reaching out to others expands joy. Incorporating simple practices into their daily lives has created a fertile ground for JOYBeing to flourish among our class participants and clients.

What are some ways that support more joy in your life?

It is essential to become aware of our emotions, how we use our energy, and how we can incorporate practices into our daily lives. We will explore these in more detail below.

How We Bury Our Emotions to Survive and How This Impacts JOYBeing

We are all born with emotions. Our feelings connect us with the essence of our soul. We begin life with an emotion—the cry that gives life to us. Children naturally experience a wide range of emotions as they explore the world. They communicate their needs and desires through emotions such as crying and yelling. They laugh and smile when they feel safe, connected, and loved. Even though children don't understand their emotions, they naturally respond and act on their feelings.

We have all had moments when the adults in our lives had different expectations of us or themselves and did not respond well to our needs and emotions. In an attempt to be loved and accepted by our parents, caregivers, teachers, and others, many of us unintentionally learned to suppress our emotions by tensing our muscles, holding our breath, and letting go of our authentic selves and needs. Others acted out their feelings. In these ways, we learned how to survive in our families and society. These ways of being helped us to cope and function in our family and community systems when we were young. Our behaviors became habitual patterns that brought us to adulthood. These same behaviors may not be serving us now.

Without awareness, we have learned to numb ourselves or to hold back from expressing our emotions; both lead to body tension or physiological blockages and stress. By contrast, some of us have learned to overreact by expressing emotions in ways detrimental to ourselves and others. Both of these ways block our life force energy and vitality and psychologically impact us, limiting our experience of JOYBeing.

As we mentioned in Chapter 2, our emotions connect us to our life energy and guide us to move away or toward things. Our emotions are essentially a guidance system and a gift. To protect ourselves, we unconsciously repress, deny, disregard, or act out our feelings. We use our intellect and rationalization to control people and situations, limit our sense of aliveness, and restrict our possibilities. However, through the guidance of emotions, we can naturally release tightness and stress, which allows us to reconnect with our natural life energy.

Pushing back or managing our emotions takes a lot of energy, much like holding a beach ball under the sea. However, when our emotions run out of control, we create pain and havoc in our lives. When we are aware and connect with our emotions, we release our energy, as if letting the beach ball flow freely along the surface. When we hold back tears or what we perceive as depleting emotions like anger, fear, and frustration, we also hold back our opportunity to experience joy. When we act them out without control, we create knots in our relationships and might move into a place of regret. Once we become aware of our emotions and choose to open the space for positive and productive expression, we create lightness and liberation and allow the emotions to move through us. We clean the clutter within and open more space to JOYBeing.

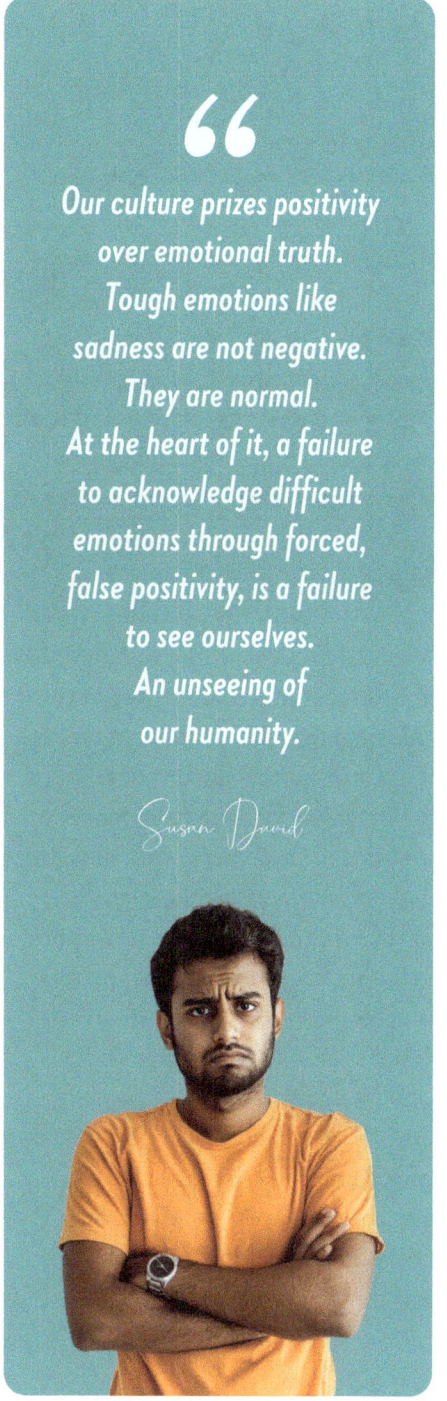

> Our culture prizes positivity over emotional truth. Tough emotions like sadness are not negative. They are normal. At the heart of it, a failure to acknowledge difficult emotions through forced, false positivity, is a failure to see ourselves. An unseeing of our humanity.
>
> Susan David

Recognizing Our Emotions and Working with Our Moods

In order to work with our emotions with awareness, it is useful to recognize and name them as they are happening. According to Harvard brain scientist Jill Bolte Taylor, an emotion lasts ninety seconds. When we experience an emotion as a reaction to our thoughts or something in our environment, there is a ninety-second chemical process that takes place in our bodies.

We have thoughts about our emotions. If we repeat these often, they become our story that then influences how we experience similar occurrences in the future. If we continue to experience an emotion, examining what thoughts may be restimulating the circuitry that causes our physiological response is useful. For example, when we feel a tightness in our solar plexus in an interaction with a colleague and continue to think, "He is against me," we are likely to continually experience anger and fear. It is important to notice what we are experiencing in the moment and the meaning we are attributing to a situation.

- ✓ Recall a situation in which you become stressed and feel yourself launching into a full fight, flight, freeze, or appease reaction.
- ✓ Try pausing your impulse to react for a full ninety seconds.
- ✓ Focus on your breathing.
- ✓ Notice what supports you and what you do to calm yourself.
- ✓ Pay attention to the duration of your emotion and notice your narrative around it.

Recall the 4A recipe for processing emotions introduced in Chapter 2. It is helpful to Awaken (notice the tightness), Attend (be with your experience), Acknowledge (identify your emotion and allow yourself to experience, accept, and appreciate the message it has for you), and Act (connect with your inner resources and choose how you will respond). We benefit from recognizing emotions are messengers informing us of what is happening in and around us and possible actions.

An effective way of working with emotions is to name them and essentially give ourselves empathy. When we name an emotion, we activate our prefrontal cortex, allowing us to be more at choice in our actions. Research shows that having a strong emotional vocabulary is useful and valuable. The more granularity we have in naming an emotion, the more accurate we can be in expanding our possibilities for action. Recognizing our emotions requires honesty with ourselves. It can feel threatening, at times, to assess and accept our feelings, making it more challenging to move with purposeful action. For example, we may find it hard to accept that we are envious when we see others' success and have not processed our emotions. Identifying and embracing our emotions is a skill that can be learned and enhanced.

> **When a person has a reaction to something in their environment, there's a 90-second chemical process that happens in the body; after that, any remaining emotional response is just the person choosing to stay in that emotional loop.**
>
> *Jill Bolte Taylor*

Emotions come and go; they can last for a short time or extend to become a mood, pattern, or way of being if our thought patterns continue. No good or bad emotions exist, but we can learn to accept and work with all of them effectively. Our emotions provide us with information and guide our actions.

The difference between an emotion and a mood lies primarily in their duration, intensity, and specificity of causes. Emotions are typically short-lived, lasting from a few seconds to a few minutes, and are generally more intense. Emotions are usually triggered by specific events or situations, such as feeling joy from hearing good news or anger from an insult. In contrast, moods last longer, ranging from hours to days or even longer, and they are generally less intense. Moods are less specific and can arise without a clear cause, influenced by various factors such as overall health, environment, or prolonged stress.

The Mood Meter developed by Marc Brackett at the Yale Center for Emotional

Intelligence is a valuable tool to expand our emotional vocabulary. It has been introduced in many school systems and is also an app called How We Feel. You can identify your level of pleasantness and energy intensity to find an emotion on the chart to clarify how you feel in the moment. Some of our clients have posted the Mood Meter around their homes and offices to practice assessing their emotions and increasing their awareness and repertoire around what they are experiencing. For example, a client who initially named all her emotions as simply feeling good or bad eventually, with practice, was able to create more clarity and connection with her inner life. She was able to identify emotions of gratefulness, hopefulness, and enthusiasm. This awareness opened her to new possibilities and allowed her to take actions aligned more closely with her purpose.

Another client, rather than just feeling "bad," realized he was frustrated since he could not say "no" to requests at work. Recognizing and naming his emotions allowed him to see his pattern and work toward making requests that gave him more energy and joy at work.

MOOD METER — How are you feeling?

ENERGY ↑↓

ENRAGED	PANICKED	STRESSED	JITTERY	SHOCKED	SUPRISED	UPBEAT	FESTIVE	EXHILARATED	ECSTATIC
LIVID	FURIOUS	FRUSTRATED	TENSE	STUNNED	HYPER	CHEERFUL	MOTIVATED	INSPIRED	ELATED
FUMING	FRIGHTENED	ANGRY	NERVOUS	RESTLESS	ENERGIZED	LIVELY	ENTHUSIASTIC	OPTIMISTIC	EXCITED
ANXIOUS	APPREHENSIVE	WORRIED	IRRITATED	ANNOYED	PLEASED	HAPPY	FOCUSED	PROUD	THRILLED
REPULSED	TROUBLED	CONCERNED	UNEASY	PEEVED	PLEASANT	JOYFUL	HOPEFUL	PLAYFUL	BLISSFUL
DISGUSTED	GLUM	DISAPPOINTED	DOWN	APATHETIC	AT EASE	EASYGOING	CONTENT	LOVING	FULFILLED
PESSIMISTIC	MOROSE	DISCOURAGED	SAD	BORED	CALM	SECURE	SATSIFIED	GRATEFUL	TOUCHED
ALIENATED	MISERABLE	LONELY	DISHEARTENED	TIRED	RELAXED	CHILL	RESTFUL	BLESSED	BALANCED
DESPONDENT	DEPRESSED	SULLEN	EXHAUSTED	FATIGUED	MELLOW	THOUGHTFUL	PEACEFUL	COMFY	CAREFREE
DESPAIR	HOPELESS	DESOLATE	SPENT	DRAINED	SLEEPY	COMPLACENT	TRANQUIL	COZY	SERENE

← PLEASANTNESS →

Mood Meter used with permission from the Yale Center for Emotional Intelligence

CHAPTER 5 Sowing the Seeds: Planting Inner Awareness

The Feelings Circle, developed by Gloria Willcox, is another tool in a different format that is useful for exploring emotions and expanding your vocabulary. This tool moves from the center with basic feelings into more granularity, creating more awareness and specificity of what we feel in the moment.

Emotions tell us something about ourselves, our stories, and the lives we choose for ourselves. Avoiding emotions does not serve us. On the contrary, the more we avoid them, the more intense they grow, as does the need to address them.

Recognizing our emotions requires being open and honest with ourselves. Once we create this ground and more freely notice what is happening within, we can make healthier choices and detach from old stories and patterns that no longer serve us.

Gila

My life's mission has always been to empower myself and others. As a child, my search for acceptance and my urge to be seen for who I was led me to develop a habit of giving and caring for others to seek love, validation, and a sense of worthiness. Unknowingly, this pattern became deeply ingrained within me, shaping my career path first as an educationalist and therapist and later as an executive coach. However, I realized while I poured energy into supporting others, I struggled to accept kindness directed toward me. Expressions of gratitude or compliments felt uncomfortable because I never truly believed I deserved them. I'd deflect, respond with kindness back to the person, or feel embarrassed, unable to embrace acknowledgment for the selfless energy I offered.

Not until my late thirties did I consciously recognize this detrimental pattern. I began creating space to accept compliments, embrace positive feedback, and acknowledge my own strengths, value, and impact. Through a profound personal journey, I learned to declare, "I deserve," allowing myself to take pride in the positive effect I had on others. Delving into my emotions, I nurtured the parts of myself that felt unseen and overshadowed, gradually moving from a sense of inferiority toward a place of empowerment. This transformation allowed me to finally acknowledge my own worth and appreciate the difference I made in people's lives.

In my work today as a coach, I draw from my personal experiences to help my clients embrace their true selves, advocating for their worth, and I encourage them to stand strong for who they are and what they deserve.

Ann

When I did not hear back from my daughter during her time away at college, I felt a pit in my stomach and a sense of contraction. My instinct was to be upset and angry and think she "should" be more responsive. I attended to my sensations and emotions. I acknowledged I felt hurt and disappointed. Additionally, a concern surfaced about how her non-responsiveness might affect her connections with others.

Reflecting on my role as a parent, I found myself frustrated with my inability to convey the importance of responsiveness. I teach people how to engage in conversations and value relationships. What was the message of my emotions, and what was I to learn from this painful experience? Recognizing that my daughter, an introvert, was in the process of forging a new life, I acknowledged our differing perspectives and needs for connection. Notably, her lack of responsiveness didn't imply a lack of care for our relationship or inefficacy in her interactions.

I shared my experience with her, and we agreed on a more satisfying communication process. This agreement eased my anxiety and supported our relationship and connection.

This experience was a learning opportunity for me to remind myself that we cannot impose change upon others unless they themselves desire it. This lesson now resonates in my personal life and in my professional work with leaders and organizations.

Uncovering Depleting Emotions and Restoring Emotional Vitality for JOYBeing

Talk to anyone these days and they will most likely say they are stressed. When we examine these experiences more closely, we become aware that we are referring to different combinations of emotions that can be identified on the Mood Meter. For example, some of us are feeling tired and frustrated, while others are experiencing grief and feeling overwhelmed.

We tend to perceive stress or pressure as negative. However, we need some level of stress to be motivated, grow, and live fully. Health psychologist Kelly McGonigal emphasizes that we benefit from eustress, energizing stress that enables us to achieve goals. For example, your sense of pressure or stress can help you focus and get it done if you have a project due. However, if you become overly stressed and feel overwhelmed, you will not be effective.

> *Stress is caused by being here but wanting to be there.*
>
> —Eckhart Tolle

Life gets challenging when we have too much pressure or stress and are overwhelmed by depleting emotions. Life circumstances and significant life changes such as having a child, losing and changing jobs, climate disruption, and losing a loved one can cause us to experience depleting emotions, which alert us to pay attention. We see these emotions as messengers and an opportunity to awaken to our reality, attend to what we are experiencing, acknowledge and accept reality, and determine how we will act—our 4A Recipe. We need to have practices to work with the emotions we face. Our stress can become overwhelming when we lose contact with our coping mechanisms.

Stress and emotional pressure are important factors that disconnect us from our life force and sense of aliveness. Buddha described stress as the gap between our expectations and reality. The larger the gap, the more stress we experience, which minimizes joy.

Stress has become a way of life in our fast-paced world. We have normalized it as we push ourselves beyond our natural limits and focus more on doing than being. Abundant research shows the consequences of stress on our health and wellbeing. When we are in a highly stressful state, we disconnect from JOYBeing. Our amygdala is activated in an elevated stress level, and our cortisol levels increase. When we are experiencing JOYBeing, our level of oxytocin increases in the body and enhances our wellbeing experience.

Our sympathetic nervous system naturally reacts to perceived threats by a fight, flight, freeze, or appease response. We are designed and have the capacity to release this response and shift into a parasympathetic "tend and befriend" response when there is no longer a perceived danger or pressure. In such cases, we are relaxed and able to fully experience aliveness. Without awareness, we can continue to activate and prolong the sympathetic response, which is unhealthy.

Emotions live in our bodies. Research shows the connection between stress

Gila

For a significant part of my life, I struggled with a persistent feeling of inadequacy, repeating to myself the belief "I am not good enough." I operated on autopilot, constantly rushing around to support others, while avoiding a deeper connection with myself. This habit of constant action allowed me to escape confronting my own emotions. I found myself overwhelmed by stress, yet unaware of what was truly happening within me. I continued this unhealthy cycle, trying to be everywhere for everyone. No matter how much I did, I felt insufficient for my children, believing "I am not a good mother." I also lacked time for friends, not meeting the expectations of my close circle, and I always fell short at work.

The intensity of these emotions drove me to move even faster, yet the more I rushed, the more inadequate I felt. Only when I had the courage to look deep inside myself did I discover the power of pausing and slowing down. Then my life took a profound turn. I realized by slowing down, I paradoxically gained more time. Slowing down for the sake of speeding up! My relationships and quality of life improved, and even though I allocated less time, the quality of my presence in my relationships flourished. Slowing down became my new pathway to a more fulfilling life.

Today, I find myself deeply connected to my inner world. By nurturing this connection, I can maintain a sense of peace and tranquility even amid numerous responsibilities. I feel attuned to the vibrant energy of life around me, and I engage with others from a more profound place of creating meaning. Transitioning from a state of simply "doing" to embracing a state of "JOYBeing" has brought me a sense of true vitality and aliveness.

and our health. After reviewing a wide range of studies, Howard Friedman, PhD and a professor at the University of California, concluded that being chronically irritated, pessimistic, depressed, or anxious doubles the risk of contracting a major disease.
A connection exists between how we experience and manage our emotions, dramatically affecting our physical health and sense of wellbeing.

When we change our mindset about the value of stress and see it as a messenger and a generative force, we can use this energy to propel us forward. We can work with this mindset for effective results and unlocking our potential. When we look deeply and feel what is happening within us, rather than getting caught in an internal conflict, we can listen and open to the wisdom within our bodies. With curiosity, we can discover the vast potential within us. When we can meet our internal experience, as if meeting a new person with compassion and curiosity, we discover new avenues that fulfill us.

Developing coping strategies to minimize stress and connect to the life force inside us is useful. Some of these include getting enough sleep, exercising, adopting healthy eating habits, drinking water, spending time in nature, and meditation.

Focusing on restoring our energy and building moments of pause into our daily lives is important for creating more meaning and connection with our life force.

Ann

I lived with my foot on the gas pedal for much of my life, and stress became a persistent companion. Being busy was a way of life and a badge of honor that led me to neglect my own needs. I operated under the misconception that I could get more done with less sleep, disregarding the essential value of rest and rejuvenation, as highlighted by recent research. Evidence now shows that, akin to animals, our systems are designed for cycles of stress followed by relaxation.

The unhealthy emphasis on doing more than being took a toll on my overall wellbeing. Now that I understand the value of unplugging, I give myself time away from work to be—whether by walks in nature, engaging in art projects, connecting with friends, or listening to music. This shift has brought about a profound transformation, fostering a renewed sense of connection to life and others. In these moments, I tap into the flow of JOYBeing, experiencing a spaciousness that paradoxically allows me to achieve more with less effort.

CHAPTER 5 Sowing the Seeds: Planting Inner Awareness

We know our muscles grow stronger after we rest, and making music relies on the pauses between the notes. We also naturally pause between our inhale and exhale. Understanding what is contributing to our stress and allowing space and relaxation is a support to us.

We can focus and pause by paying attention to the traps that pull us away from our life force, emotional vitality, and JOYBeing. When we are aware, awake, and open, we can connect with our natural sense of aliveness and JOYBeing.

Many of the leaders we work with are stressed and reactive at work and with their families. These leaders feel they need to keep a rigorous pace. Some tell us the only real time they have for themselves is in our coaching sessions. Jim, a leader in a technology company, thought he was doomed to a life of stress, plus the possibility of losing his marriage and his relationship with his children. When he became aware it is natural to experience stress and that he needed to unplug at times and breathe, he began to connect with himself and become more aware.

He was shocked by how simply slowing down, reconnecting with himself, and centering could make such a difference. He experienced deeper relationships with others and began to experience a sense of JOYBeing. He found his productivity was actually enhanced. Many other leaders have had similar experiences.

Janice, another coaching client, could not understand why she was not being promoted. She worked hard and thought she was achieving her business goals. Her boss said she was "transactional." With her high-stress level, she focused on the task and failed to build relationships with her colleagues, managers, and clients. Only when she became more centered and calmer within and recognized and worked with her emotions could she more fully create the relationships that allowed for a smoother way of working and getting things done. She connected with her sense of JOYBeing and began to receive the recognition and results she desired, which included a promotion to the next level in her organization.

Recognizing Our Traps

Since each moment offers so many things to pay attention to, we often fail to see what is available to us; that may cause us at times to react or feel emotionally down. Different events around us create mood fluctuations in us. For example, trying to complete a task, attending a meeting, having to check emails, or a critical comment by another person may pull our mood down. However, playing with or spending time with our children, reading a book, or taking a walk in nature may uplift our mood.

Whenever we are pressured and experiencing a depleting mood, there's a narrative behind it.

> We tend to fall into three basic traps focusing on:
>
> ✓ A memory based on our past.
>
> ✓ A worry about the future which is not yet lived.
>
> ✓ A desire to change the external circumstances or the people around us.

To walk through the door of unlimited possibility, we have to leave behind the story we tell about our past.

— Joe Dispenza

We use a lot of energy when we fall into any of these three traps. Our thoughts and emotions are manifestations of our different parts that talk to us internally. When the stories we create persist without awareness, they can become our consistent moods and way of being, which may not serve us.

How would life be different if we were to use this energy that doesn't serve us for a positive outcome? How would this affect us physically and emotionally?

We fall into these traps when we do not recognize and process our thoughts and emotions, and we put our energy into things we cannot change.

We all fall into these traps. However, with awareness, we can learn to make different choices.

Trap 1: Focusing on the Past

We all have experiences that condition how we interpret our interactions and our present experiences. Through repetition, we form habitual patterns that influence who we are and who we become. For example, if we believe people will mistreat us, we are likely to interpret many interactions negatively and experience people mistreating us. Our background shapes how we see and make meaning of our world. Our expectations become self-fulfilling prophecies.

We don't see the world as it is but as we are. When we are experiencing an emotion based on our experience of the past, we fail to fully embrace the present moment and move away from JOYBeing. By staying with a past memory, we enliven and strengthen its intensity and tend to see it as our current reality. This can then become our mood. This is the trap we fall into. With this trap, we carry the past into the present moment. For example, when receiving feedback, we may interpret it as being criticized and feel disappointed by enlivening the stories of our early years. We may feel upset and not good enough. We are living the current moment with the emotional energy of our past experiences, which affects our mood. With awareness, using the E-MRI tool we will introduce in this chapter, we can recognize our thoughts and stories from the past and notice how they are influencing our interpretations and our experience in the moment. This allows us to take new actions that serve us.

We want to use the past as a resource to inform us and guide us to increase

Ann

I have experienced challenges, disappointments, betrayals, aloneness, and sadness like everyone. Something that has helped me to connect with JOYBeing is practicing forgiveness for myself and others. We are each conditioned by our experiences, and we tend to do the best we can at any given moment based on our perceptions. There are times when we, and those around us, are fatigued, preoccupied, overwhelmed, stressed, and simply unaware, not embodying our best selves. I know there are multiple realities and many ways to perceive a situation.

Embracing the notion that I am a "good enough" parent, partner, coach, and friend has been a journey in self-acceptance. I forgive my younger self for lacking awareness and making mistakes just as I endeavor to grant the same to others. My openness to forgiveness does not mean I forget how others have behaved; I still express concerns and take necessary actions. However, I am empowered to forgive by accepting that learning is an inherent part of life and we all grapple with challenges while often succumbing to habitual patterns that may not be productive. I recognize this process may take time, and through forgiveness, I create space to be more present with myself and others, fostering a richer experience of joy.

our learning, choices, and growth for the current moment.

Trap 2: Worrying About the Future

Our emotional state is also influenced by our thoughts about the future. We generally focus on the future with excitement or worry. When we put our energy into negative anticipation, we create a stressful emotional experience. For example, we could worry about completing a project on time. If worrying is embodied in who we are, it can turn into a pattern that does not serve us. We can deplete ourselves by constantly chewing on the same issues without nourishment. Perseverating or repeating words and thoughts about what could happen over and over again takes energy from the present moment. We often speak about what we intend to do or need to do while we are in a situation rather than acting upon it. Once we are aware of the truth of the current moment and what we are doing to ourselves, we can make better choices.

Sometimes our energy is focused on what we need to do in the future. In that case, we are not fully in the present moment and are unaware of the cost of how we are using our energy in ways that don't serve us. Worrying about what may come in the future is easy. For example, we could be worrying about a project due the coming week while trying to enjoy time with a friend. When our energy is focused on the future, we tend to miss the moment we are experiencing. If we are really worried about the project, perhaps we could choose to work on it rather than being with our friend or schedule a different time to work on the project. However, since we have chosen to be with a friend, which is our reality at the moment, we can catch ourselves and notice the trap of worrying about

---

Ann

I have been future-oriented, focusing on all that needs doing to make life better for everyone. I always have a long list of projects and goals. This future focus has caused me to miss moments of joy. Instead of fully experiencing the joy, I think about what needs to be done next. For example, I have gone outside for a walk and spent the whole time planning a project rather than enjoying the beauty and experiencing rejuvenation.

Instead of staying in my head and ongoing narrative, I have practiced creating more spaciousness and attending to my sensations and emotions. When I embrace the present moment without judgment rather than focusing on the future, I find more joy throughout my days, feeling liberated from preconceived notions and open to new experiences.

It is such a simple and unexpected discovery. It requires me to slow down and appreciate the gift of living. I embrace what is happening around me and within me. We each have a river of aliveness flowing through us. I am learning to connect with this energy, a process both fascinating and rewarding, and trust the process.

CHAPTER 5 Sowing the Seeds: Planting Inner Awareness

the future. Then we can choose to be fully present, knowing we plan to work on the project at a more convenient time.

Our society trains us to focus on the future. Especially during these times of great uncertainty, worrying or putting our energy on what may happen in the future moves us away from JOYBeing.

Trap 3: The Desire to Change External Circumstances and the People Around Us

We often have the experience of reacting when someone does something differently than we would like or expect. This can be as simple as how someone dresses, eats, or talks. Our attention goes to trying to change people and situations because we have our own expectations, and we might naturally try to impose our shoulds on others.

While it can be tempting to want to control things in our lives, it often comes at the cost of our joy. Being overly controlling can lead to stress and anxiety. The urge to control comes from our desire to feel secure and safe. However, it can prevent us from allowing ourselves to be present and take in the beauty and joy the world has to offer.

Of course, we cannot control or change many things. For example, we can't control the weather, traffic, or other people's decisions, yet we often resort to feeling like a victim or blaming others when we experience such events. When it rains on a day we have planned a picnic, we complain. Yet can we stop the rain? We can only manage how we respond to the rain. We cannot control a global pandemic, but we can control our response to it. How can we adapt to situations in ways that serve us? Ironically, when we change ourselves, we inspire others to change.

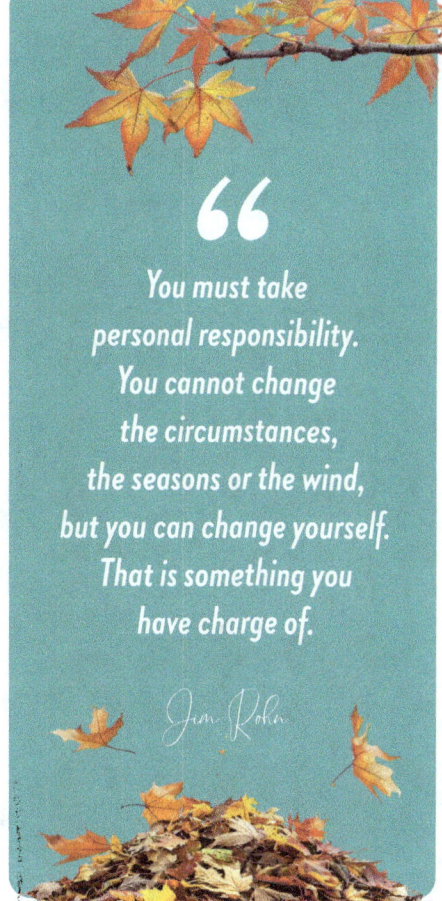

> "You must take personal responsibility. You cannot change the circumstances, the seasons or the wind, but you can change yourself. That is something you have charge of.
>
> — Jim Rohn

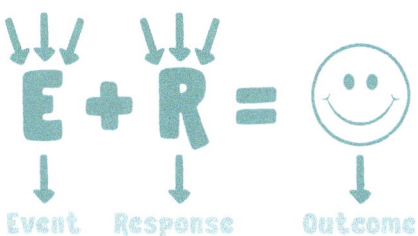 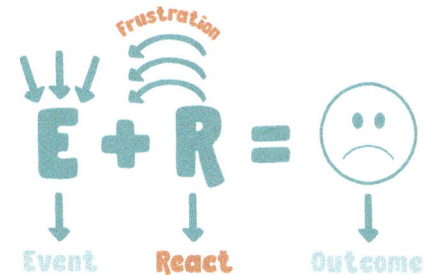

The way we react or respond to events and circumstances in our lives greatly impacts the outcomes we experience. Our choices and actions shape the results we achieve. A fundamental principle for success in the personal development field is:
Event + Response = Outcome

It is an empowering equation for work and life. We cannot change the events in our lives. The only thing we can change is our responses to events, which changes the outcomes.

When we focus our energy on trying to change things beyond our control, we can easily experience burnout and depletion. Rather than responding with intention, our energy drains, and we tend to become more reactive to others' requests or conversations, often leading to adverse outcomes and frustration.

To live an empowered life of JOYBeing, we need to acknowledge we can become aware and make choices that serve us. We can choose different thoughts and take different actions, which will influence our emotions and the lives we live. Our biggest trap is to miss this idea and use our energy to try to change people and events that are unchangeable.

As coaches, we have learned not to try to change our clients but to create awareness so they can make the choices that serve them and the greater environment. You will know you are experiencing this trap when you blame yourself or others and when you feel helpless in changing situations and experience a lack of results or outcomes. It is easy to blame circumstances and people and to feel like a victim. In such moments, experiment with questioning your reaction, connect with your sense of aliveness and power to act differently, and change how you respond to that event.

> *Life is 10 percent what happens to me and 90 percent of how I react to it.*
>
> — Charles R. Swindoll

JOYBeing

Ann

There was a time when I felt detached from the vibrancy and joy within, lacking a true zest for life. I was too focused on obligations and responsibilities. I worked long hours, took care of a young child, and supported aging parents and neighbors while managing a business and traveling for work internationally. I did not recognize how depleted I became, but I kept pushing forward. Sometimes, life requires this of us. Regrettably, I lost touch with the inner garden of JOYBeing that is always available.

In a moment of introspection, I began to ask myself what gives me joy and amplifies my energy. It turned out to be simple things—immersing myself in nature, connecting with friends, and engaging in meaningful conversations. Recalling the childhood joys of art, bike rides, and card games, I deliberately reintroduced these activities into my life, allowing myself to have fun more often. I looked for small moments of joy, such as the smile of a friend, a sunny day, or hearing an inspiring song, and learned to savor the experiences in the moment.

I confronted the trap of equating productivity with self-worth and shouldering the responsibility for so many people. I realized I could be a source of support without bearing the entire burden. Although I yearned for joy, I initially doubted it was within my grasp. A turning point came when I recognized I could significantly influence others by being more alive and connected with myself. By prioritizing my awareness of moments of joy and experiencing the essence and joy of being alive, JOYBeing became a conscious decision I am profoundly grateful for today.

When our attention is on changing events and people we cannot change, we are using up our energy and can experience frustration, resentment, and burnout. With these low-frequency emotions, we deplete our energy, feel like a victim, and react rather than respond. We can easily hurt our relationships when we are in this trap. For example, when you are stuck in unexpected traffic on your way to a meeting, it is easy to blame yourself for not leaving earlier, blame the slow drivers, experience stress, and dump your frustration on others. When you become aware of your reaction, you can choose to take a few breaths and surrender to the situation. You can choose a different response. For example, you can make a call informing the people in your meeting that you will be late, and rather than swim in an aggressive mood, listen to music and calm yourself to change your mood. You will likely enter your meeting with a more centered presence and be more productive when you accept and make peace with your current reality.

When you become aware of your trap of trying to change people and circumstances, you will be at choice to take responsibility, be open to new possibilities, and identify actions that enable you to experience JOYBeing. You will have confidence in leading your life rather than being led. You will be more

CHAPTER 5 Sowing the Seeds: Planting Inner Awareness

proactive in identifying solutions and be more innovative. Rather than trying to be perfect, you can accept and appreciate the challenges of life and be open to responding, experimenting, and learning.

In summary, the outside world we live in is full of disappointments, suffering, and trauma, making it easy to feel overwhelmed and helpless. However, the key to coping with these external challenges lies in our ability to choose our responses deliberately. Rather than reacting impulsively or succumbing to fear, we can take an Open Stance and cultivate a mindful awareness that allows us to notice our internal experiences and emotions. By connecting to our inner sense of aliveness, we empower ourselves to respond in ways more aligned with our values and aspirations. This conscious choice in how we respond, rather than merely react, enables us to create a new way of being that is resilient and grounded in our inner truth.

Being responsible for our responses to uncontrollable external events is a profound act of self-empowerment. JOYBeing, or the ability to find joy and meaning in the midst of suffering, is rooted in this responsibility. It involves recognizing that, despite the hardships we face, we can still contribute to life from a place of inner aliveness and possibility. This internal way of being allows us to transcend the limitations imposed by external circumstances and remain connected to a sense of purpose and fulfillment. By choosing to respond from this place of aliveness, we not only enhance our own wellbeing but also inspire and uplift those around us, creating a ripple effect of positive change.

Gila

Being called "Gila" multiple times a day, which means "joy," paradoxically serves as a continual reminder for me to reconnect with my joy—a facet of myself I had long been disconnected from. During my search for joy, I often got caught in traps. At times, I was fixated on recreating moments from the past, while in other instances I was attempting to move myself forward to the future, not living in the moment but in an unrealistic space that nurtured expectations that led to inevitable disappointments. Alternatively, I allocated my energy into attempting to change events or even the people around me, triggered by my achiever pattern. These unhealthy patterns became the focal point of my awareness as I put my attention into what wasn't working, seeking a pathway to embody the true essence of my name.

Through this exploration, I crafted a new narrative for myself—one rooted in experiencing JOYBeing. This personal evolution led me to develop the E-MRI tool of awareness, which has been a steadfast companion on my journey for almost a decade and a half. Not only have I been using this tool in my own growth, but I've also shared it with countless clients, each of whom has found it to be an invaluable instrument for cleansing our inner emotional landscape.

Emotion Mood Reflection Indicator (E-MRI)

For decades, our work has been in coaching leaders to open new windows of simple, usable, practical awareness tools to cope with and manage day-to-day challenges. We see ourselves as awareness agents. Awareness exists at the moment, which is where the potential to change lives. We want to embrace and integrate all aspects of ourselves to experience wholeness. Not using and honoring all of our parts is like living half a life. It's like looking at life from a narrow-angle rather than a 360 perspective. We are the leaders of our lives, and our choices and our use of self influence who we become, what we evoke in others, and our effect on the world.

We use a lot of energy and contract when we fall into our traps. How would life be different if we used this depleting energy in the opposite direction with awareness? How would this affect us physically and emotionally?

As previously explained, whenever we feel stuck, there's a narrative behind it. Our emotions are connected to stories that keep our emotions alive. When we continue to hold on to our old stories, we limit our mindset and narrow our possibilities.

The narratives we create are usually either about a fear in the past, an anxiety in the future, or a desire to change the people or circumstances outside of us. We are not accepting the reality of the moment. Our suffering occurs when we resist our true reality or *what is*.

Emotions are messengers that provide guidance for our wellbeing. When we are in our traps, we often experience low-frequency emotions and use our energy in ways that drain us, and we are not present in the moment. With the E-MRI awareness tool, we can be more aware of the stories we are telling ourselves and how we treat ourselves, and thus be more at choice and open ourselves to possibilities. Dorothy Siminovitch, author of *A Gestalt Coaching Primer*, says that our presence and awareness of the moment say a lot about who we are. Once we are aware, our use of self determines the influence we can make.

> "Presence is our GPS where the data of the moment is registered.
>
> *Dorothy Siminovitch*

E-MRI, developed by Gila Ancel Seritcioglu, has been used with hundreds of clients as a way of becoming aware of our emotions in the moment, addressing traps, and enhancing JOYBeing.

Similar to a medical MRI scan, this E-MRI tool is a magnifying glass to scan our emotional landscape, which provides us with the data of the moment.

To use this tool, simply notice your mood in the moment and identify whether you are experiencing a low-frequency or high-frequency mood, whether your mood is enlivening or depleting. Notice where you are experiencing this mood in your body.

If you are experiencing a high-frequency mood where you feel more alive and positive, rather than taking it for granted, appreciate this moment and what you are doing to foster this experience. This awareness indicates you are present and embracing the moment and experiencing JOYBeing. You are open in your body. The more experiences we have like this, the more fulfilled we are. We are strengthening the neural pathways that, at a cellular level, create regulation and reinforce JOYBeing.

> ### Gila
>
> Years ago, I worked with a client who was preparing for a job interview and deeply fearful and self-sabotaging. She was extremely anxious about the possibility of failure or rejection. When I asked her about her past experiences with rejection or failure, she couldn't recall any. This realization sparked a profound awareness within her—she recognized the pattern wasn't rooted in her reality. She was artificially generating anxiety for herself.
>
> This incident made me consider the origins of all of our narratives. Do these stories stem from our lived history? If so, the crucial work lies in revisiting and reframing those past experiences. However, if these stories aren't rooted in our personal histories, we still need to foster awareness in our clients. Often, we invent narratives. Helping individuals uncover the truth behind their narratives—whether they're based on genuine experiences or fabricated—can be a powerful tool in guiding them toward a more authentic and empowered perspective.

When we experience high-frequency moods, we are expanding our wellbeing. We are investing in ourselves, like adding coins to our internal bank account, and we become more resourceful and resilient and invest in our future. An enlivening mood check tells us we are doing well. We create more self-confidence and self-worth and are emotionally centered. A positive mood is a confirmation that we are continuing to nurture ourselves. We have gotten into the habit of doing a mood check during the day. When we feel peaceful, excited, and engaged, we notice we are much more effective and have a greater effect on whatever we are doing.

If you are experiencing a low-frequency mood, such as disappointment, despair, anxiety, boredom, or frustration, you may feel down with low energy. This indicates that you may have fallen into one of the three traps. You are likely to feel contracted and tense with shallow breath. Notice where this emotion lives in your body.

Consider whether you are visiting a memory of the past, are ahead of yourself worrying about the future, or are using your energy for wanting to change a person or a situation. When our mood is low, we are often in one of these three traps. Once we have identified the trap, we can take a pause or a breath to notice the reality of our present moment.

Once we notice our trap, we can make an intentional choice to bring us into the reality of the present moment. With this awareness, we can be more at choice and move into purposeful actions that serve us to come back to center and access JOYBeing.

Intention and practice are required to shift from low-frequency emotions and contraction to openness, curiosity, compassion, and JOYBeing. When we cultivate a way of being that focuses on opportunities in life, we open our hearts to living fully. When we understand that we naturally fall into traps and experience low frequency, we can open our hearts and be more compassionate with ourselves and others. It's possible to train our hearts and minds and access the wisdom of our bodies to experience JOYBeing.

> ***In low moments notice:***
>
> ✓ **What is your low-frequency mood?**
>
> ✓ **What are your sensations related to this low mood? Where do you notice them in your body?**
>
> ✓ **What is your narrative around this mood?**
>
> ✓ **Where does this narrative come from? How old is it? Is it familiar?**
>
> ✓ **Which trap have you fallen into that is hijacking your energy?**

CHAPTER 5 Sowing the Seeds: Planting Inner Awareness

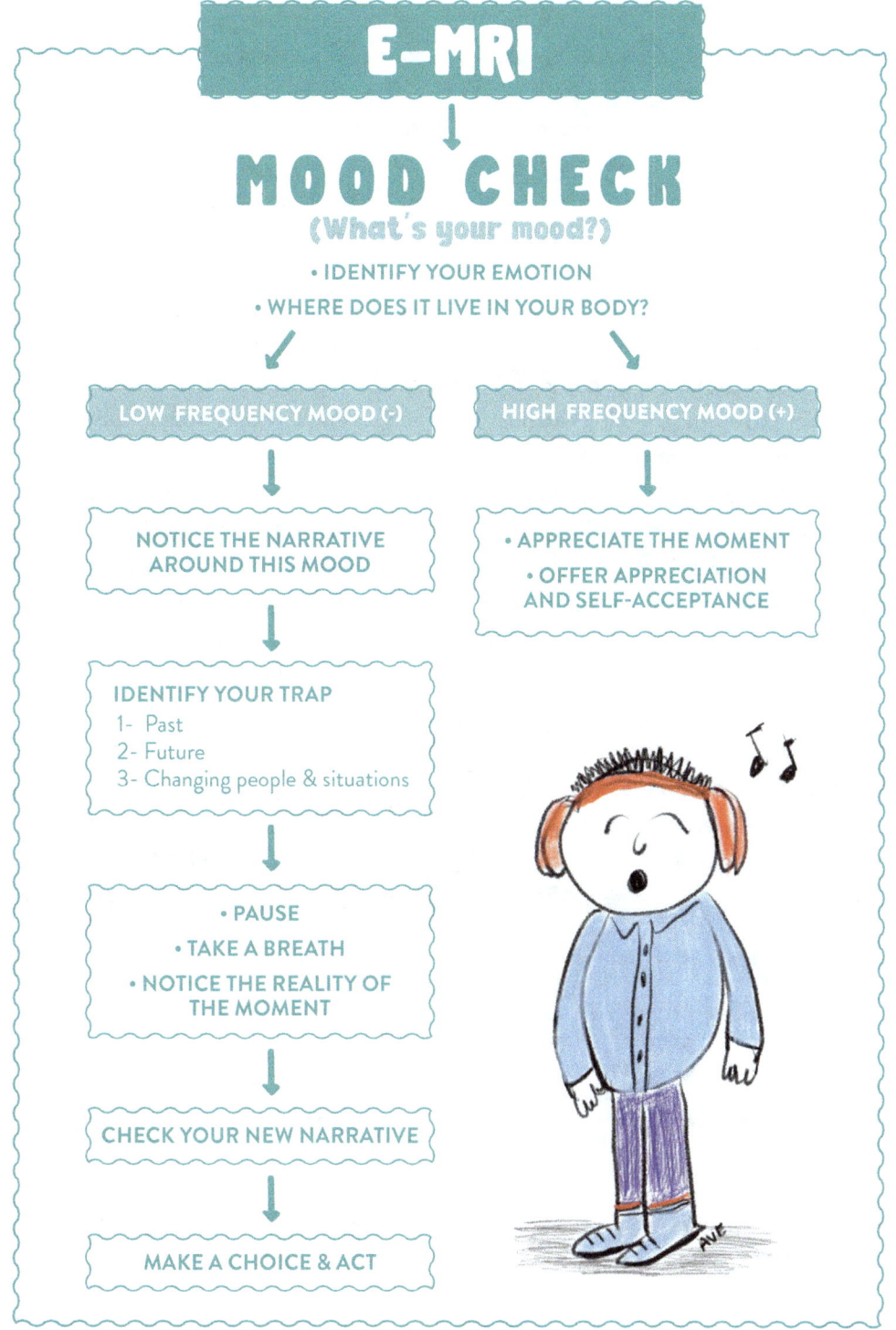

E-MRI

MOOD CHECK
(What's your mood?)

- IDENTIFY YOUR EMOTION
- WHERE DOES IT LIVE IN YOUR BODY?

LOW FREQUENCY MOOD (−)

NOTICE THE NARRATIVE AROUND THIS MOOD

IDENTIFY YOUR TRAP
1- Past
2- Future
3- Changing people & situations

- PAUSE
- TAKE A BREATH
- NOTICE THE REALITY OF THE MOMENT

CHECK YOUR NEW NARRATIVE

MAKE A CHOICE & ACT

HIGH FREQUENCY MOOD (+)

- APPRECIATE THE MOMENT
- OFFER APPRECIATION AND SELF-ACCEPTANCE

When doing a mood check, George noticed he was experiencing worry and identified this as a low-frequency mood that frustrated him. He wanted to make a request that would make him more effective and feel better at work. His narrative was that he would not be heard or would be misunderstood. He felt a tightness in his chest. He became aware of the trap of putting his energy into the future, making him not present in the moment but anticipating rejection. He noticed how his thoughts were negatively affecting him. With this awareness, he was able to understand he had made up a scenario that wasn't serving him; therefore, he created a new narrative that he had the skills and the right to ask for this request. He took a few breaths, calmed himself, recalled positive experiences, and connected to his resources. He took an Open Stance to express himself with a new mindset and had a successful interaction.

Another client, Wendy, was upset that her daughter complained and did not move forward with her life. Her daughter was unsatisfied with her job and her relationships. When doing a mood check, Wendy noticed her sadness about her daughter's situation and that her daughter did not take action according to her advice. She recognized she had constantly been telling her daughter what to do to no avail. She was caught in the trap of trying to change her daughter and her daughter's life. Once she awakened and attended to the contraction and tension in her heart, she could acknowledge her own fears and effort to control. She adopted

Ann

My natural propensity is to focus on others and prioritize their needs. Intentionally cultivating the practice of turning inward, I embarked on a journey of noticing my sensations, emotional moods, and intertwined narratives. It didn't take me long to become aware of my ingrained patterns. For example, I tried to fix things—especially when others were unhappy or hurting. The desire to engage, include everyone, and care for others was a driving force, accompanied by expectations about how things "should" be.

While these patterns have not entirely vanished, the pull to react impulsively has diminished. I can see how my conditioning and the stories I tell myself are influencing me. This heightened awareness has fostered a greater acceptance of life's challenges and an enhanced ability to exercise choice in my responses. Understanding the intricate dance between my conditioning and my reactions has brought clarity and empowered me to navigate life's complexities with a greater sense of resilience, wellbeing, and joy. I am grateful to be alive.

CHAPTER 5 Sowing the Seeds: Planting Inner Awareness

an Open Stance and created new strategies to relate to her daughter. Then she was able to relax and accept her adult daughter's choices. Changing her perspective and her way of interacting with her daughter created a more peaceful environment and a more fulfilling relationship. She and her daughter both experienced a more positive way of being. Ironically, her daughter became more open to her mother's perspective and even, at times, asked for her opinion.

Sara, an older client who was entering menopause, noticed her anger while doing a mood check. She was upset that she did not look and feel as fit as she once did. Looking into her anger, she noticed her trap of trying to recreate the past with her previous body in her thirties. Her trap was that she did not let go of the past and accept the reality of the present moment. When she awoke to her story, she noticed her longing for her past life. When she was able to be self-compassionate and acknowledge her emotions, she could connect with her true essence, appreciate the wisdom of this time of her life, and accept the challenges and reality of aging.

Tom noticed his low mood as he entered his coaching session and expressed his emotion, "I'm tired." Using the E-MRI Awareness Tool, he acknowledged that he was in a low mood because he had not gotten enough rest and had been overworking. In our conversation, it became clear he was trapped in his past perception that everything had to be completed by him before he could rest. Noticing this "should" pattern and realizing he could not change the past, he made contact with his present need for rest, relaxation, and more fun. He honored his humanness and committed to taking a walk and watching a movie with his family rather than focusing on work that evening. He reported that he was refreshed and had more energy the next day.

Once we acknowledge and create a shift in our mood, we start self-regulating and come to a place of attunement within. We are then positioned to more effectively attune with others. As collective trauma expert Thomas Hübl

158

says, once we self-regulate, we can prepare ourselves to coregulate with others, and by listening, we see and feel others more clearly and grow in relational wisdom. This kind of attunement with ourselves and others is essential for connection. How we connect with others is essential to our wellbeing because it literally determines whether we survive or thrive.

Research shows that stress creates inflammation and leads to illness. We can support our health by checking in and continually clearing our emotional clutter. If we were to spill coffee on our desk, without hesitation, we would immediately clean it. If not, it would leave a stain or negatively affect our computers and papers. If we don't take out the garbage regularly, our home will not be habitable. Likewise, the E-MRI is a tool to clear away our internal emotional clutter and create a healthy, clean environment of JOYBeing. The sooner we catch and identify our traps, the sooner we can clear our internal emotional landscape and experience JOYBeing.

The E-MRI awareness tool allows us to examine our stories and live life fully in the present moment, appreciating the realities and rhythm of life. It requires the practice of checking in with ourselves regularly for a mood check to create a life of balance and wellbeing. Attending to our inner life and prioritizing keeping it clean is important so we can live our external life with ease and JOYBeing.

The 4A recipe and the Open Stance mindset enable us to explore and integrate our emotions when we are trapped, creating deeper awareness, new understanding, and positive action.

Gila

Checking my mood multiple times a day has become a regular practice. Once I scan my body and assess how I'm feeling, I can instantly sense my mood's impact on me through various sensations. A high positive mood often manifests as an opening in my chest, which I always remember to acknowledge, while a low mood tends to signal contractions in my stomach or throat, and heaviness on my upper back.

Following these sensations and delving into the narratives around them, I often have an aha moment. When I fall into one of the traps, usually being ahead of the present moment, it fosters disconnections. Becoming aware of this pattern has created an immediate shift in me. I feel it in my breath becoming slower and deeper, and in my body, which gradually de-contracts and returns to its natural relaxed state. These instances serve as special moments of awakening, bringing me back to my center and strengthening my connection to JOYBeing.

Practices

1. MOOD CHECK

We suggest identifying specific times of the day or setting the timer on your phone (every thirty or sixty minutes) to regularly check in with yourself regarding your mood and the emotions you are experiencing to provide data on your internal emotional landscape. Consider using the "How We Feel" app.

- ✓ What is your mood right now? Is it high or low?
- ✓ Name the emotion you are experiencing. (Refer to the Mood Meter above.)
- ✓ If you're in a high mood, notice your sensations and where this mood lives in your body, and enjoy and appreciate the moment. Say "bravo" to yourself.
- ✓ If you are experiencing a low mood, give yourself empathy and self-compassion.
- ✓ What are your sensations related to this mood? Notice where it lives in your body.
- ✓ Identify the narrative around it. Where does it come from? Is it familiar?
- ✓ Identify which trap you have fallen into. Consider, are you present in the moment, or have you fallen into one of the traps of focusing on the past, the future, or trying to change a person or a situation?
- ✓ Ask yourself the following questions:
  - What is the truth of this present moment?
  - Where do I have control in this situation? What is my response to what I can't control? What choices do I have today that will serve me?
  - What outcome do I want to create?
  - What can I do differently now?
- ✓ Notice your new narrative after responding to these questions.
- ✓ What action will you take?
- ✓ What can you say differently to yourself? Is there a positive affirmation you can give yourself?
- ✓ What is your mood now after this process?
  You may keep a mood journal to notice the pattern of moods and emotions.

Practices

E-MRI DAILY TEMPLATE

Time	Mood (+ or -)	Emotion & Place in the Body	Narrative	Identify Trap	Action Taken	Self-Appreciation

2. SELF-APPRECIATION PRACTICE

Every evening or at a prescribed time of the day, take five to ten minutes of "me time" to reflect on what you appreciate about yourself and how you have lived your day in alignment with your values. For example, you may appreciate yourself for the decisions you made, for actions you took that supported you, and for what is important to you that is in line with your values. You may appreciate that you did mood checks and cleared your emotional clutter. By doing this practice, we are investing in our JOYBeing bank account. Be sure to focus on what is going well. Recall that energy follows attention.

We don't see the world as it is. We see it as we are.

— Anaïs Nin

3. FOCUSING EXERCISE TO STRENGTHEN JOYBEING CONNECTION

We are not advocating avoiding pain or negative emotions. On the contrary, JOYBeing is about being aware, accepting, and meeting sensations and emotions as they are. By exploring the messages behind them, we create space for understanding and connection. This act of being "with" creates the transformation.

Take a moment to scan your body and notice sensations. Is there a part that invites you to be more understanding? For example, you may notice tension in your back or neck or a headache, or you may be aware of an emotion such as excitement or worry. Notice any symptom that creates some curiosity or energy for exploration that might open the door for insight. Keep focused attention on this part. Simply notice and allow it without trying to change it.

Consider having a conversation with this part to learn more. Ask any questions you are curious about. Here are some examples:

✓ Who are you?
✓ What do you look like? What's your color and shape?
✓ What is your purpose? How are you serving me?
✓ What is important to you?
✓ What is your message to me?
✓ What do you need from me?
✓ How can we work together?
✓ What do you need?

Allow time for self-reflection and journal the answers.

Notice if there is a new awareness and if something has shifted or changed. How did this conversation support your sense of JOYBeing?

Practices

4. REDUCE CLUTTER AND CREATE SPACE

When we are unaware, we create clutter. We accumulate stress when we have things that are undone, and that gets in our way of JOYBeing. Unfinished items take our energy and reduce our joy. When we experience a sense of completion or closure, we are more in touch with JOYBeing. Making mindful choices, slowing down, and having ways to address our priorities with awareness support us to create more space for JOYBeing. Spaciousness allows us to be more relaxed and in touch with our sensations. Spaciousness within ourselves allows more connection and freedom on the outside, which supports us in taking purposeful action and experiencing more satisfaction.

Ironically, less allows us to experience more joy. When we let go of things we feel lighter. When we don't close issues, it is like leaving many windows open on our computer, which siphons energy.

- ✓ Notice how you accumulate clutter (physical and emotional), such as overbooking appointments, not putting things away in your home, and having a messy space.
- ✓ How is your pattern serving you? What is the emotion you are experiencing?
- ✓ What can you do differently to create a greater sense of space internally and externally?

> ❝ When we no longer are afraid of who we are, we act from integrity and authenticity.
>
> *Richard Strozzi-Heckler*

CHAPTER 5 Sowing the Seeds: Planting Inner Awareness

> "Joy arises when we open to both the beauty and suffering inherent in living. Like a great sky that includes all different types of weather, joy is an expansive quality of presence. It says yes to life, no matter what!
>
> — Tara Brach

Ann

Integrating the Open Stance process internally and externally has significantly influenced my experience of JOYBeing. The reminder to "stop, step back to cool down, and shift to being open" has become a guiding light. I regularly check in, keenly observing the reactions and judgments of others and myself. A tangible instance involves stopping when I sense a tightening and contracting in my stomach and hear my internal dialogue saying, "That is not right. They should be more considerate." Then I step back and cool down. I allow myself time to breathe and give myself empathy. "You are disappointed and frustrated." I allow myself to shift into an open, curious, and compassionate state. I may recall positive feelings with the person or how I feel open and alive in nature.

Operating from an Open Stance provides me with the necessary space to comprehend others' intentions and see other perspectives and possibilities. I can be kind to myself, recalling my conditioning and past expectations, including the natural desire for inclusion. This openness allows for generosity toward myself and others, fostering a profound sense of JOYBeing. I have come to appreciate that life is full of challenges and opportunities. Most of us are doing the best we can at the moment, given our unique history and experiences.

By consistently noticing our moods, adopting an Open Stance, and noticing our narratives, we can develop the neural pathways that enable us to be more open to ourselves and others more frequently. Consequently, joy and possibility become readily available, even in the face of life's myriad challenges.

CHAPTER 6

Sprouting and Growing Our Inner Garden: Nurturing JOYBeing

> "Dear Inner Child,
> It's okay if you've built walls to protect yourself.
> You can always open windows on those walls to let the light in."
>
> *Anonymous*

As children, we eagerly anticipate growing older, dreaming of the freedom and opportunities that adulthood seems to promise. However, as the years pass and we face life's complexities, a sense of longing often emerges. Many of us find ourselves wishing for the simplicity and joy of childhood days, longing for the innocence and spirit of those earlier years.

Joy is a birthright. In the depth of our being lies a child whose laughter is free and spirit wild. This inner child, with eyes full of wonder and an unscarred heart, serves as a beacon of light in a world often marked by hardships. When life's burdens become heavy, it is essential to remember this inner child filled with hopes and dreams, embodying innocence. Embracing the joy and playfulness of our inner child can rekindle a spark within us, providing a source of strength and guidance. By allowing our inner child to thrive, we can face the world with renewed energy and a heart that remains open to wonder, transforming life's challenges into opportunities for growth, resilience, and discovery.

When we are overwhelmed by responsibilities, stress, and societal pressures that dictate our behavior, we can unconsciously repress or lose touch with the liveliness of our inner child. In some ways, growing up asks us to become responsible and focused on results. The paradox is that once we are adults, we yearn for the natural aliveness of a child. Sometimes when we become parents or engage with children or pets, we reconnect with our inner aliveness and vibrancy. And often, the search for reconnection can be a journey. Many different ways exist to reconnect with our inner child's joy and aliveness, and it's well worth the effort to find what works for us. In this chapter, we will explore connecting with our inner child.

Just as we all have unique handprints, we have developed unique patterns of engaging in the world. These patterns are shaped by our experiences, beliefs, and behaviors. Our work is to create more awareness to discover what our patterns are so we can embrace those unique parts of ourselves and reconnect with our inner child. This involves recognizing and nurturing the playful, creative, and authentic parts of ourselves that may have been overshadowed by the demands of growing up. As we integrate these aspects into our daily lives, we foster a more harmonious relationship with ourselves, enriching our overall experience for greater fulfillment.

Reconnecting with Our Inner Child

We know that laughter is a natural and magical expression of joy and delight. It has the power to uplift our spirits, create connections, and foster a sense of ease and vitality. According to Jennifer Aaker and Naomi Bagdonas in their book *Humor Seriously*, studies suggest that, on average, children laugh around 300 times a day, while adults only manage to laugh five times. What happens along our journey from childhood to adulthood that causes us to lose touch with our laughter and its abundant benefits?

Deep within each of us lies an inner child, a seed of potential waiting to sprout and grow into a magnificent oak tree. Just as an acorn carries the blueprint of a mighty tree within its tiny shell, our inner child holds the essence of who we truly are, our authentic self. Nurturing this inner child is like tending to the acorn, providing it with the right conditions for growth, nourishment, and care. As we embark on a journey of self-discovery and healing, we learn to reconnect with our inner child, acknowledging its needs, fears, and dreams. By honoring and nurturing this precious part of ourselves, we create the fertile ground necessary for our inner garden to flourish.

> "Some day, you will be old enough to start reading fairy tales again."
>
> — C. S. Lewis

JOYBeing

The concept of the inner child was first introduced by Carl Jung, the famous psychotherapist. We know children naturally experience joy and aliveness. They don't think about being joyful; they automatically live it. They are excited to learn and enjoy playing. Connecting with the essence of our inner child allows us to experience joy and creative flow.

We often observe children's natural and spontaneous expressions of joy, curiosity, and delight. They find joy in the simplest things—seeing a pet, the sound of laughter, or the taste of a cookie. They experience wonder and awe and live fully in the present moment, unburdened by past regrets or future worries.

As we grow older and navigate adulthood's complexities, we often distance ourselves from the natural joy of our inner child. The weight of responsibilities, societal expectations, and life's challenges can dull our sense of wonder and limit our capacity to experience aliveness. However, the joy of our inner child never truly fades away; it continues to be a core part of who we are, even if it feels hidden at times.

The inner child within allows us to see the world through wonder-filled eyes and a sense of aliveness. We can reconnect with the joy of our inner child by embracing moments of playfulness, curiosity, and spontaneity. Cultivating a JOYBeing mindset and engaging in activities that bring us joy and a sense of aliveness nurture our passion and infuse our lives with vitality and wonder.

Reconnecting with our inner child allows us to experience the playfulness, creativity, wonder, and curiosity that naturally lives inside us. It is never too late to reconnect with this free-spirited part that can reignite our emotional vitality through JOYBeing.

Up to around the age of six, we were in a receptive brain state where we were profoundly affected by our experiences and our environment. As a child, we simply inhaled the beliefs and ways of being of our caregivers and the people around us. We naturally formed beliefs that shape how we live and interact in the world today. We were unconsciously impacted by our environment and experiences, which included intergenerational

> **"The most sophisticated people I know—inside, they are all children.**
>
> *Jim Henson*

beliefs, traumas, traditions, and ways of functioning.

We made assumptions about what we needed to do to survive in our families and communities. We formed scripts for how life and we "should" be. For example, if our parents believed "Children should be seen and not heard," we may have adopted a quiet disposition.

Sara, one of our coaching clients, expressed difficulty connecting with her inner child. "I don't really get how to connect with my inner child. I hear the voice of my inner critic but not my younger self." Sara is not alone. Most of us were not encouraged to listen to our inner parts. Many of our Cultivating JOYBeing course participants and coaching clients learned to focus primarily on external needs and demands. In an effort of self-preservation, some learned to numb themselves and cut off their inner connection with these young selves. Adopting patterns that protected us was more efficient and safer than truly listening within. It takes commitment to pay conscious attention to our inner yearnings and reconnect with our inner child's vibrant energy.

Sara benefitted from having a photo of herself at a young age on her desk, which allowed her to stop ignoring and

Ann

As the eldest in a large family, the weight of responsibility thrust me into adulthood prematurely, bringing about early encounters with stress, worry, and an overwhelming sense of responsibility. To fulfill these duties, I unintentionally let go of laughter, fun, and the awareness of my own needs, channeling my focus onto work, productivity, and others.

After becoming aware of the importance of tending to my inner child, I deliberately decided to carve out space for this neglected aspect of myself. Admittedly, I found it easy to forget and neglect my inner child, requiring a conscious effort to establish a practice of reconnecting, nurturing, and caring for this younger part of me that yearned for playfulness and connection to a sense of liveliness. Consistently creating space and engaging in drawing, art, moving, or exploring new places has proven particularly effective for this inner child to emerge. This ongoing process of offering care to this neglected part has strengthened my ability to connect with joy and vitality.

With practice, I have become more attuned to this inner child, learning to set boundaries, identify my needs, and assertively say "yes" more often to myself when necessary. Building and nurturing this relationship continues to be an ongoing process, and with each step, I experience an increasing sense of JOYBeing. As the connection strengthens, I receive feedback from others who sense my lightness and joy, inspiring them to reconnect with their own sense of aliveness. I am grateful that my effort to connect with my inner joy and aliveness has supported my goal of contributing to others' wellbeing.

reconnect and appreciate her younger self. She also kept a stuffed animal to remind her to allow space for play and connection. By journaling and sensing what her younger self would say about a particular issue, Sara noticed patterns she adopted as a young child, such as working hard for external validation and failing to take time for herself. Through this process, Sara felt a more profound connection within herself. Over time, Sara experienced a greater flow and a sense of JOYBeing.

> *The joy we feel has little to do with the circumstances of our lives and everything to do with the focus of our lives.*
>
> *Russell M. Nelson*

We all have habitual patterns that influence how we interact in the world.

- ✓ What habitual patterns limit your connection with your inner child and sense of joy and aliveness? (For example, overworking, being externally focused, being overly responsible, worrying.)
- ✓ When do you notice connecting with your sense of aliveness, creativity, play, and joy? (For example, being with a child or a pet, engaging in art, dancing.)
- ✓ Where do you experience joy and playfulness in your body?
- ✓ How would life be different if you connected to this part every day?

Our scripts from our backgrounds unconsciously affect our interactions and can create or inhibit joy. Many of us have silenced or failed to listen and give attention to our inner child in our effort to survive, fit in, and be successful in our environments. Whether we attend to it or not, our inner child yearns for attention, understanding, care, and support.

Gila

I've always felt compelled to be a giver, striving to improve life for all and make a difference in the world. I believed I had much to offer, often overextending myself in the pursuit of helping others. However, in doing so, I lost focus on some important people in my life and neglected my own wellbeing. I failed to carve out time to simply be with myself.

Realizing I had ignored my inner child, I made a conscious decision to give that part of me the attention it deserved. Reconnecting with my child within has been a journey—a continuous effort to prioritize that relationship as much as my relationships with others. It hasn't been easy; distractions often pulled me away. Yet dedicating myself to this reunion has infused me with newfound energy and vitality. Nature and the arts have become my channels for rekindling that connection.

In this process, I've learned that nurturing my inner child doesn't mean sacrificing my desire to make a positive difference. It's about finding a balance between giving to others and giving to myself. By honoring both aspects, I've found a deeper well of strength and fulfillment to share with the world.

Cultivating Play, Creativity, and Flow

Children naturally play. They are the innate masters of play, effortlessly planting the seeds of creativity as they navigate their world. Their natural inclination to explore, experiment, and learn nurtures creativity. In the realm of play, there's no room for apprehension about mistakes. Children dive into their surroundings with enthusiasm, embracing new experiences, taking risks, and crafting their own narratives. Play opens a sense of flow, which is life-giving.

Often as adults, we forget how to play and focus on productivity and performance. However, this mindset overlooks a profound truth: Play is an essential ingredient for a sense of vibrancy. It's easy to believe play has no place in a world driven by outcomes. Our experience working with teams has illuminated that the introduction of playful elements—such as games or humor—unleashes our dormant inner child. This assumes our inner critic does not dampen the fun.

When we are able to be in the natural flow of life, we experience a lack of worry about time and are often more creative and productive. This flow serves as a pathway to our intrinsic sense of joy, where creativity and productivity intertwine harmoniously for a life of aliveness and JOYBeing.

For us, play gives us a sense of freedom of exploration. When engaging in play, boundaries dissolve, and the realm of possibilities expands. Play sets our spirits free, letting us venture where imagination has no bounds.

It is important to nurture our inner child with regular opportunities for play and creativity as we move to adulthood. The joy of play is available in our ability to have a sense of curiosity and to perceive and appreciate the beauty in all aspects of life. Whether through a stroke of a paintbrush on a canvas, the melody of a song, the grace of a dancer's movement, or the power of a heartfelt story, we can cultivate a unique connection to the world around us, transforming the ordinary into the inspiring extraordinary.

> " *Mindfulness is the paintbrush in the art of happiness. When we are mindful, we are more artful, and happiness blooms.*
>
> — Thich Nhat Hanh

CHAPTER 6 Sprouting and Growing Our Inner Garden: Nurturing JOYBeing

By giving permission to ourselves to play and paying attention to details around us, whether a flower, a piece of art, a pet, a car, or a book, we can experience awe and recognize the beauty and potential in everything. What is invisible becomes visible. This connects us with our creative energy that comes from the core of play and gives our life meaning.

Engaging with the arts, whether through observation or creation, can be calming for the mind. In *Your Brain on Art: How the Arts Transform Us*, authors Susan Magsamen and Ivy Ross encourage having an aesthetic mindset where simply observing or engaging in some art form promotes joy, health, and overall wellbeing. Drawing or creating something with our hands and engaging in art can calm and restore us at a physiological level. Studies show that the arts can lower stress hormones and elevate inner equilibrium. The level of artistic skill is not important. On the contrary, being present to sensations and being engaged creates a sense of flow, connection, and meaning. Many studies show that arts—whether sound, colors, drawing, painting, movement, or narrative—can reduce stress and prolong life. Engaging or enjoying the arts is a practice that connects us with our inner child and enhances mindfulness and JOYBeing.

In writing this book, we took a stance of play and opened to our creativity. We were not focused on getting things "right" or "perfect" but on listening within, exploring together, experiencing fun and connection, and allowing the book to emerge. We hope you enjoy this roadmap of connecting to your aliveness and vibrancy of life and take it as your invitation to play and experience JOYBeing.

Ann

I recollect playing as a child, exploring the neighborhood with siblings and friends, engaging in imaginative and often silly plays that made time seemingly expand. However, as an adult, I had to permit myself to reconnect with joy and play consciously. This journey led me to infuse play into my work with leaders and teams, incorporating elements like riddles, jokes, funny videos, and interactive sharing.

Leaders have reported that introducing check-in questions, allowing individuals to share about themselves, and fostering spaces for connection independent of outcomes enhance their work experience and significantly increase joy and success. I've discovered that allowing myself to embrace the messiness, whether in facilitating a workshop or meeting, results in a more playful, present, and enlivened version of myself. This playful approach brings me into a deeper connection with JOYBeing, creating an environment where joy and creativity thrive.

Integrating Our Inner Voices

At times, it can feel as though our inner child and inner critic are in conflict, pulling us in different directions due to their distinct and often opposing needs and agendas. It is important to recognize that both voices originate from within us and are driven by what they perceive as our best interests. Our inner child embodies our creativity, curiosity, and desire for play and self-expression, while our inner critic, as mentioned before, aims to protect us by adhering to societal standards, avoiding potential risks, and maintaining a sense of control.

Each voice has its own perspective and approach to life, which can lead to conflicts and internal tension. When the inner child and inner critic strongly disagree, we may experience an inner struggle and heightened stress. The inner critic's dominant voice may overshadow the creative child's voice, stifling our sense of joy, spontaneity, and vibrancy.

Our desire to be loved, belong, and be accepted allows us to unconsciously dim the inner child's life energy and expand the inner critic's voice. In our effort to receive acknowledgment, acceptance, and perceived success, we tend to adopt the belief that we are not enough. Our inner voice chimes in with its messages in an attempt to guide and protect us. If not managed, our inner critic and related habitual patterns can dominate our lives, diminish the fire of aliveness within us, and cut off our inner child's natural flow of energy.

The inner critic's voice drowns out the spontaneity, flow, and joy of the inner child. This is costly to our sense of aliveness and freedom. In moments when we are overly pressured or feel challenged by assimilated high expectations, this inner voice can unfold as a harsh inner critic. We are often unaware of where our beliefs originated or how we unconsciously continue to feed them. This voice's presence eventually becomes a habitual pattern and part of our identity.

> *Perhaps the only contact we've had with our inner child for a long time is to scold it, criticize it. Then we wonder why we are unhappy.*
>
> — Louise Hay

For example, we often learn in school to conform and achieve to gain acceptance. When we overemphasize this focus, we narrow access to our inner child and sense of aliveness. Focusing on achievement and success can become a habitual pattern that society often rewards.

However, it is important to assess our internal dynamic. Creating space for both the critical and inner child voices and learning how to integrate and harmonize them is crucial. Acknowledging our inner critic's valid concerns while also honoring our inner child's desires and needs allows for a more balanced internal dialogue. Developing self-awareness is required to identify when the critical voice becomes overpowering and to intentionally invite the inner child's voice to be heard.

By fostering a compassionate and supportive relationship with our inner critic, we can address its concerns without allowing it to diminish the playful and creative spirit of our inner child. Learning to work together means finding common ground where both the inner child and inner critic can coexist in harmony. This involves fostering self-compassion, challenging self-limiting beliefs, and consciously choosing actions that align with our authentic desires while acknowledging the importance of responsible decision-making.

> The genius of life is to carry the spirit of childhood into old age.
>
> *Aldous Huxley*

JOYBeing

Connecting with Our Wise Self

Not all of us learned the tools to cope and experience self-love in the face of perceived challenges. However, it is never too late to begin. In addition to connecting with our inner child and managing our inner critic, we can call on our wise selves.

Within each of us resides a wise self, a source of wisdom, guidance, and deep understanding. This wise inner self embodies our innate wisdom, intuition, and experience, offering valuable insights and support as we navigate life's challenges and pursue personal growth. Our wise self is the compassionate and wise voice that encourages us to embrace our strengths, acknowledge our limitations, and trust in our own abilities. It gently reminds us to be kind to ourselves, to practice self-care, and to approach setbacks as learning opportunities. This wise guide empowers us to tap into our potential, make aligned decisions, and take intentional actions that align with our values and aspirations. By cultivating a connection with our wise self, we access a wellspring of wisdom that guides us on our journey, fostering self-belief, resilience, and a sense of purpose. With our wise self's guidance, we can navigate life's twists and turns with greater clarity, confidence, and a deep understanding that we have the wisdom within us to create the fulfilling and meaningful life we desire.

> *Joy is the deepest invoker of possibility, novelty, vitality, intimacy, and hope.*
>
> — Amy Elizabeth Fox

Carl Jung introduced the practice of listening to our wise guides through active imagination into modern psychology. He believed we could all access the reservoir of collective unconscious wisdom. Most scientific researchers believe our inner wise self or guide is accessing the creative right hemisphere of our brain or our intuition. We find that connecting with this resource offers ease and confidence.

Richard Schwartz, founder of Internal Family Systems (IFS), is convinced that everyone, without exception, has the capacity for self-leadership. After years of working with

CHAPTER 6 Sprouting and Growing Our Inner Garden: Nurturing JOYBeing

people from all walks of life who have experienced all levels of trauma, he believes we all have a Self, or what we call a wise self, that persists and can be uncovered. According to Schwartz, our Self is characterized by curiosity, compassion, confidence, calmness, clarity, creativity, connectedness, and courage.

Our wise self, which is a mindful, centered, and open presence, can ignite our inner child's aliveness and creativity. It can serve as a loving source to listen to and appreciate our inner child as well as our inner critic with curiosity and nonjudgment. From the lens of the open wise self, we can see opportunities and possibilities and connect to JOYBeing.

Connecting with the inner child in the safe space of the wise self activates the loving and nourishing self in us. In this space, we can find the resources to grow with love and acceptance and realize our potential.

When we are in judgment or closed, the inner critic predominates and takes charge of our perspective. This

Gila

My inner critic has played a strong significant role, often drowning out my true desires with its inhibiting voice. Seeking affirmation externally, I grew up feeling inadequate, especially as a girl in a family that valued boys. This situation pushed me into a relentless cycle of overworking and doing to gain recognition. Recalling childhood attempts to imitate my older brother by excelling in traditionally masculine activities like playing football, cowboy with guns, or playing with Ken dolls rather than Barbies, I found myself sacrificing my feminine identity at the expense of meeting expectations and being accepted for who I was.

These external pressures led to shame, making it difficult for me to accept the acknowledgments I genuinely deserved. Consistently, I reached out to my inner child, sensing a deep yearning. The journey to transform this inner voice into a supportive companion was very difficult. Eventually, I reframed it, connecting with my little girl inside and embracing my femininity, and even by creating a two-day workshop on becoming friends with our inner critic. Instead of being a saboteur, eventually my inner critic became a protector and ally.

This transformative process allowed me to shift toward a mindset of "I am enough." Connecting with my inner wise self and embracing all aspects of myself, including my femininity, led me to a state of reconnecting with my *joie de vivre*, which I call JOYBeing today—a profound realization that I am complete just as I am.

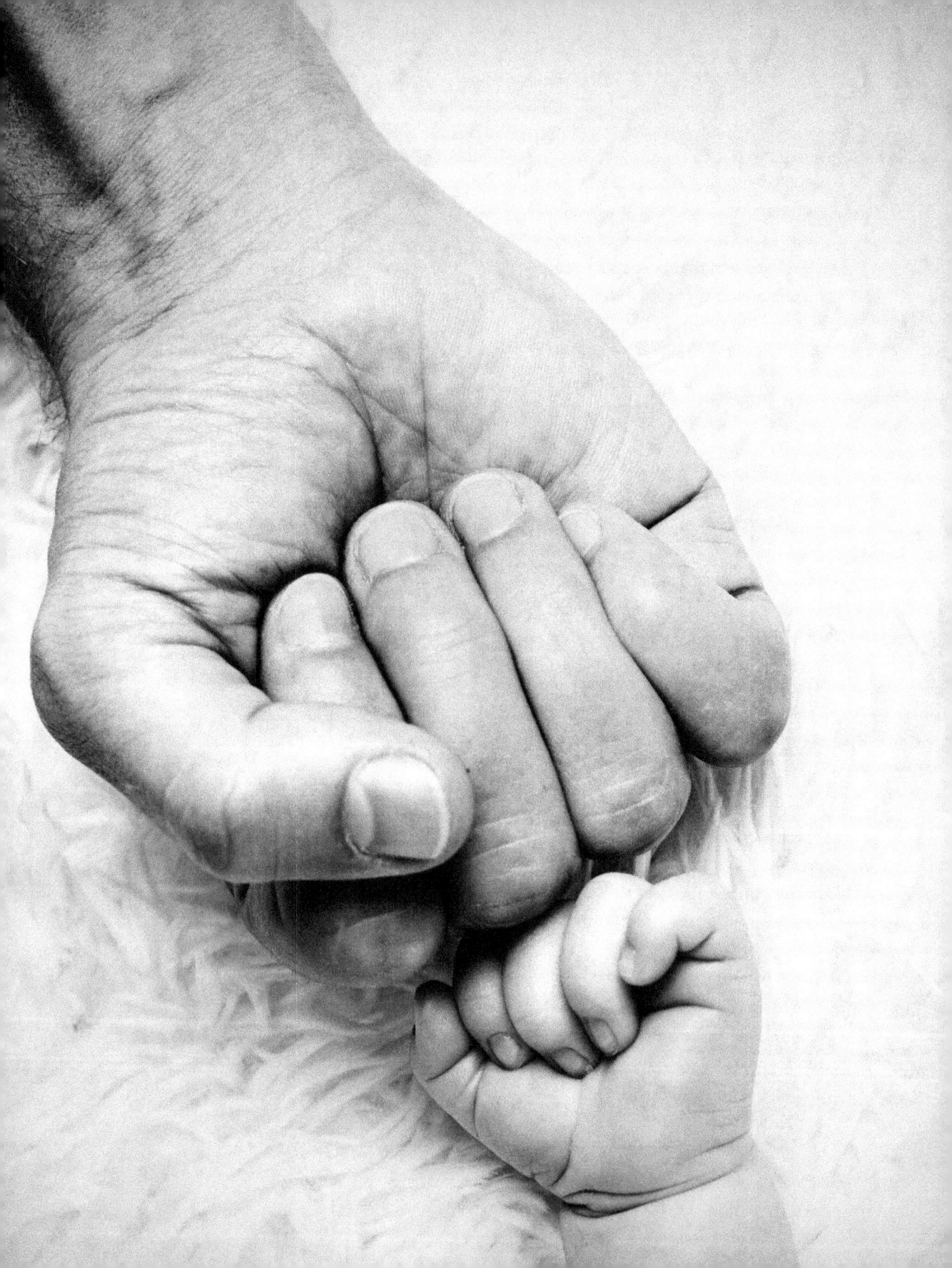

influences how we see and act. We can become aware and choose to shift to being in an Open Stance. By connecting with our wise self, we can invite our inner child to reclaim its power, freedom, creativity, and joy.

It's important to support our inner child to experience JOYBeing. One way of supporting our inner child is to be a loving caregiver and friend who takes a wider and hopeful perspective. Our wise self easily serves this purpose. Many of us did not receive the loving care we might have wished for as children. However, it's not too late to be the loving and caring support to ourselves that we need. In fact, it's our responsibility to be a friend and care for ourselves. We will then be better equipped to live fully than if we expect others to meet our needs. When we take responsibility for ourselves, we increase our emotional capacity for connection and attunement and for living a more fulfilled life.

By adopting an open mindset and connecting with our wise selves, we not only enhance our own lives, but we inspire others to do the same. This transformation ripples through our relationships, making life better for all involved.

Ann

Each of us harbors parts within ourselves that grapple with feelings of inadequacy and recurring issues throughout our lives. Connecting with these internal facets is always available through conscious effort. For instance, I occasionally encounter a part of me that feels uncared for and alone. In response, I've deliberately chosen to reconnect with this wounded aspect rather than deny or harbor anger toward it. Like an ideal loving parent, my wise self can be open and compassionate without judgment, providing assurance and companionship to these challenging inner parts. This intentional process has proven transformative, bolstering my hurt part's confidence and fostering a reconnection with a sense of playfulness and JOYBeing.

My work assisting leaders in recognizing and managing judgment and facilitating a shift toward openness, curiosity, and compassion in their conversations has concurrently supported my connection with the wise self. When I discern contraction and judgment within myself, I can intercept it and transition into an open, curious, compassionate, and kind state. Through practice, I've discovered that from this vantage point, a broader perspective unfolds, revealing an array of possibilities.

Transforming Challenges into Opportunities for Growth and Enhanced JOYBeing

> Everyone who wills can hear their inner voice. It is within everyone.
>
> — *Mahatma Gandhi*

We all experience challenges as we go forward in life. Working through the challenges is what supports our growth and sense of joy. While we may want to suppress or avoid contact with disturbing and painful experiences, it is life-giving to address and work through our wounds and challenges. Some are obvious, such as the loss of a loved one, lack of financial security, rejection, or physical and emotional hurt. We carry traumas that have been with us since childhood, some that have been passed down through generations. Wounds that have been with us since our early years shape how we experience and interact in the world and our connection with our inner child. For example, not being seen or valued as a child can create habitual patterns that continue to influence our daily experiences. We tend to perpetuate these challenging experiences in our own styles to cope with life until we learn ways to heal and transform them.

The impact of trauma and our childhood wounds can be profound, causing significant barriers to experiencing joy and aliveness in our lives. How we respond to traumatic experiences can leave deep emotional wounds that affect our sense of safety, trust, and wellbeing. They can create a protective armor around our hearts, blocking our ability to fully embrace joy and feel truly alive. Trauma can manifest as hyper-vigilance, where we experience fear and anxiety or depression, or it can manifest as numbing and a disconnection from ourselves and others. To address the impact of trauma and restore a sense of joy and aliveness, it is important to prioritize healing, including often seeking professional support. Cultivating self-compassion, self-care practices, and engaging in practices that bring ease and connection can also help gradually dissolve the blocks and create space for JOYBeing and aliveness to resurface. Healing our wounds is a courageous journey, but with the right support and self-compassion, it can lead to a renewed capacity for joy and an authentic sense of aliveness.

JOYbeing is not about running away from difficult issues and inner wounds but connecting with what is inside us to create more space and transform pain into something that will serve us. We want to make intentional connections between painful experiences and our reality in a safe environment. We have the capacity to make contact with all of our emotions and our narratives when the conditions are supportive. We can trust that our inner selves were once reacting in a way they thought was best to protect us. When we are able to reconnect with our inner child, we can heal and experience vitality.

JOYBeing is giving ourselves a sense of ease, expansion, and spaciousness and becoming aware of how we block the energy inside us and our sense of aliveness. When we become aware of the tightness and blockages inside us, we can choose to engage in dialogue with our inner parts in order to expand and give more space to our inner child's energy. That opens us to experience JOYBeing, which is an excitement for and higher engagement in life. We want to enjoy and experience the fullness and aliveness of life. We want to make life a celebration of who we are.

> *The wound is not my fault. But the healing is my responsibility.*
>
> — Marianne Williamson

Meet Sara—A Leader Focused on Self-Improvement

In our fast-paced world, it's not uncommon to feel the weight of being overwhelmed pressing down on us, suffocating our sense of joy and vitality. Meet Sara, a dedicated leader who is passionate about personal growth and self-improvement. As she navigates her professional life's demanding landscape, she often finds herself teetering on the edge of burnout, yearning for a sense of aliveness that seems just out of reach. In her own words, Sara vulnerably shared, "The constant juggle between my demanding job and the pursuit of personal growth sometimes leaves me feeling overwhelmed, craving for more joy and a deeper connection to life."

Sara had a belief: "I must constantly achieve more to be worthy of joy and fulfillment." This belief created a perpetual cycle of striving for perfection and external validation; she never felt "enough" and believed she was falling short of expectations. She felt an overwhelming sense of pressure to excel in her professional and personal endeavors, leaving little room for rest, self-care, and genuine moments of joy.

With her constant focus on future goals and accomplishments, Sara was missing the present moment and the beauty in the here and now. By challenging her beliefs and understanding that self-worth is inherent and not solely based on achievements, Sara cultivated a mindset of self-compassion, allowing herself to experience joy, aliveness, and wellbeing in the midst of her demanding professional life. She prioritized self-care, setting boundaries, and celebrating small victories.

Sara envisioned an inner "rejuvenating garden" to nourish her spirit and reconnect with her inner energy and vitality to bloom. She planted seeds of connecting with her inner voices and made it a practice of checking in on her inner child regularly. She spent more time in nature and dancing. She called on her wise self to create more balance and open space for her inner child and a sense of calm. She noticed her inner critic's demands more often. She was able to release her constant focus on self-improvement and let her path unfold with more ease by using breathing and centering practices.

After her coaching journey, Sara reported: "I am enjoying my life now. I am more aware of my needs and have more energy. I notice more moments of joy, and I am actually more productive."

Practices

1. MEET YOUR INNER CHILD

Take a pencil or marker and paper, and with your non-dominant hand, draw a picture of yourself that represents your inner child. Keep it nearby to remind you to connect with this part. While you are drawing, notice your inner voice and its messages. (Are the messages encouraging or diminishing?) Practice acknowledging yourself with the voice of your wise self and drawing as a way of connecting to your inner child.

2. CONNECT WITH YOUR CHILDHOOD PHOTO

a) Find a childhood photo of when you were small. Put it somewhere you can see it often. As you look at the photo, allow yourself to connect with your inner child and notice your sensations. Notice what memories come to you.

In your journal, answer these questions:
- ✓ What are some moments of joy that you recall as you are looking at the photo?
- ✓ What were the sufferings?
- ✓ What do you long for?
- ✓ Notice what is a way you can address this longing today?

b) Take a moment to send love to this child.
- ✓ Notice what it has been longing to hear.
- ✓ What can you say to it, starting with the sentence "You are…"? (You are enough. You are beautiful. You are loved. You are successful.)
- ✓ Notice your emotions and what gets evoked in you.

c) What is an affirmation you can create and tell yourself that will support your inner child every day? For example, "I am safe and enough. I am loved."

With such affirmations, speak kindly to your inner child. Continue to contact your childhood photo regularly to ensure you are connecting with your life energy.

3. ALLOW SPACE FOR PLAYFULNESS

Children who feel cared for and supported naturally engage in play. We need to remind ourselves to be playful as adults. For children, play is an automatic and natural response and a creative way to explore the world. How can you allow yourself to create more space for playfulness?

We don't give the inner child enough space to live or allow and accept this part to do silly and fun things. Notice the critical voice that stops you from connecting with this lively, creative energy. Experiment and connect to your child part to stretch your boundaries.

Plan some time to engage in activities that you may not usually give yourself permission to do because you consider it a waste of time or childlike. Some options include coloring, painting, drawing, biking, playing with children, singing, playing ball, playing cards or a game, and dancing. Have a date with yourself—do something creative that could connect you to JOYBeing.

> We don't stop playing because we grow old; we grow old because we stop playing.
>
> *George Bernard Shaw*

4. FIND AN OBJECT TO RECONNECT WITH YOUR INNER CHILD

Find a childhood toy or purchase a stuffed animal, doll, toy, or object that will reconnect you with your inner child. Put it on your desk or a place where you will see it often to remind you to connect with JOYBeing.

Practices

5. BREATHE TO CONNECT WITH YOUR INNER CHILD

In Thich Nhat Hahn's book *Reconciliation*, he says that in each of us is a young, suffering child. To protect ourselves from future suffering, we try to forget the pain. We try to ignore this part by being overly busy, overeating, drinking, etc. However, forgetting the pain results in more pain.

Thich Nhat Hahn suggests breathing in and saying, "I go back to my inner child," and breathing out, saying, "I take care of my inner child." Most of us have negative childhood experiences. When we bring nurturing support from our wise self to our inner child, we can reconnect with JOYBeing.

6. SPEAK KINDLY

Start speaking kindly to yourself. Try speaking in a loving, soothing voice facing a mirror. Be a nurturing, supportive, wise self to your inner child. Tell your inner child that they are valued and loved by you. Tell your inner child that they do not need to prove themselves to anyone.

- ✓ What words has your inner child been longing to hear?
- ✓ You can say things like: "I love you. I hear you. I am with you."
- ✓ Tell your inner critic that you appreciate its role in supporting you, but it can take a break.

7. TREAT YOURSELF AS YOU WOULD TREAT A FRIEND

A loving parent would ensure you eat healthy food, get enough sleep, and exercise. Treat yourself and your inner child with a bath, a massage, time outdoors, or a delicious and healthy meal. Set clear boundaries, and don't let others treat you poorly. Do nice things for yourself, like preparing a cup of tea or taking a walk in nature.

Have compassion for yourself and treat yourself the way you would a good friend. Accept your humanity and that we all have flaws and have made mistakes. Reassure yourself and accept that you are growing and developing.

8. CONNECT WITH YOUR WISE SELF

Go to a comfortable, safe place, and take some quiet breaths. Invite your wise self to become known to you. Trust the image or sensation that emerges. It could be a clear image of a person, place, or sensation, an awareness, or a metaphor. Introduce yourself and get to know your wise self. Ask if this part has a message for you. Then listen. You may continue the inner dialogue. You may ask this part, "What will more deeply connect me to joy and aliveness?" Begin to build a relationship and take the time to frequently connect with this part.

Invite your wise self to be a source of love and support for your inner child. Perhaps they meet in your inner garden. This part of you appreciates your inner child's challenges and wounds and can offer compassion and insight that may be missing for this part. Befriend your wise self and call on it often to offer guidance.

Practices

9. CREATE ALIGNMENT BETWEEN THE INNER CHILD AND THE INNER CRITIC

Ultimately, by cultivating a cooperative relationship between our inner child and inner critic, we can harness the strengths of both voices. This integration allows us to tap into our creativity, experience aliveness, and live authentically while navigating daily life's practicalities and challenges.

Engaging in a dialogue between your inner critic and inner child can help foster understanding, empathy, and a cooperative relationship. With a sense of curiosity and compassion, you open the space for your wise self to become visible in the process.

Here are some questions to support the dialogue:
- ✓ What are you experiencing?
- ✓ What are your sensations and emotions?
- ✓ What is the narrative of each part?
- ✓ What are your fears and concerns?
- ✓ What is most important to each part?
- ✓ What does each part need to feel understood?
- ✓ What I need from you is....?
- ✓ What are our common needs?
- ✓ What actions can we take that will serve us?
- ✓ What can we agree on?

These questions are meant to initiate a dialogue and foster understanding between your inner critic and inner child. Approach this process from the wise self perspective with curiosity, compassion, and an open mind, allowing all voices to be heard and respected. This dialogue can help you find a more harmonious and cooperative relationship between these internal aspects of yourself. You may also choose to work with a coach to support you.

10. DO INNER PARTS WORK

We are comprised of multiple parts. Richard Schwartz's book *No Bad Parts* finds value in all of our parts. Rather than seeing them as obstacles, each part has an intention to protect us and can be valuable to our overall system. The Internal Family Systems model encourages getting to know our parts and working with them.

We suggest a simple process, based on Gestalt Psychology and coaching. Literally or figuratively, allow an empty chair to represent each of your parts. You can then engage in dialogue by inviting each part to express their experience, sensations, emotions, needs, and messages to you. Often, simply becoming aware and giving empathy to your parts enables a shift in energy and a greater sense of aliveness.

CHAPTER 7

Thriving and Flourishing in Our Garden: Expanding JOYBeing in Different Parts of Our Lives

> "The most visible creators are those artists whose medium is life itself. The ones who express the inexpressible—without brush, hammer, clay, or guitar. They neither paint nor sculpt. Their medium is simply being. Whatever their presence touches has increased life. They see but don't have to draw... Because they are the artists of being alive..."

Donna J. Stone

JOYBeing

Talking about joy is easy, but living a life of JOYBeing requires commitment and practice. Embracing a life of JOYBeing demands perseverance and a deep nurturing relationship with ourselves. This adventurous and fulfilling journey challenges us to grow continually. JOYBeing allows us to connect with the innate beauty and creativity within us as well as with the rhythm of life. Through this connection, we can find a profound sense of purpose and contentment, enriching our lives in ways we never imagined possible.

We may not have good role models of people experiencing vibrancy and joy, and we may not think it is available to us. However, we know it is possible because we are born with this energy, and we want to encourage you to rediscover it on this journey. As shared in Chapter 1, JOYBeing requires consistency of intention, awareness, choice, and practice. This process is like planting seeds and establishing strong roots in a garden that allows us to grow and support a fulfilling life.

We each need to be the gardeners of our lives and take good care of ourselves. By using the practices in this book, we can reinforce our higher-frequency, thereby enlivening emotions; be aware; and let go of our weeds and the depleting behaviors that no longer support us. Then we will flourish and be better positioned to nourish and influence others, given that emotions are contagious.

Life's challenges can easily uproot us just like when a storm strikes a garden. To keep our commitment to JOYBeing, we need strong roots to keep us grounded. Rather than resist or fight the storm, we want to experience it fully and appreciate the rain, which supports growth.

We need to trust that the seed of JOYBeing is within us and we have the natural capacity for vibrancy. We need to nurture and strengthen the seed within. As we do so, we naturally have the capacity to spread this enlivening energy to others so it feeds relationships, grows our potential, and moves us toward a beautiful quality of life. When we collectively spread JOYBeing, we strengthen our roots, survive, and flourish together.

CHAPTER 7 Thriving and Flourishing in Our Garden: Expanding JOYBeing in Different Parts of Our Lives

Given the polarization, inequities, and great disruptions occurring in our world, an even greater need exists for us to make the commitment to live a life of JOYBeing.

While life will continue to offer challenges, we can manage ourselves and be more resilient by setting an intention for JOYBeing and adopting a hopeful outlook.

Integrating JOYBeing into different parts of our lives requires recognizing the importance of relationships, work, service, and community. Nurturing positive relationships allows us to experience joy through shared experiences, deep connections, and moments of love and understanding.

Similarly, work plays a significant role and time commitment in our lives, so finding joy in our professional endeavors is crucial. When we feel a sense of purpose, accomplishment, and fulfillment in our work, it not only enhances our wellbeing but contributes to a greater sense of joy.

Lastly, the community we belong to, whether it's our local neighborhood or a broader social network, offers opportunities for shared experiences and acts of service, support, and collaboration. Engaging with our community allows us to cultivate a sense of belonging, contribute to others' wellbeing, and

Gila

I've discovered that tuning into my inner world and maintaining the clarity of my internal emotional landscape brings a profound sense of contentment. When I'm attuned to what's happening within me, I connect to my JOYBeing and can effortlessly radiate the energy of joy into my interactions with family, friends, and those around me.

During my younger years, the fear of solitude constantly drove me to engage in activities, travel, and collaborate with others. Being alone with my thoughts and emotions was daunting because it meant confronting the hidden aspects of myself. I became reliant on the company of others, considering them my antidote to loneliness.

As the years unfolded, I turned the mirror inward, forging a connection with my essence. This transformative process empowered me to nurture healthier relationships within various circles, sowing the seeds for personal growth. Nowadays, I often receive comments about the perceptible shift in my energy—whether it's reflected in my voice, posture, or approach to life.

Embracing JOYBeing has not only changed my individual outlook but has also allowed me to cultivate robust, trust-rooting friendships and work relationships. This newfound way of being has become a container for my authenticity and positivity, influencing the dynamics of the connections I build.

experience the joy of making a positive difference. By recognizing the importance of relationships, work, and community, we can intentionally integrate joy into various aspects of our lives, creating a harmonious and fulfilling existence.

We all want to live an integrated and joyful life. Living a full, happy life depends on how we integrate performance (success in life in terms of our job or work), learning (growing and being open to new learning), healthy relationships, and wellbeing (being comfortable and healthy in our body and engaging in self-care). When we integrate these into our lives and create an inner balance that works for us, it enhances our life of JOYBeing. We need to be able to confront the challenges in our relationships, work, and community. JOYBeing is about how we experience and respond to life—the opportunities and challenges. JOYBeing is a choice and the music of our soul.

In his book *Happier*, Tal Ben-Shahar cites research by Sonja Lyubomirsky, Laura King, and Ed Diener that shows happy individuals are successful and happy across multiple domains, including marriage, friendships, finances, work performance, and health. The relationship between happiness and success is found to be reciprocal. Happy people have better relationships, thrive at work, and live better and longer.

> "Don't ask yourself what the world needs. Ask yourself what makes you come alive, and go do that, because what the world needs is people who have come alive.
>
> *Howard Thurman*

CHAPTER 7 Thriving and Flourishing in Our Garden: Expanding JOYBeing in Different Parts of Our Lives

Sowing JOYBeing Seeds in Relationships

Relationships are the fertile ground that fosters joy. Healthy connections have the power to nourish and amplify joy within each of us. They provide support, encouragement, and a sense of belonging, enhancing our overall wellbeing. In these connections, we find the strength to face challenges, the inspiration to pursue our dreams, and the comfort of knowing we are not alone. When we build meaningful, heartfelt connections with others, even those we have just met for the first time, joy blooms. Strong relationships, whether with romantic partners, family members, friends, or colleagues, create a healthy environment for joy to thrive. These genuine interactions create a sense of warmth and understanding, allowing JOYBeing to spread naturally. Thus, joy and relationships are symbiotic; each element enhances and enriches the other.

We experience joy in relationships when we are open, curious, and compassionate and we approach the other with a sense of discovery. When we are able to accept people as they are and appreciate their strengths and uniqueness, we create a sense of trust and openness. When we are present with a sense of JOYBeing, joy expands in our friendships and families.

> *In the long run, we shape our lives and we shape ourselves. The process never ends until we die. And the choices we make are ultimately our own responsibility.*
>
> — Eleanor Roosevelt

Gila

Since my mid-thirties, I've made a conscious effort to invest significantly in my relationships, whether with family or friends. One indispensable routine that holds profound importance for me is our Thursday afternoon gatherings. This group of close girlfriends, who have become my chosen family, is a source of joy and connection.

During these meetings, we check in with each other, sharing vulnerable moments, and offer support when needed. These get-togethers are not just about companionship. They're also about having fun, playing games, and sometimes dancing like little girls to music. These cherished moments of JOYBeing are a testament to the strength and beauty found in nurturing deep connections with those who matter most.

The Harvard Study of Adult Development, one of the longest-running longitudinal studies on happiness, demonstrates that relationships with others are highly correlated with happiness and satisfaction. Led by Robert Waldinger, the study found a strong link between happiness and close relationships with family and friends. Indisputably, connections and a sense of belonging with others are crucial for a sense of joy and happiness.

Loneliness and disconnection are significant barriers to joy. US Surgeon General Vivek Murthy has called it a public health epidemic, citing that loneliness increased by 181 percent during the pandemic and continues to be an issue. Be aware that people can be lonely even when surrounded by others. We need to reach out to others and ensure we are building strong friendships and connections.

Human connections need to be developed beyond just social media "friends." Heavy social media users are three times more likely to feel socially isolated than casual readers. With the emergence of working from home, the increased possibility of loneliness exists as does the need to invest in building relationships.

We each need to take responsibility for our own joy. When we stop trying to change or blame others and focus on listening and caring with an open heart, we have more access to JOYBeing and the ability to flourish. We need to invest in relationships and inspire others to experience joy and be open to JOYBeing.

Christina Bethell, a national leader in the development of policy, practice, and research, has been instrumental in creating frameworks for assessing and improving the health and wellbeing of children and families. Rather than assuming that adverse childhood experiences limit our ability for relationships and wellbeing, she provides a hopeful perspective and believes we can address trauma. Her paradigm is centered on the concept of flourishing that emphasizes the importance of social, emotional, and relational wellbeing as key components of overall health. We must have a sense of seven criteria to promote our natural capacity to flourish and meet adversity with more resilience.

> *Personal connection creates emotional stimulation, which is an automatic mood booster, while isolation is a mood buster.*
>
> —Robert Waldinger

CHAPTER 7 Thriving and Flourishing in Our Garden: Expanding JOYBeing in Different Parts of Our Lives

They are:

- ✓ Meaning and purpose
- ✓ Engagement in life
- ✓ Positive relationships
- ✓ Positive outlook
- ✓ Noticing what's going well
- ✓ Contribution to others
- ✓ Self-worth

Take a moment to reflect on the questions below:

- ✓ Who are the most important people in your life?
- ✓ What makes you value these relationships?
- ✓ What kinds of relationships are you building intentionally?
- ✓ What relationship do you want to invest in more? How?
- ✓ How are you being empathetic in caring and understanding others?
- ✓ How do you create a safe and non-judgmental space for people to express themselves?
- ✓ How do you honor your commitments and agreements with your relationships?
- ✓ Who will you call in a challenging moment? Who will feel comfortable calling you?
- ✓ Where in your life do you want to cultivate more flourishing relationships with JOYBeing?

Ann

As I have worked to cultivate openness and connection with my inner self, I have felt more grounded and joyful. Before, my intention was primarily to focus on others and make a meaningful difference. However, when I included a connection with myself and created space for inner joy, I realized I could make a more significant difference with less effort and greater ease. People comment on sensing my presence, joy, and aliveness, often expressing inspiration to connect with their inner joy.

I have become more deliberate in the relationships I form and invest in. Cultivating friendships with regularly scheduled conversations where we share experiences and learning has been delightful. In these exchanges, we listen attentively and give each other empathy and care. Building these connections has been enjoyable and heightens my aliveness and joy. I am equally grateful for the groups I am a part of, where collective learning and growth unfold. Experiencing a sense of belonging and connection is critical in leading a joyful life.

Observing an elderly friend surrounded by companions with whom she shared history and mutual care, I recognized the sustaining power of rich connections in later years. I aspire to nurture such profound connections as I age and navigate the later phases of life.

Connecting to JOYBeing in the Workplace

What is your reaction when you see the words joy and work together? Most of us have been conditioned to see work and joy as two different entities. Many of us don't associate joy with work. In fact, we have been conditioned to believe work should be hard and, thus, not joyful. Most of us spend much of our lives working without joy unless we notice and choose joy. However, when we allow joy and aliveness to flow through us, we are more engaged and productive.

For generations, we have heard from our elders that "work is work" and "play is play," and the two shall never meet. We are often expected to differentiate work from play and fun. Interestingly, if laughter and fun exist in the workplace, it can be regarded as not "working." We are expected to be serious and hard-driving about work and focus on productivity and results. We cannot be successful if we are not devoted and serious about our work. In this scenario, there is no room for joy. Today, considering how much of our lives we spend at work, in sleep, and on busy weekends with chores, where does joy fit into the equation? How much time do we have for joy? Based on our experiences, we believe that thinking we don't have time or space for joy is an unsatisfactory way to live that does not serve our wellbeing.

> *A soul-based workplace asks things of me that I did not even know that I had. It is constantly telling me that I belong to something larger in the world.*
>
> — David Whyte

Today, world conditions challenge our sense of joy, and many in the workplace are unengaged. Technological advancements have caused the focus to be primarily on productivity and increasing output. Recent global circumstances have caused people to reflect on what is most important. People are leaving their managers and workplaces because they don't feel valued and do not experience engagement and a sense of aliveness and joy. What increases and supports engagement and retains talent and motivation is paying attention to an organization's mood or environment. Humans excel and are open to creativity when they experience psychological safety, are joyful, and connect with one another, which allows them to bring out their best attributes and selves.

Younger generations are more sensitive about bringing joy and aliveness to all facets of their lives, including work. In fact, they and others are demanding work environments that are more human, incorporating empathy, compassion, play, joy and aliveness. According to a 2022 Gallup poll, those organizations that emphasize cultures of heartful connection and wellbeing are experiencing greater performance and productivity. When teams are engaged and experiencing fun and joy, they are more innovative and inclusive. While people want to experience more joy at work, they often don't know how to do so. Those organizations that emphasize joy are often financially more successful.

What is your prevailing mindset about work? Rate each statement below on a scale of 1-5, with one being low and five being high. Notice what gets evoked in your body as you respond. What are you aware of? Which of these mindsets would you like to strengthen?

✓ **Work is hard or stressful.**

✓ **Work never ends and is something to be endured.**

✓ **Work is meaningful.**

✓ **Work is an opportunity to experience challenges and grow.**

✓ **Work is fulfilling and contributes to my purpose.**

✓ **Work is separate from fun or play.**

✓ **Work can be fun and joyful.**

✓ **Work can be enjoyable when aligned with my values.**

✓ **A positive work environment fosters creativity.**

✓ **I can make work fun and joyful.**

JOYBeing

> We are shaped by our thoughts; we become what we think. When the mind is pure, joy follows like a shadow that never leaves.
>
> — Buddha

Usually, we see the work environment as a place to be productive and create results. Research shows that we do actually experience joy at work. A 2010 study by Killingsworth and Gilbert that asked people to report on their level of satisfaction at different times of the day showed that people were often joyful while engaged at work. Joy can be missing in the workplace and in teams when all of the attention is focused on results and performance rather than joy and wellbeing. Jennifer Moss, in a Harvard Business Review article, presents research that suggests those who are satisfied with their work are more productive.

For us, JOYBeing is a way to be present and open to experiencing the fullness of work. This includes all emotions and experiences, such as disappointments, challenges, uncertainties, opportunities, and achievements. With the JOYBeing mindset, we are open and ready to face and explore whatever is present. JOYBeing is being in the flow and being present in a nonjudgmental way. It is about connecting with ourselves, others, and our surroundings.

In the work environment, it is easy to be pulled out of our center. We automatically contract, react, numb ourselves, resist, or move away from what we perceive as challenging. This could be our reaction to people and situations in the workplace. JOYBeing is our ability to see what pulls us down, notice what triggers us, and take purposeful action.

When we are able to be in the JOYBeing presence, we connect with our internal resources to digest and integrate the reality of the present and create new meaning and possibilities. When we are not aware, we are carrying an emotional load, based on our past and habitual patterns, that affects our productivity and interactions with people at work. On the contrary, when we are aware and awake, we are able to handle challenges more effectively, connect with possibilities, and experience joy.

One of our clients, Can, had a habitual pattern of reacting and pouting. He would often not follow through, complain that he was not consulted, and grumble that his boss always told him what to do. He was not aware of his assumptions and judgments or the story he created. He believed he was not respected and valued and not considered worthy of making his own choices. He was frustrated and not connected with JOYBeing.

Through coaching, he became aware of his habitual reaction pattern, which came from his need to be seen as independent and competent. Over time, he could stop, step back, and cool down, and then shift to being open and curious and engage in a conversation with his manager. He learned his manager was under pressure and his only intention was to support Can to prepare him for a new project that would enable career progression. With this new understanding, Can transformed his way of being and connected to JOYBeing.

When we make contact with the narrative that creates the imaginary weight we create for ourselves, we can soften, release, and liberate energy for new possibilities. We can reconnect to the flow of life, our aliveness, and JOYBeing.

It is important to be intentional and process the full experiences and emotions generated in the workplace. JOYBeing can become the ground for positive and productive workplaces and cultures, allowing integration, inclusion, and a sense of belonging. We believe JOYBeing, which encompasses wellbeing, should become a foundational priority at work.

By creating environments that allow us to bring our embodied selves into the workplace, we can ensure more openness and connection and ignite the energy of innovation.

A culture that supports JOYBeing has outcomes that include better teamwork, stronger communication, creativity, and an open mindset to overcome challenges and enable greater resilience and sustainability. Burnout is reduced, and psychological safety, a critical component for engagement, is enhanced.

Recall that emotions are contagious. When we embody JOYBeing, we positively influence our teams and work outcomes. We need to trust that our JOYBeing presence can make a difference.

We each bring to work our background experiences and our past stories that shape our work, lives, and workplaces. We need to recognize that each person has experienced challenges and traumas and be kind and open to one another. We need to be aware of our own patterns and connect to JOYBeing.

Being aware of, respecting, and being open to all the differences people bring to the workplace can make a significant difference in our relationships with others. Ann refers to this as adopting an Open Stance. When we appreciate our past and present situation and are open to what is unknown, we enhance our capacity for JOYBeing.

We are constantly experiencing disruption and uncertainty in the workplace and in life. Through this disruption, we can create something new. JOYBeing allows us to awaken, attend, acknowledge, and act during these times.

Ann

In my decades of work with organizational leaders, I've witnessed the transformative power of adopting an Open Stance, engaging in open-minded conversations, and infusing the potential for joy into teams and organizational cultures. The shift from a closed and contracted state to an open and joyful one doesn't just impact the internal dynamics; it's a catalyst for change in the entire environment. Emotions, as we know, are contagious, and the shift ripples through the fabric of the workplace and beyond. When teams and organizations agree to assume positive intent, the environment inspires innovation, psychological safety, open-minded conversations, co-creative solutions, and joy.

The outcomes are profound: a surge in commitment, elevated levels of collaboration, and increased productivity. I encourage managers and leaders to take responsibility for the cultural landscape they cultivate through their own openness and JOYBeing. The ripple effect is tangible—people find greater enjoyment in their work, and positive influence radiates into their personal lives and extends to clients and their more extensive systems. Focusing on enhancing JOYBeing in the workplace is clearly valuable.

Leading with JOYBeing

We need leaders who embody JOYBeing. According to a 2022 Gallup poll, only 32 percent of people are engaged at work in the United States. More than half indicate they are working without energy or passion. Eighteen percent are actively disengaged and report being unhappy with work. A similar trend is seen across the globe.

In our experience and work with organizations worldwide, when people are more engaged and love what they do, they feel physically and psychologically safe, appreciate the purpose and meaning of their work, and do the best work of their lives. They enjoy more choice and autonomy over their work. They experience real connection with others, connect with their sense of JOYBeing, and celebrate success.

Conscious leaders recognize the significance of their own evolution and growth journey. They appreciate the positive and challenging experiences that have shaped them. Being a leader who inspires JOYBeing requires a commitment to embodying joy and aliveness. This involves personal awareness, reflection, and self-development. By engaging in personal development work and embracing vulnerability, leaders demonstrate their humanity, which encourages others to feel comfortable in sharing their thoughts, ideas, and concerns. This sharing fosters a culture of open communication, belonging, and JOYBeing, and it builds a sense of community, increased engagement, and a sense of aliveness, energy, and resilience.

> "Joy is a net of love by which you can catch souls. A joyful leader is an extraordinary leader."
>
> — Mother Teresa

By opening space for sharing and vulnerability, leaders bring in their human selves, which inspires a

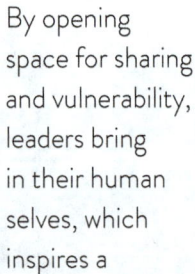

sense of trust, aliveness, and joy. In this space of energy, people can be more innovative, creative, and collaborative.

Amy Elizabeth Fox, CEO of Mobius Executive Leadership, highlights how unprocessed emotions and unresolved memories can become embedded in the psyche of leaders, manifesting as unconscious habits, beliefs, and even physical tension in the body. These "emotional loads" shape how leaders act and respond and affect their overall presence and energy. When unexamined, these trauma patterns can obstruct a leader's ability to effectively guide others, as they restrict access to their full life force, vitality, and joy.

Fox suggests that leaders often carry these burdens unknowingly, which can lead to behaviors that block their authenticity, responsiveness, and capacity to inspire others. The inner dissonance caused by unaddressed emotional baggage cuts them off from their natural sense of energy and connection. Leaders, in essence, operate with diminished capacity because these unresolved issues restrict their life energy.

However, once leaders develop the awareness and courage to confront these hidden aspects of themselves,

Gila

In my experience of more than fifteen years working with leaders and organizations, I've frequently observed the sidelining of joy within the workplace. Leveraging my background as a facilitator with a creative foundation, I've consistently introduced practices and processes that seamlessly integrate joy and fun into the fabric of organizational work. I firmly believe it's during moments of shared laughter and fun that we create space for our inner child to emerge and that genuine transformation, connection, and change can occur.

Injecting the energy of play into the professional sphere has proven to be a catalyst for significant shifts. I have often experienced that these moments of joy not only break down barriers but inspire trust and bring a vibrant liveliness to the workplace. The fusion of fun, play, and being open to creativity with organizational endeavors has, in turn, unlocked new avenues for collaboration and heightened productivity. By infusing a sense of playfulness, I have seen leaders open doors to joy, creativity, and innovation, fostering an environment where individuals feel not only engaged but empowered to contribute their best. I have also witnessed that my holistic approach to work not only enhances the workplace atmosphere but also sets the stage for meaningful and impactful transformations within the organizational structure.

they can unlock a deeper level of emotional intelligence. By embracing emotional clarity and integrating these unprocessed elements, they regain access to their full life force. This enables them to lead with more vitality, presence, effectiveness, and JOYBeing. They become not just managers but guides capable of inspiring others, fostering authentic connections, and creating environments where both individuals and organizations thrive.

In doing so, they tap into a more expansive and alive version of themselves, transforming their leadership style and the very culture they cultivate. The journey toward emotional awareness becomes a key step in reclaiming their ability to influence with integrity and impact.

When people are more joyful and playful at work, they are more curious and alert. They are more open to learning. They are more open to asking for help. They are more generous, and they focus on the vitality of the workplace. When people are given the opportunity for open dialogue, they experience more wellbeing and joy. JOYBeing is a natural inner resource that enhances connection, productivity, and results.

Making JOYBeing a strategic priority can positively affect an organization's culture. This result enables people to show up with their full selves and inspire meaningful connections.

Our path for creating JOYBeing at the personal level can be applied at the work or organizational level. This includes:

✓ **Setting the intention to create a culture of JOYBeing.**

✓ **Enhancing awareness and choice for JOYBeing.**

✓ **Introducing practices that support cultivating JOYBeing.**

The key is developing leaders who embody JOYBeing, demonstrate care, create moments of joy, inspire others, and celebrate success.

Creating a Culture of JOYBeing at Work

Here are ten essential areas of focus that support leaders in integrating JOYBeing into the workplace:

1. Connecting and aligning around a meaningful purpose

2. Regular check-ins that inspire energy and heartfelt connections

3. Clarifying norms and expectations, which include fun and play

4. Having open-minded conversations focused on finding common ground and co-creating shared solutions

5. Creating a respectful environment with a sense of belonging and meaningful connections

6. Showing appreciation and recognition

7. Engaging in compassion and care for others

8. Inspiring wellbeing to plant positive energy and healthy habits

9. Implementing systems and processes that support ease and joy

10. Evaluating continual growth and celebrating success

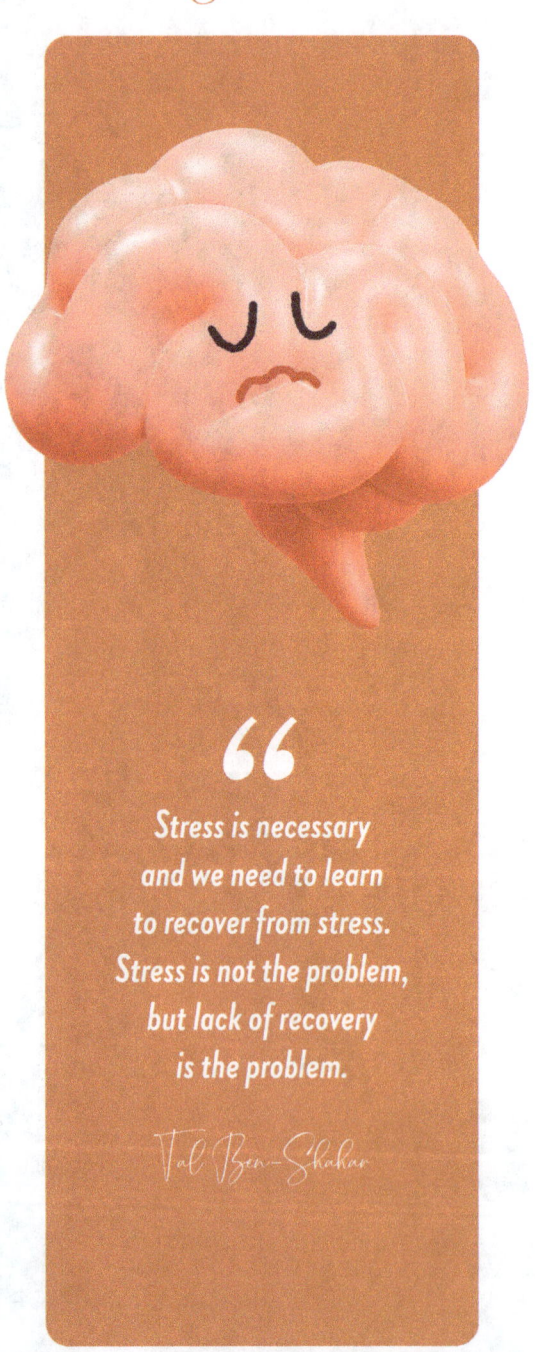

> *Stress is necessary and we need to learn to recover from stress. Stress is not the problem, but lack of recovery is the problem.*
>
> — Tal Ben-Shahar

1. Connecting and Aligning Around a Meaningful Purpose

What inspires you to come to work every day?

How do you see your personal goals and values aligning with your organization's purpose?

What aspects of your work do you find most meaningful?

Research consistently shows the importance of having a clear purpose and a sense of meaning. The most effective leaders inspire alignment around a shared purpose and set of values. When we have a clear sense of purpose, we feel our actions and endeavors align with our values, and we contribute to something larger than ourselves, it brings a profound sense of fulfillment and satisfaction. When people feel they are contributing to something that benefits others and the planet, they are likely to experience more meaning, joy, and energy to move forward.

Being aware of what is most important to us and knowing "for the sake of what" creates excitement and inspires positive energy for action. Moving to what's important to us with a sense of purpose enables the embodiment of joy and aliveness. Without alignment around a shared purpose, a sense of uncertainty, frustration, and being lost can exist.

Leaders and organizations must continually emphasize their organization's values, vision, and meaningful purpose.

According to McKinsey, research shows that about 70 percent of people say they define their purpose through work. Increasingly, especially after the COVID-19 pandemic, people are leaving workplaces where they do not experience a sense of purpose. This is especially true for millennials and Generation Z, who are entering the workplace. We must align our individual purposes with the organization's purpose to create harmony and generate energy within the system. This alignment enables people to feel at home in the workplace.

> *The best leaders are those who can bring people together toward a common goal and ignite a sense of joy and purpose.*
>
> — Simon Sinek

Emphasizing JOYBeing in the workplace could totally change the energy of the work environment. Considering that a large portion of our life is focused on work, how would life be different in the work environment if more attention were paid to encouraging JOYBeing?

2. Regular Check-Ins That Inspire Energy and Heartfelt Connections

Do you check in and share your thoughts and feelings with your team members on a regular basis?

How are these conversations serving you?

What is the cost of not having check-ins?

Building a practice where team members connect regularly to share their experiences and aspirations can make a huge difference. Creating the opportunity for heartful, genuine sharing supports team members in building meaningful relationships based on empathy, understanding, and compassion.

Sharing reflections and ideas at a personal and professional level creates a sense of aliveness and harmony in a team. When each team member brings in their voice, it supports further dialogue and an enhanced quality of energy that builds the team spirit. Heartfelt connections involve acknowledging each individual's humanity and uniqueness, relating to motivations, emotions, and challenges.

By showing empathy, listening actively, and genuinely caring about others' wellbeing, the team fosters a relationship built on respect, trust, and support. In such an environment, team members feel valued and a part of the team. They feel appreciated for who they are, not just for what they do professionally.

Regular check-ins allow team members to recognize and share their moods, which allows them to become more present with others. It also helps team members understand more deeply the invisible parts of each other that they might not otherwise recognize. This recognition sets the opening ground and tone for team members to relate to each other and work more productively together. Hearing each other's moods creates awareness and collective understanding. Also, by naming emotions, we can release the energy we hold and create the space for possibilities and JOYBeing.

The E-MRI tool and the Mood Meter, shared in Chapter 5, are useful resources for identifying more granular emotions.

3. Clarifying Norms and Expectations, Including Fun and Play

Does your team agree it is okay to have fun at work?

What resources or support do you need to feel comfortable engaging in fun at work?

What activities will foster a sense of fun and play at work?

How can you inspire and invite others to have fun?

Teams and organizations need to define how they choose to operate and the kind of culture they want to create. When a set of values and behaviors is clarified and agreed upon, team members understand what is expected. In addition to agreeing to listen to one another, assuming positive intent and being inclusive, specifying joy, fun, and play as a norm will make a huge difference in creating a positive culture.

A simple practice for an organization and individual teams is to clarify the norms around what people hope to see, hear, and experience and what they desire not to hear, see, or experience. With dialogue, the team and organization can specify the norms to create success.

Some believe fun and play may be a distraction at work. However, play is positively associated with job satisfaction, a sense of competence, and creativity. More fun and play are linked with less fatigue, boredom, stress, and burnout. When people have a sense of joy at work, they experience flow and are more creative, innovative, and productive. Pleasurable activities release dopamine, which creates a positive environment, deepens bonds, and enhances collaboration. Once play becomes habitual and part of the culture, JOYBeing is sustained and supports productivity.

4. Having Open-Minded Conversations Focused on Finding Common Ground and Co-Creating Shared Solutions

Are you encouraged to have real conversations at work?

How do you manage different perspectives and uncertainty?

What will support you in engaging in open-minded conversations?

How do you address and resolve conflicts in a way that enhances your sense of joy and connection?

How do you ensure all voices are heard and valued to create workplace joy?

Team members need to commit to engaging in open-minded conversations where they can notice their assumptions and judgments and then shift to being open, finding common ground, and creating agreements. Being open-minded requires practicing listening, giving empathy, and being flexible and receptive to one another. Change happens through one conversation at a time.

When team members understand we naturally become closed and contract in the face of differences, uncertainties, and challenges, they can learn to take an Open Stance and find more joy.

A leader's ability to face and address difficult circumstances sets the ground for openness and transparency.

> *Leadership is not about being in charge. It's about taking care of those in your charge and creating an environment where joy can flourish.*
>
> *Max DePree*

Openness is contagious. By being open and engaging in meaningful conversations, leaders inspire JOYBeing. Resilience and thriving for teams is then supported. The OASIS Conversations process, developed by Ann Van Eron, offers tips for engaging in open-minded conversations.

5. Creating a Respectful Environment with a Sense of Belonging and Meaningful Connections

Do you feel a sense of connection and belonging at work?

What does respect in the workplace look like for you and others?

What practices can you implement to create a psychologically safe environment where people feel included?

CHAPTER 7 Thriving and Flourishing in Our Garden: Expanding JOYBeing in Different Parts of Our Lives

As humans, we naturally wish to be respected and valued. According to Christine Porath in a *Harvard Business Review* article, we are more creative, productive, positive, and healthy in respectful environments where we can engage in meaningful relationships. We need to build positive and productive connections and feel accepted by our colleagues. Respect is what employees all over the world want. However, half of employees don't feel respected by their bosses.

Respect and belonging enable people to bring their best authentic selves to work. A sense of belonging is critical for life satisfaction, mental and physical health, and longevity. Too much energy is depleted when people do not feel included. Belonging is the feeling of being valued in a community, and it is essential for psychological safety. The Aristotle research conducted by Google demonstrates that respect and psychological safety are the critical ingredients for high-performing teams.[8]

Experiencing meaningful connections and being respected with a sense of belonging unites team members around a shared purpose and ownership. Nonjudgmental heart-to-heart conversations in the workplace lead to more authenticity and openness among employees.

Gallup Research from 2022 reports that having a good friend at work is correlated with high engagement and a sense of belonging. Disengaged employees have lower productivity, more absenteeism, and a lower quality of work, which adds to the cost of doing business. With a sense of joy and belonging, engagement is enhanced.

Genuine connections start with ourselves and how we manage our energy. When we are self-aware of what is happening within us and manage our emotions, we can open the door to meaningful connections that reflect and

> *The most basic and powerful way to connect to another person is to listen. Just listen. The most important thing we can give each other is our attention.*
>
> — Rachel Naomi Remen

---

[8] Duhigg, Charles. "What Google Learned From Its Quest to Build the Perfect Team"

inspire JOYBeing. When respect exists, we can open ourselves to others in the workplace, be seen with our full range of emotions, and invest in a culture of JOYBeing.

6. Showing Appreciation and Recognition

When was the last time you felt appreciated and recognized in your work?

What emotions were evoked in you?

How did it influence your energy and productivity?

How can you celebrate and acknowledge the contributions of all team members?

In the workplace, appreciation is essential for creating a positive environment and strengthening relationships. More than 35 percent of employees consider lack of recognition a significant hindrance to productivity. MIT research from 2022 shows that toxic culture, poorly managed change, and lack of recognition are the top factors for the exodus of people from organizations.

Employees say they are leaving organizations where they don't receive recognition and don't feel their leaders are compassionate and care for them. Creating moments where people feel seen greatly affects energy mobilization and creates a sense of gratitude and joy.

Appreciation makes a difference when people are recognized not only for what they do but for who they are.

7. Engaging in Compassion and Care for Others

What are some small acts of kindness you can incorporate into your daily routines to show care for others?

When we feel compassion for others and a sense of being cared for, we experience a sense of JOYBeing.

Compassion comes from a Latin word that means "co-suffering." Compassion involves being empathetic and caring for others as well as taking action to care for and be of support.

CHAPTER 7 Thriving and Flourishing in Our Garden: Expanding JOYBeing in Different Parts of Our Lives

Research recognizes compassion as an essential aspect of a productive work environment.[9] Showing compassion to colleagues is critical for enhancing job satisfaction and work-related motivation.

Compassion in the workplace is associated with many important outcomes. For example, employees report less stress and greater satisfaction.[10] People are more loyal and dedicated to organizations where they experience compassion.

Work cultures that advocate compassion enjoy more cooperation and retention as well as more focused efforts that benefit the organization.[11]

Jon Kabat-Zinn emphasizes the importance of compassionate leadership as a way to reduce work stress and increase peace among professionals. He proposes that anyone is capable of building the skill of compassion if they choose.

> *Great leaders create a culture where joy is not an absence of problems, but the presence of resilience, courage and compassion in the face of challenges.*
>
> *Brené Brown*

8. Inspiring Wellbeing to Plant Positive Energy and Healthy Habits

What are some ways you can integrate moments of positivity and relaxation into your daily work routines?

What small changes can you make to your work environment to enhance comfort and wellbeing?

How are you modeling and encouraging others to focus on wellbeing?

In a 2023 Deloitte study, 84 percent said that improving their wellbeing was a top priority and that wellbeing is important for organizational success. However, 80 percent said they were facing obstacles related to work, including heavy workloads and stress.

According to Deloitte, "the future of workforce wellbeing depends on a significant mindset shift and a long-term approach—one that extends beyond the walls of the organization. Executives have an opportunity to rewrite this story—for their employees, for their managers, and

---

[9] Jane E. Dutton, Kristina M. Workman, and Ashley E. Hardin. "Compassion at Work."
[10] Stephen Fineman, ed. *Emotions in Organizations.*
[11] T. Van Bommel. *The Power of Empathy in Times of Crisis and Beyond.*

JOYBeing

also for themselves. Work shouldn't be the reason people feel exhausted, stressed, and isolated from friends and family."

Today, our sense of wellbeing has expanded beyond physical wellbeing to focus on creating a culture of holistic wellbeing that takes into consideration individuals' emotional lives. When people feel a sense of groundedness and meaning in their work, they experience positive emotions, which are contagious and lead to a life of JOYBeing. Organizations are prioritizing wellbeing in the workplace, recognizing it as a critical factor for success, energy, and health.

Many factors are causing employees to feel depleted and burned out. By emphasizing building healthy habits and wellbeing, individuals can feel supported and healthy and amplify joy.

Often, people feel pressured by their workloads and the pattern of "do more with less" work cultures. In this mechanical way of being, which we have seen with many of our clients, joy is hidden. Instead, organizations can purposely emphasize the benefits of practices that increase awareness, positive emotions, and meaning. It is the leaders' responsibility to model and inspire JOYBeing.

The importance of wellbeing needs to be emphasized and finding ways to replenish energy and increase positivity need to be encouraged. A sense of wellbeing and positive energy can open the space for aliveness, JOYBeing, and possibilities.

9. Implementing Systems and Processes That Support Ease and Joy

How do your current systems affect employee job satisfaction and joy?

Are there processes that can be enhanced to inspire more connection and joy?

Too often, people complain that organizational processes, such as making decisions, take too long, inhibit passion and excitement about work, and drain energy by causing frustration. It is valuable to consider how to simplify bureaucracy, reduce political agendas, and make processes easier and more effective, which are conducive to JOYBeing.

Clear guidelines, procedures, and access to resources reduce confusion and minimize stress, which contributes to a sense of joy in the workplace. Effective systems promote collaboration, enabling teams to work more productively together, share knowledge, and leverage each other's strengths. By establishing a culture of continuous improvement and feedback, organizations can refine their systems and processes to address challenges, optimize workflows, and create an environment that supports JOYBeing.

10. *Evaluating Continual Growth and Celebrating Success*

What responsibility are you taking to create a JOYBeing culture at work?

What is currently working well?

What needs to be modified?

How do you celebrate successes?

What could be different if JOYBeing were enhanced in your workplace? Creating a culture of joy requires commitment, practice, and continual assessment of progress. Simple conversations and qualitative evaluation of what makes the work experience positive and what supports a sense of meaning, playfulness, and fun keep the focus on creating a culture of JOYBeing.

We observe that teams and leaders often jump from one project to another and miss the opportunity to celebrate the hard work and savor the joy and successes they achieve. Sharing success stories can inspire joy and motivate people to contribute to ongoing achievements. Recognizing individual and team efforts and successes boosts morale and creates a sense of community and wellbeing.

Ann

Over my years of working with leaders, teams, and organizations to foster inclusive cultures of collaboration and engagement, I've realized that hope and joy are vital catalysts in this transformative process. Whether coaching an executive, facilitating a team, or working with an organization, I emphasize the power of adopting an Open Stance, a process centered on managing reactions and judgments while fostering a connection with our innate sense of aliveness and joy. A clear intention and a focus on the desired environment are essential.

We position ourselves and others to cocreate innovative solutions when we engage in meaningful conversations with a sense of gratitude and openness. By collectively recognizing our shared humanity, sharing laughter, and engaging in the creative process, the entire system's energy undergoes a remarkable shift. I've witnessed powerful ripple effects, manifesting as dramatic transformations, in leaders, teams, organizations, and communities. Through shared presence, an acknowledgment of our aliveness, and the infusion of joy, we envision possibilities and realize our potential.

Meet Raj—A CEO

Meet Raj, a CEO with a packed schedule both at work and in the community. He is deeply concerned about the culture within his organization. Striving for more engagement and collaboration, Raj faces myriad pressures and market demands, necessitating continual innovation. Driven and results-focused, he understands the expectations of stakeholders and the board. However, in his pursuit of success, he finds little time for himself or his family, a struggle that many CEOs and leaders can relate to.

Upon receiving feedback that his staff were not highly engaged and many reported feeling stressed, Raj embarked on a journey of self-discovery through coaching. The feedback highlighted that his leadership style hindered open communication and collaboration within the organization. He learned of the power of emotional intelligence, open-minded conversations, and taking an Open Stance. While initially hesitant about incorporating joy into his leadership approach due to time constraints and unaware of how to do so, he gradually embraced the concept of JOYBeing. Through introspection and mindfulness, Raj began noticing what energized or depleted his spirit, making conscious efforts to enhance his wellbeing and emotional management.

Through his journey of self-discovery, Raj underwent a significant transformation in his leadership style. By embracing vulnerability and sharing JOYBeing practices with his team, he initiated a shift toward a culture of joy, openness, and collaboration within the organization. This new approach, with more check-ins that encouraged moments of joy and connection, was warmly embraced by his leadership team. Their more open and engaging leadership style had a profound and positive impact on their teams, creating a ripple effect of JOYBeing throughout the organization.

Raj envisioned a collaborative inner garden that bore an abundance of different kinds of produce that fed the community. As Raj's journey progressed, he incorporated JOYBeing into his daily life in more tangible ways. He expanded his wellbeing practices, incorporating physical health routines such

CHAPTER 7 Thriving and Flourishing in Our Garden: Expanding JOYBeing in Different Parts of Our Lives

as morning walks and strength training, and nurturing reflective moments during walking meetings. He built the habit of doing regular mood checks to increase self-awareness and manage emotional traps. By fostering genuine connections and purpose-driven interactions, Raj prioritized meaningful conversations and laughter among his team members. Despite the challenges that came his way, Raj remained steadfast in his commitment to JOYBeing, fostering a culture of connection, engagement, and open-minded dialogue within the organization.

As Raj and his team embraced joy and collaboration, a ripple effect of positivity cascaded throughout the organization. Enhanced connection, engagement, and enjoyment in their work led to improved results and a thriving organizational culture. The organization flourished through Raj's commitment to JOYBeing, with teams united in purpose, innovation, and shared joy. Engagement scores increased and employees reported a greater sense of belonging and more joy at work.

Nurturing Communities of JOYBeing

Connecting in social networks and being a part of a community are essential for JOYBeing.

In *The Upswing: How America Came Together a Century Ago and How We Can Do It Again*, Robert Putnam provides research on social capital that shows how forming and being part of communities is critical for our mental health and a well-functioning society. Being a part of what is referred to as "third places" outside of work and home where we feel seen and part of a community is crucial for JOYBeing. Outside of work and family, we can each belong to various communal spaces, such as our social, spiritual, educational, health, cultural, virtual groups, neighbors, organizations, and others. Creating a community that experiences JOYBeing is important in today's fast-paced and often stressful

> "The next frontier of human advancement—personally and collectively—is the emotional frontier. Your task and the task of humanity is to learn how to intelligently resolve feelings for your own and others' benefit, in order to enrich your experience of life and create a better future.
>
> *Doc Childre*

world. Such a community provides a sanctuary where individuals can come together to celebrate the joy of being alive, connect with each other, and support each other's wellbeing.

In a world that can sometimes feel disconnected and isolating, establishing a community that cultivates JOYBeing fosters a sense of belonging and unity. It creates an environment where individuals can share their joys, inspire one another, and navigate life's challenges together. By prioritizing joy and wellbeing, communities become a source of rejuvenation, inspiration, and resilience. They serve as a reminder that life is meant to be lived with joy and that through connection and support, we can uplift each other on the journey of embracing and savoring the joy of life. We each can do our part to inspire this kind of connection and community. Through our presence, we can make a difference.

> *Here are some questions to consider and reflect upon to enhance your communities:*
>
> ✓ **What social groups or communities support your sense of JOYBeing and how?**
>
> ✓ **How are you being kind, positive, and inclusive in your interactions with these groups?**
>
> ✓ **How can you inspire and spread more joy in your communities?**

In our courses, we have found that when people connect with the goal of enhancing JOYBeing, an energy arises that inspires and supports growth. Being part of a community helps us feel as though we are part of something greater than ourselves. Together, we can create environments of belonging and JOYBeing. The seeds we plant as a community will sprout and grow over time.

Gila

Elevating joy to larger spheres has become a focal point for me, and I'm eager to invest more energy in this pursuit. Recognizing the profound impact and far-reaching ripple effects that come from engaging with larger communities, I am dedicated to expanding the spirit of JOYBeing to make a tangible difference in the world. I hold this responsibility with utmost seriousness, and I am committed to actively practicing and promoting JOYBeing in larger communities.

Understanding the transformative power inherent in spreading joy on a grand scale, my goal is to contribute to creating a positive shift in collective consciousness. By fostering environments where joy is not just a fleeting experience but a sustained way of being, I aim to influence communities toward greater harmony, collaboration, and wellbeing. I believe the practice of joy has the potential to create a ripple effect, inspiring individuals within these larger spheres to embrace a more joyful and fulfilling existence.

In essence, my commitment to amplifying JOYBeing is not just a personal endeavor; it's a conscious effort to contribute to a world where the cultivation of it becomes a shared responsibility and a source of empowerment for individuals and communities alike.

CHAPTER 7 Thriving and Flourishing in Our Garden: Expanding JOYBeing in Different Parts of Our Lives

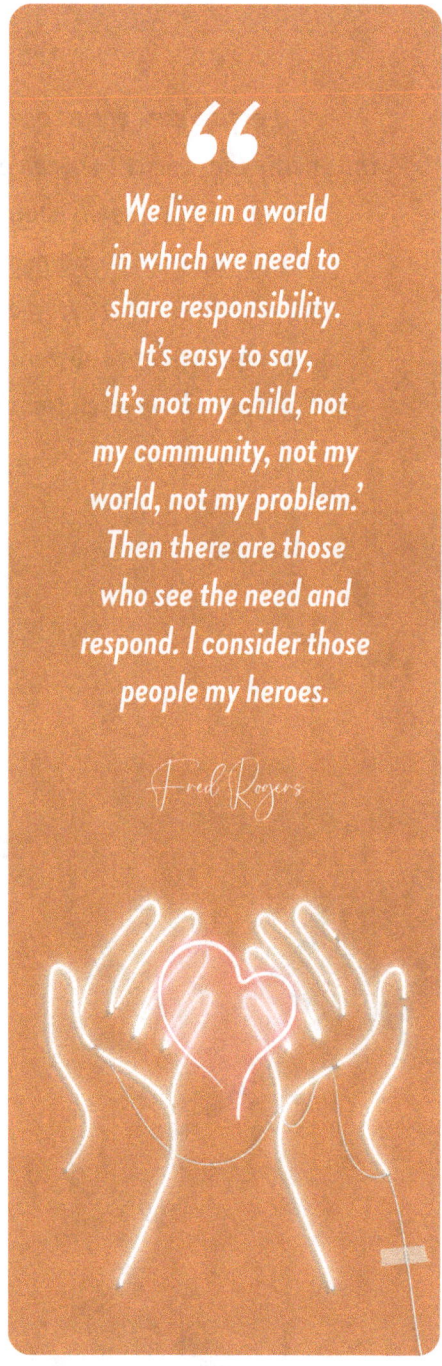

> "We live in a world in which we need to share responsibility. It's easy to say, 'It's not my child, not my community, not my world, not my problem.' Then there are those who see the need and respond. I consider those people my heroes."
>
> *Fred Rogers*

Ann

With a conscious and resolute intention, I am dedicated to infusing the spirit of openness and JOYBeing into the communities I am part of, those I am instrumental in forming, and those I can influence. My commitment extends beyond personal practice; it involves modeling JOYBeing and sharing its profound process and benefits with others. I have been offering and training facilitators to lead Open Stance Circles, where people share their commitment, experiences, and joy related to being open to others and themselves and how they influence their environments. In addition to sharing as a community, participants engage in a peer coaching process to support one another.[12]

Recognizing the contagious nature of emotions, I understand we are constantly influencing and inspiring one another. As a collective, we have the remarkable ability to amplify joy. Envision the possibilities if more of us deeply connect with our inner sense of joy and aliveness. This connection would pave the way for engaging conversations, co-creating innovative solutions, and positively influencing our world.

JOYBeing transforms our relational dynamics and sense of connection. When we are present and experiencing joy, we become less needy and expand our capacity to be present with others. Naturally, this enhanced state allows us to be more generous and giving. In essence, each of us can become a carrier of JOYBeing. My profound commitment lies in sharing the transformative power of connecting through openness and JOYBeing, sparking a ripple effect of positive transformation.

---

[12] For more information on Open Stance Circles, visit https://potentials.com/open-stance-community

> I define connection as the energy that exists between people when they feel seen, heard and valued; when they can give and receive without judgment and when they derive sustenance and strength from a relationship.
>
> Brené Brown

Practices

1. SHOW APPRECIATION FOR WHAT PEOPLE DO AND WHO THEY ARE

As you thank a person for what they do, mention their effect on you and appreciate who they are. For example, "Thanks for the extra effort you took to get the project done. You enabled us to achieve our goal on time and keep positive relationships with our stakeholders. I appreciate your thoughtfulness and generosity."

We are interconnected, and value exists in appreciating things often taken for granted, as well as more visible issues. Don't wait until conditions are perfect; appreciation is what fosters a positive environment.

2. PRACTICE ACTS OF KINDNESS

Turn to the people you see daily—your family, colleagues, and people in the community, such as shopkeepers and taxi drivers, who make our lives better. Give them a smile, and in your heart, wish them positive energy. Consider buying coffee for a stranger and practice acts of kindness. Inspire others to engage in acts of kindness and service to one another by fostering a spirit of giving and selflessness to deepen the sense of JOYBeing.

3. THROUGHOUT THE DAY, IN YOUR INTERACTIONS, RECONNECT WITH A SENSE OF JOYBEING

When you are at work, with family, or in a community, take one to two minutes a few times a day to pause, breathe, and quiet yourself by reconnecting with a sense of care and compassion for yourself and others. Remember that emotions are contagious, and our presence influences others.

CHAPTER 8

Committing to Our Path of JOYBeing: Embracing Our Future Self

> "I'm an artist at living,
> and my work of art is my life."
>
> — D. T. Suzuki

JOYBeing

JOYBeing can be seen as a metaphor for a garden. Many factors influence our garden's sustainability, including weather conditions, insects, and fertilizers. We each need to tend to our garden and weed it or to let go of what is hindering its growth, as well as take care of it through our rituals and practices. Tending a garden is a continual process, just like tending and cultivating the self. It requires faith, patience, and perseverance. We experience gratitude and joy as we reap the nourishment and beauty of the endeavor.

Imagine yourself at a future time; it could be one year from now, three years, or longer. Envision a future where your dreams have taken root and flourished, where you have become the best version of yourself. In this future, you radiate the essence of JOYBeing—a state of profound joy, fulfillment, and authentic living.

> **As you envision yourself in the future, ask yourself:**
>
> - What am I doing?
> - ✓ Where am I?
> - ✓ What emotions am I experiencing?
> - ✓ What types of relationships have I cultivated?
> - ✓ Have my core beliefs or priorities changed, and how are they reflected in my actions?
> - ✓ How is my life different?
> - ✓ What daily activities bring me joy, fulfillment, and a sense of purpose?

One aspect of experiencing life with excitement requires possessing a powerful connection with our future selves. Knowing where we want to go and how we want to live creates a clear path to what excites us. This clarity fuels our passion and guides our choices and actions, bringing us closer to our goals and dreams. Embodying our vision of the future is a key to unlocking our full potential. This concept is not merely wishful thinking. The act of forming a relationship with our future self propels us toward becoming

our ideal self, realizing our aspirations, and living our most authentic life.

Our future self is not a distant figure waiting to be discovered; it is who we actively choose to become. Visualization is a potent tool that bridges the gap between our present and future states. The clearer and more vivid our vision of our best self, the more effortlessly we can align our present actions and choices to support the manifestation of that future.

Today, at this very moment, you are crafting your future self. Embrace this perspective, for it infuses your choices, actions, and habits with purpose and meaning. Just as a gardener nurtures seeds for a bountiful harvest, the choices you make today are the seeds that will blossom into the reality of your future. By consciously cultivating a profound connection with your future self, you empower yourself to create the life you envision—one of expanded joy, growth, and authenticity. As you continue on this journey, allow the seeds of transformation to bloom into the reality of your brightest future.

We are always in the process of becoming, and within each of us lies the power to shape the person we aspire to be. The more aware we are of who we want to become, the more we will make choices that allow us to experience the essence of JOYBeing. It's not about searching for JOYBeing externally; rather, it's about fostering practices that allow us to experience it from within. We need to create an open mindset in our lives for more joy.

Many of us feel busy and have full schedules. We feel we have little time reserved for ourselves to enjoy life alone and with others to do what we love and what brings us joy.

To experience a life of JOYBeing in the future, as we stated in Chapter 1, we need to stay on the path of JOYBeing and be guided by our intentions, awareness, choices, and practices.

As we live and walk in the garden of life, we benefit from connecting with our purpose, setting our intentions, and identifying what we need to weed out and let go of. We need to choose and enact rituals and practices, like regular watering, that will nourish the garden and sustain us. Being grateful enables us to enjoy our garden's fruits and beauty.

We need to take responsibility for creating the life we want. By prioritizing moments of joy, we are nurturing our wellbeing and unlocking the potential for growth and fulfillment.

JOYBeing

As we venture forth into this journey, we embark on a path of self-discovery and empowerment. By embracing the power within us, we sow the seeds of JOYBeing, and as they take root, we blossom into the fullest expression of ourselves—living a life of purpose, joy, and authenticity.

A useful practice for becoming our ideal future self, a self that embraces JOYBeing, is to reflect daily on:

- ✓ Our Commitments
- ✓ What we choose to Let Go that does not serve us anymore
- ✓ What we choose to Call In as new energy
- ✓ Noticing and experiencing our Sense of Gratitude

These components originated in a somatic movement process, the "Commitment Practice," developed by Gila Ancel Seritcioglu and Giulio Brunini for their Coming Back to Center workshop leadership series in Tuscany.

This empowering framework serves as a guiding light, anchoring us in the present moment and infusing our days with heightened awareness. By incorporating the practice of daily review and somatically experiencing each of these four components, we embark on a transformative journey. Embracing this ritual at the beginning of each day creates the intention and supports us in connecting with pragmatic wisdom, engaging in skillful actions, and radiating heartfelt compassion.

We each have an inner garden.

For a moment, pause, take a breath, and envision the kind of garden you are and wish to be.

- ✓ What do you need to cultivate more JOYBeing?
- ✓ What do you need to let go of that does not serve you in this moment?
- ✓ What are you calling in that will move you toward your desired future self?
- ✓ What are you grateful for?
- ✓ Can you envision a more expansive, colorful, and fruitful garden where JOYBeing blooms?

Now, let's explore each of these steps.

Hoeing Purpose and Commitment

Having a meaningful purpose creates a sense of joy. Our purpose is what we desire to create. For example, we want to make a difference in people's lives. Our joy is magnified when our purpose benefits others.

Our commitments are the promises we make to actualize our purpose. Realizing our purpose becomes more attainable when we wholeheartedly set our intention and commit to embracing JOYBeing. Our commitments act as guiding stars, illuminating the path ahead and infusing us with the energy to forge ahead on our purposeful journey. By dedicating ourselves to the experience of JOYBeing, we enhance the trajectory of our future self, propelling it toward the full realization of its profound potential. Each intentional step toward JOYBeing nourishes and enables our purpose to bloom, creating a garden of opportunities awaiting our embrace.

To ensure our future self experiences a life of JOYBeing, we must commit to pursuing it on our path toward purpose and fulfillment.

Purpose starts with knowing who you are, your values, what you want, and building clarity on how you will get it. It originates from a place of longing. It is about ensuring alignment with who you are and what you want. A compelling purpose supports your choices and provides energy to draw you toward your future.

Declaring our purpose and commitment is valuable because we create the future through language and energy. When we make a declaration, we create future possibilities.

A commitment is about living our dream rather than simply speaking about it. When we declare a commitment, we awaken the energy to move toward it. This requires energy, awareness, and devotion. As we craft

> **"** Happiness is not something you postpone for the future; it is something you design for the present.
>
> *Jim Rohn*

our commitments, we can include them in our daily practices. One suggestion is to daily recall your purpose and envision actualizing your vision. For example, an aspect of Ann and Gila's purpose is to enjoy life and inspire others to do the same. This purpose and commitment have compelled us to work together in writing this book and facilitating related workshops.

When we move toward our purpose and commitments, we naturally face challenges, joys, moments of sadness, delight, stress, and awe. Our purpose enables us to move through all sorts of weather with equanimity. Purpose provides perspective and a sense of meaning that supports our desire to live and move forward. No matter what our purpose is, JOYBeing is the oxygen that enables us to move through life with more ease toward actualization.

Pause for a moment and connect with your purpose.

What can you commit to after reading this book that will incorporate more JOYBeing, excitement, and aliveness to support you on your journey toward realizing your purpose?

For example, Ann's purpose is to be all that she can be and to connect leaders with themselves, others, and their creative energy to enjoy and make life better for others. Ann's commitment is to take an Open Stance, live a life of JOYBeing, and inspire others with her presence to make a difference. Frequent review of her purpose and this commitment creates a sense of accountability and influences daily choices.

Gila's purpose is to grow herself and others and to make a difference in the world. Her commitment is to stay connected with her creativity, passion, and joy; to grow herself and others; and to live life from a place of JOYBeing. She wants to make a difference in this world through her work and presence.

> *If you carry joy in your heart, you can heal any moment.*
>
> — Carlos Santana

Letting Go

To flourish and embrace our best future selves, it is essential to shift our focus toward letting go of certain aspects of our lives. With numerous demands competing for our attention, it becomes crucial to discern which elements no longer serve our growth and progress. As we walk on our path of life, we recognize that certain baggage can hinder our journey, thus necessitating us to release these burdens. By choosing to fully shed what no longer serves us, we make space for new opportunities and fresh energy to propel us forward on our path toward personal fulfillment and growth. Embracing this process of letting go is a powerful act of self-nurturing and enables us to welcome the enriching possibilities that lie ahead.

It's a paradox that we believe we need to add to our lives to make things better. In our relentless pursuit of growth and development, our focus often remains fixed on what we lack, what we must acquire, and what we need to develop in our lives. The very fabric of developmental theories is woven with the idea of accumulation—doing more, achieving more. Undoubtedly, growth is essential for our progress, but we must also recognize the transformative power of releasing and letting go. By shedding old patterns, beliefs, and attachments, we create space for something new to be born. Our upbringing has instilled in us a pattern of constantly seeking more, yet the secret lies in discerning what no longer serves us. We must courageously let go of the burdens that weigh us down and the habits that hinder our growth. Instead of focusing solely on what we can add, we benefit from embracing the liberation that comes from what we can let go of.

By cultivating the muscle of releasing, we find the freedom to forge new paths, unburdened by the constraints of the past, and to be open to the infinite possibilities that await us. A gift we can give to our future self is to develop the habit of eliminating things that are draining energy and burdening us. These are often things that may have once served us but are no longer needed when we move toward our future.

JOYBeing

Gila

As mentioned in previous chapters, establishing a preschool was a source of immense joy, shaping the person I am today and reconnecting me to my personal power, self-confidence, and self-trust. However, two years ago, I reached a pivotal moment when what started as a passion project evolved into a burden. The school, once a metaphorical "baby," had grown into adulthood, and the weight of its responsibilities became evident. Despite the thousands of children, including my own, who had benefited from it, I sensed a shift—my past passion was transforming into a bodily contraction, cutting off my energy and obstructing my path to the future.

The decision to let go of a well-functioning business was emotionally challenging. However, I prioritized choosing myself, recognizing that my JOYBeing was irreplaceable. This act of releasing what was no longer serving my personal growth was a necessary step, creating space for new possibilities to unfold.

In another facet of my recent life, I faced the difficulty of letting go of relationships that, despite my efforts, no longer served my wellbeing. The pain of letting go was undeniable, yet it was a crucial act in aligning with my authentic self and pursuing a life rooted in JOYBeing.

Moreover, I underwent a significant personal transformation through a major operation, shedding parts of myself that were hindering my health and connection to what truly mattered to me. Letting go was essential for my heart's longing, for allowing and opening new space for what wanted to come to life and paving the way for a life centered around JOYBeing where I could embrace vitality and welcome new experiences.

Lately, the act of letting go has woven its way into various aspects of my life. It is manifested in decluttering wardrobes and creating breathing room within my home, a deliberate effort to foster a sense of spaciousness. My journey isn't merely about discarding belongings; it's a conscious step toward embracing a simpler life.

In this process, I've found myself drawn to the elegance inherent in the possessions I already have, recognizing the value in appreciating what surrounds me. Letting go for me today extends beyond the physical realm; it's a mindful choice to release the unnecessary, paving the way for a more meaningful and uncluttered existence. This intentional simplification becomes a canvas upon which I paint the strokes of a life filled with purpose and JOYBeing.

We can also benefit from decluttering our homes and our work environment, getting rid of all the stuff we keep and don't use. When we overstuff ourselves, we bury joy and the life energy inherent in us. We know people feel lighter, with less stress and more joy, after cleaning out closets, houses, and belongings. Decluttering and simplifying our environment sparks joy and creates space for possibilities. People have less of the stress hormone cortisol when they describe their homes as being less cluttered. According to Alice Boyes, PhD in "6 Benefits of an Uncluttered Space," after decluttering, people report better focus, higher self-esteem, better relationships, and improved wellbeing. Letting go is not simply getting rid of things but experiencing gratitude for what once served us in life and does not do so now.

For a moment, stop and take a breath.

What are you currently carrying that you would like to let go of, which emotionally might create an obstacle to your purpose and a sense of JOYBeing?

How is what you are letting go of no longer serving you with regard to your commitment?

What you let go of could be a limiting belief, a "should," a judgment, a story from the past that drains your energy, or an old habit you are holding onto that no longer serves you. For example, you may believe you are not good enough, or you overwork and don't take time for yourself. You may believe you are only of value if you are serving others, and you may say yes to all requests to please people. With awareness and practice, we can consciously choose to put our energy and attention into different choices that serve us.

Just as we may choose to let go of some of the plants in our garden to create room for others, we can consciously choose to release old patterns to strengthen our wellbeing. We may choose to let go of unrealistic expectations that lead to chronic disappointment and frustration. We can let go of past regrets, missed opportunities, and mistakes we and others have made in our lives. We may let go of our fear of failure to bring in more creativity and risk-taking. Perhaps you choose to let go of your focus on attaining material possessions to appreciate the simplicity around you. You may even let go of relationships that drain you to create healthier boundaries and space for nourishing relationships.

Ann

Making a firm commitment to release the tight grip of worry and over-responsibility has been a profound journey of shedding the familiar weight of these longtime companions and well-worn grooves. It has demanded a sustained and conscious effort to stay acutely aware and to let go of deeply ingrained patterns where I acted without deliberate reflection.

Before hastily agreeing to any request, I've embraced pausing to check in with myself. I intentionally delay the reflex to respond promptly, allowing time to consider what is important in addition to others' needs. While not easy, this intentional pause creates space and reduces the noise of commitments and obligations.

Furthermore, simplifying my life has become a deliberate effort to be more present and connected with JOYBeing. This effort involves releasing commitments and parting ways with possessions. I've become more discerning about how I spend my time, recognizing that simplicity is a lifestyle and a conscious choice to nurture a deeper inner connection of JOYBeing.

Calling In

In addition to letting go of what is no longer serving us, it is useful to be mindful of what thoughts, actions, and practices will serve us as we move toward our purpose and commitments to enhance our experience of JOYBeing as our future self.

We each have many seeds of possibility. When we water those seeds, they sprout and grow into fullness. The thoughts we nurture in our minds blossom into the beliefs we hold. Our actions cultivate the seeds of potential within us, gifting us with their fruits over time. The emotions we feed become the soil from which our experiences grow. The attention we give to certain ideas shapes the reality we perceive and live in. The habits we cultivate sow the seeds of our future.

Calling in involves inviting in something new or something we have not yet experienced regularly. It can be a new mindset, action, attitude, way of being, or attribute that has been hidden or forgotten in us. It could be something that will support us in honoring and serving our commitment. For example, if we let go of worry, we can call in more breathing, silence, time in nature, and ease.

By practicing this new attribute, we fuel our motivation to evolve and unlock our true potential. When we are calling in, we cultivate the capacity for being open, we connect to positivity, and we connect with our desires and longings. Calling in is remembering and inviting what is important to us. It is about opening new doors to ourselves and experiencing new discoveries. It is about connecting to our passion and what we love. It's about making a conscious choice to live in alignment with our heart's deepest longings. It creates an opening inside us that grants space for our true essence, which craves expression and fulfillment. It is taking steps to live a full life of purpose and JOYBeing.

Calling in is a step toward becoming our best selves and taking action to live our values. We are moving toward what we truly care about and being who we are meant to be.

For a moment, take a breath and reflect on what you desire to call in that will serve you on your journey toward your purpose and JOYBeing.

What will you do differently?

How will this new behavior affect you?

Laurie, a participant in our Cultivating JOYBeing course, called in moving her body to support her health and wellbeing. She added walking to her days and had the extra benefit of time outside. We know that being physically active is important for our vitality and overall health and wellbeing. Didem, another participant, called in being on a more regular sleep schedule and creating time for rest as a way of creating more life energy at work.

We can, over time, call in the facets that support our wellbeing. In addition to physical health, we can focus on our mental, spiritual, emotional, and relational health. For example, our client Cindy created a savings plan for her retirement, Lisa added joining a community for meditation and reflection, and Pia added the process of finding three things that went well each day. Tony started doing mood checks to create more awareness, dim his inner critic, and ensure emotional wellbeing.

What can you add to your life to support your overall wellbeing? Do not overwhelm yourself by trying to change many things at once. Instead, build habits that support you by tying new behaviors with current habitual patterns.

Ann

Over the years, I have embraced numerous practices that enhance my ability to be present and savor moments of joy. To foster wellbeing, I have adopted the following habits that bolster my health:

✓ **Physical health:** exercising, strength training, healthy eating

✓ **Mental health:** meditating, doing mood checks, immersing in nature, listening to music, drawing

✓ **Spiritual health:** participating in groups, exploring ways of being

✓ **Relational health:** spending quality time with friends and family, joining communities

✓ **Service:** volunteering and supporting people

✓ **Learning:** studying, reading and taking courses

✓ **Professionally:** developing new skills and creating programs

As I integrate these new habits, I elevate my overall JOYBeing and fulfillment. It's inspiring to envision success in each domain and take continuous action. Reinforcing your identity as a person who experiences JOYBeing, as someone who is healthy and fulfilled, is empowering. Of course, introducing a few practices at a time is beneficial. I have found it enriching to explore a variety of practices. Enjoy the journey.

Gratitude

On our profound journey of realizing our purpose and embracing the essence of JOYBeing in every aspect of our lives and future self, gratitude stands as our essential companion and true friend. Ideally, we continually want to experience gratitude for our awareness of who we are in the moment, our circumstances, and who we are becoming. Gratitude serves as our compass, leading us to trust the intricate rhythm of life and its abundant experiences.

Gratitude is particularly imperative during times of inner and outer turmoil. Amid personal struggles, acknowledging our blessings, big and small, can bring hope and perspective and the possibility of seeing challenges as growth opportunities. Gratitude acts as a shield against despair in the face of global uncertainties and can act as a guiding light and energize us to see possibilities. A mindset of gratitude bolsters us from despair to hope and JOYBeing.

Gratitude is acknowledging our personal effort, or others' efforts, that supports us in our commitment. As the gold standard for JOYBeing, gratitude is not merely an abstract notion; it flows within us, resonating in our thoughts, hearts, and guts, filling us with an invigorating sense of aliveness. Being steeped in gratitude empowers us to center our emotions, fortify our willpower, and propel us forward, unwaveringly embracing our purpose and commitments with renewed determination.

For example, I am grateful to myself for prioritizing joy. I am grateful for others who bring joy to my life. I am grateful for the beautiful sunny day that allows me to take a walk and enjoy nature.

Notice how you experience gratitude and where you feel it in your body.

What are you grateful for?

What are ways you express gratitude in your walk of life?

Embodying gratitude throughout our day is a habit that becomes even more crucial during uncertain and challenging

times. While it's easier when things are going well, it's the practice during these times that truly strengthens this habit. By reminding ourselves to be grateful for all we have, including our current breath and living experience, we can overcome the challenges we face. We can even appreciate our natural negativity bias that aims to protect us and all the patterns we created to survive.

Ann

I find it useful to remind myself of my purpose and intention, the patterns I intend to let go of, and those I want to develop.

Daily, I reflect on the following:

- ✓ My **purpose** is to be all I can be and to connect leaders with themselves, others, and their creative energy to enjoy and make life better for others. I am committed to taking an Open Stance and living a life of JOYBeing, inspiring others with my presence, and making a difference.

- ✓ In addition to simplifying and decluttering, I am **letting go** of worry and over-responsibility.

- ✓ I am **calling in** more conscious breathing, joy, and openness.

- ✓ I am **grateful** for the journey of JOYBeing and expanding my appreciation and gratitude for life.

Gila

I've been incorporating the commitment practice into my morning routine. This practice combines movement meditation with a breathing pattern accompanied by a piece of soul-transforming music. Each morning, I set an intention for the day, focusing on my commitments, what I am letting go and calling in, and what I'm grateful for. This practice has significantly influenced my life in several positive ways.

Firstly, it has helped me start each day with a clear sense of purpose and direction. By setting an intention, I can prioritize my tasks and maintain focus throughout the day. This clarity has improved my productivity and efficiency, allowing me to accomplish more with a calm and centered mindset.

Secondly, the focus on gratitude has cultivated a more positive outlook on life. By acknowledging the things I'm thankful for, I find myself more resilient in the face of challenges and better able to appreciate the small joys in everyday life. This shift in perspective has enhanced my overall wellbeing and happiness.

Additionally, the integration of movement meditation and breathing patterns has had profound effects on my physical and mental health. The gentle movements and deep, rhythmic breathing help reduce stress and promote relaxation. This practice has improved my flexibility, balance, and overall physical health while also providing a mental reset that keeps me grounded and focused.

I have been teaching this practice to organizational teams and individual coaching clients for many years. The feedback I've received highlights that starting the day with this level of awareness is a powerful tool for cultivating a new self. Many have reported increased productivity, enhanced wellbeing, and a greater sense of fulfillment in their personal and professional lives.

Practices

1. USE THE COMMITMENT PRACTICE AS A DAILY ROUTINE

To move toward your JOYBeing future self, reflect on the following questions:

✓ What's my purpose? What is meaningful to me?
✓ What is my commitment?
✓ Why is this important to me?
✓ How will I know I am practicing my commitment? What will I be doing differently?
✓ What might get in the way that I would like to let go of?
✓ What support can I call in to strengthen and sustain my commitment?
✓ What am I grateful for?
✓ Who are the people who will hold me accountable? How often will I check in with them?
✓ What daily practices will I incorporate to support my purpose and allow me to experience more JOYBeing and aliveness?

Complete the following statements. Repeat them daily, and put them into action during your day.

> My purpose/commitment is….
> I am letting go of….
> I am calling in….
> I am grateful for….

You can use this practice daily to support you by formulating simple intentions to serve your purpose and create more JOYBeing. For example, you can affirm:

"Today, I will take better care of myself. I will let go of responding immediately to others' needs or being in a hurry. I am calling in, slowing down, and reflecting before I respond to a request, pausing and checking in with myself. I am grateful to be aware of my needs and for having the ability to make choices that support me."

At the end of the day, reflect on how this practice has served you.

2. WRITE A LETTER FROM YOUR FUTURE SELF TO YOUR CURRENT SELF

Connect with your future self through writing.

Listen as your future self thanks and appreciates you for the energy and courage you took to realize your potential.

Savor the encouragement, insight, and positive guidance of your future self.

What did your future self learn that can support you now?

3. CREATE MOMENTS OF PAUSE FOR AWE

Take a ten-minute walk, focusing on what brings you "awe" that you would like to continue and carry into your future self. It may be a walk in nature or your neighborhood. Just pay attention and savor the beauty and wonder around you. Reflect on how you can trust life and its offerings. Notice the magic that lies in the ordinary.

4. ENVISION THE LIFE OF YOUR FUTURE SELF

Reflect and somatically connect with your future self:
- ✓ Where are you, and at what phase of life?
- ✓ Who are the people around you? How are you interacting with them?
- ✓ How is your health and wellbeing?
- ✓ What work or service are you doing? How are you making a difference?
- ✓ What practices are supporting your spiritual development?

CHAPTER 9

The Ripple Effect: Impacting the World Through JOYBeing

> "Love only grows by sharing. You can only have more for yourself by giving it away to others."
>
> — Brian Tracy

As we step into the final chapter of this journey, let's imagine the boundless possibilities that arise from appreciating our interconnection. Imagine the ancient redwood forest in California, where towering giants touch the sky with their majestic canopies. At first glance, each redwood appears to stand in solitary grandeur, a testament to individual strength and resilience. But beneath the surface lies a hidden secret—a mystical network of roots intertwining just a few feet underground.

In this enchanted forest, the roots of each tree reach out to one another, forming an intricate web of connection and support. These roots share nutrients, wisdom, and strength, creating an unbreakable bond that sustains them all. When one tree faces adversity, the entire forest unites, holding it up and ensuring its survival. Together, they thrive as a unified organism, their collective strength far surpassing what they could achieve alone.

> **May you experience each day as a sacred gift woven around the heart of wonder.**
>
> *John O'Donohue*

This magical story of the redwoods is a powerful metaphor for our own lives. It reminds us that our greatest potential is realized not in isolation but in the connections we forge and the communities we build through JOYBeing. As we reflect on the lessons in this book, let us embrace the beauty of our interconnectedness and strive to live a life filled with joy, purpose, and the boundless possibilities that arise when we stand together.

Scientific research increasingly supports the idea that all life forms are interconnected. This interdependence isn't just a poetic notion; it's a fundamental reality of our existence. By appreciating our interconnectivity, we can better understand how our actions influence one another, fostering a more cooperative and compassionate world.

Imagine a world where we fully embrace this interconnectedness. We would be more inclined

CHAPTER 9 The Ripple Effect: Impacting the World Through JOYBeing

to support each other, work together toward common goals, and celebrate our shared humanity. This could lead to personal growth as we learn from each other's experiences and to social harmony as we respect and understand each other's perspectives. Like the redwoods, we can stand tall and strong, not as isolated entities but as a unified force, thriving together.

Today, we are encountering numerous collective challenges as a world society, often referred to as the metacrisis. We are experiencing polarization, environmental disruptions, political divides, wars, inequities, and more. Life is challenging on so many levels, from the personal to global. While it may seem counterintuitive, enhancing our sense of joy and aliveness or JOYBeing can be a powerful service that supports others and our planet during these turbulent times.

Reaping the Benefits of JOYBeing

Just as the redwoods in the enchanted forest thrive through their deep, interconnected roots, so too can we reap the profound benefits of JOYBeing by nurturing our connections with others. When we embrace a life filled with joy and purpose, we, like the trees, create a network of support and enrichment. By sharing our joy and strength with those around us, even admitting challenges, we build a vibrant community that sustains and uplifts us all. This interconnectedness not only amplifies our individual joy but also fortifies our collective wellbeing, allowing us to flourish together in a harmonious dance of mutual support and shared success.

Our emotions and energy are undeniably contagious. When we connect with our joy and sense of aliveness, we inspire others to be hopeful and see possibilities. Adopting a JOYBeing mindset and maintaining and managing our energy with an Open Stance equips us to better face uncertainty. This can be engaging in the many practices offered in this book, such as the mood check (E-MRI), noticing and savoring moments of joy, and practicing gratitude. When doing so, we are taking a step toward regulating our nervous system. We not only experience calmness and aliveness ourselves, but we influence others from a centered presence. Fostering joy and openness amid challenge, turmoil, and uncertainty is not just beneficial for individual wellbeing but also critical for societal resilience and cohesion.

JOYBeing can be a powerful antidote to anxiety and depression, especially during challenging times. Embracing joy boosts our resilience, enhances our immune function, and promotes overall physical health. It fosters a profound sense of belonging and community, equipping us to handle crises with greater strength. By nurturing JOYBeing, we deepen our empathy, compassion, and sense of interconnectedness while also cultivating gratitude and inner peace. This heightened awareness and aliveness not only enrich our daily experiences but ignite creativity and innovation, enabling us to engage in meaningful conversations and cocreate solutions.

JOYBeing, in its essence, is a transformative force that touches every aspect of our being, leading us to a more vibrant, connected, and purposeful rhythm of life. Just as a healthy garden goes through fallow periods without bearing fruit, we can trust in our resilience. Together, we can navigate the myriad challenges before us. We understand that challenges are an inherent part of life, and with collective effort, we can manage uncertainty, learn, and experience post-traumatic growth. By embracing JOYBeing, we become part of a collective effort, empowering us to contribute to societal resilience and thriving.

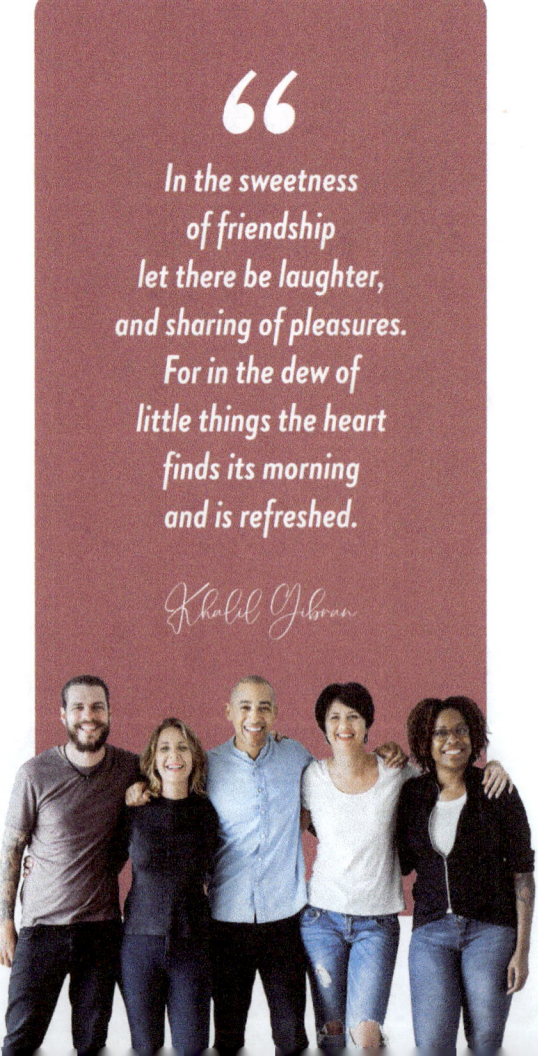

> In the sweetness of friendship let there be laughter, and sharing of pleasures. For in the dew of little things the heart finds its morning and is refreshed.
>
> *Khalil Gibran*

Our Wish for You

Spread joy and watch the world bloom with hope and aliveness. Envisioning a world transformed by JOYBeing is a vision of a world where kindness, empathy, compassion, and love are the driving forces behind our actions. It's a world where people prioritize the wellbeing of not only themselves but their fellow human beings, creating a ripple effect of joy and positivity that can reshape and restore the fabric of society. In this world of interconnectedness, joy becomes a shared currency, and together, we can create a brighter future for all.

Like a resilient seed, the essence of JOYBeing lies inherently within each of us. Similar to the seed that bravely breaks free from its sturdy shell, our capacity for joy withstands the tests of life's thunderstorms and basks in the warmth of sunshine during our personal growth. Much like the seed expresses gratitude for the nurturing touch of warm sunshine and the rejuvenating presence of refreshing dew, JOYBeing flourishes as we acknowledge and appreciate the diverse experiences that contribute to our inner growth and wellbeing. Embracing JOYBeing is a transformative journey, much like the seed's evolution into a flourishing plant.

As you complete this journey with us, and look at the garden of your life:

- ✓ **What do you see, and how do you feel?**

- ✓ **How are you accessing JOYBeing, and what difference is it making in your life?**

- ✓ **What do you need to focus on and practice to strengthen and flourish your inner garden of JOYBeing?**

- ✓ **How would your life be different if you had more access to joy, allowing you to live and spread the energy of JOYBeing?**

CHAPTER 9 The Ripple Effect: Impacting the World Through JOYBeing

Throughout this book, we have demonstrated how to create a path toward cultivating a life of JOYBeing. Using the metaphor of the garden as a way of creating a world of JOYBeing, we know it is crucial to plant, tend, nourish, and care for our inner garden so that we can be ready for the miracle to grow and reap abundance.

We continue our daily practices of connecting with JOYBeing. In addition, we have created a live online course and are building a community committed to living and spreading the power of JOYBeing. We are honoring our commitment to staying connected to joy and influencing others to do so too. We believe the world will be better if more of us notice and savor joy and aliveness.

Nature is our teacher, and JOYBeing is our guide, whispering to us every moment the formula for creating a fulfilled life. Within the environment of a positive and open mindset, conscious use of energy, and a focus on living a healthy life of wellbeing, we create and tend the garden of our life growing toward JOYBeing.

This path of JOYBeing, as shared in the first chapter, is created with four steps:

1. **Intention** is the creative power that activates the energy of possibility, trust, and excitement toward making contact with our aliveness and manifesting our passion.

2. **Awareness** of our internal life as well as the world outside us shines a light on what is needed.

3. **Choice** is about making decisions and taking actions that align with our values so that JOYBeing can be embraced each day. Joy is a choice and is available to all of us. It is not only available in grand achievements but in the smallest of decisions that align with our values.

4. **Practices** are the habits that keep the garden well and support us in cultivating a new self—a life of JOYBeing.

We encourage you to experiment with the practices and adapt those that are most meaningful to you.

In life's rhythm, our garden sometimes lies fallow, not constantly flourishing. During these times of storms, uncertainty, and suffering, we can discover our true resilience, finding strength and our life energy in the midst of adversity and cultivating our inner essence needed to weather life's challenges. Even in moments when joy is hidden from us, JOYBeing remains within our reach. During these times of retreat, we turn inward, clearing the way for new growth in our lives. Each phase of life invites us to revisit and nurture our soil, allowing new plants to flourish in the garden of our existence. This cyclical process enriches our journey, reminding

> "Spread love everywhere you go, let no one ever come to you without leaving happier.
>
> *Mother Teresa*

Gila

Today, my life is devoted to empowering both myself and those on a quest for their inner strength, both personally and professionally. It revolves around the profound journey of self-exploration, understanding our essence, finding our core, and navigating life with purpose, intention, and a vibrant sense of aliveness. My fundamental journey has always been centered on awareness—how to guide others toward choosing a similar transformative nourishing path once I've embarked on it myself.

I've consistently delved into self-exploration, sharpening the essence of my being to seek more joy, vitality, and connection. My focus has been on using my own journey and resources to create a difference and contribute to positive change in the world. Witnessing my personal transformation, I've cherished a deep longing to share this awareness globally, making it accessible to anyone in search of themselves and seeking pathways to reconnect with their inner power, joy, and vitality.

The birth of JOYBeing emerged during a time when I yearned for a way of being that would restore my sense of belonging, becoming, and purpose. Today, I am profoundly grateful for the unexpectedly fortunate encounters, friends, colleagues, teachers, clients, and inspirations that have shaped my journey. Ann, whose path intersected with mine, played a crucial role by encouraging me to pen this book together with her—an offering to those who have entered and touched my life at the perfect juncture for the right reasons. My gratitude extends to my history, my family, and life itself. As I now step into an unknown future with faith and trust in the process, may life unfold with all its magic, marvelous surprises, and opportunities for growth.

CHAPTER 9 The Ripple Effect: Impacting the World Through JOYBeing

us that joy, like nature, has its seasons and will blossom anew.

JOYBeing is not a destination but a journey to be lived in the present moment. We can illuminate the path for those who are suffering and not in contact with joy by offering compassion, fostering greater awareness, and creating supportive communities where individuals feel valued, connected, and empowered to connect with their inner essence.

Throughout this book, we have explored numerous practices and tools that guide you on the path to JOYBeing. As you embark on this journey of self-cultivation, we would like to share and offer you the seeds that have supported us in our journey. By nurturing these seeds, you will cultivate an enriching journey that allows your life to blossom and flourish in the rhythm of life.

In summary, here are the seeds of JOYBeing we have planted in our garden that have assisted us throughout this journey. We would like to offer these to you to tend your inner garden and flourish in the rhythm of life. May you pass these on to the people you meet on your JOYBeing journey.

Ann

From the moment life begins until our final breath, connection has the power to shape every experience. How we connect with ourselves, others, and our environment determines our capacity to thrive, to love deeply, and the nature of the successes we enjoy. Imagine your inner self as a garden where JOYBeing is the most beautiful and vibrant flowers and fruits. Nurture this garden and you will discover the expansiveness of joy richly rewarded.

May your garden blossom with abundance to nourish you and others as you experiment and incorporate awareness, choice, and practices to open and connect with the inherent joy of being alive.

As I continue this journey of learning, growing, and embodying JOYBeing, I am committed to sharing what I discover to support openness and connection. I hope that, together, we can make a meaningful difference with our presence, spreading the transformative power of JOYBeing to enrich the lives of others.

I am deeply grateful to you, the reader, for your commitment to experiencing the joy of aliveness. Your partnership in this journey is truly appreciated. I am also thankful to all who have joined and supported me on this inner garden journey, especially Gila, colleagues, clients, family, and friends. I look forward to continued learning, growth, and joy.

- **Make choices that honor your values and purpose.** Move toward what is important to you where joy flourishes. Pursue your passions and contribute to the wellbeing of others to expand aliveness.

- **Connect to yourself, others, and your environment.** Notice that joy is not isolated but available to you wherever you go. Like the weather, life is full of challenges and uncertainties, yet joy can be a companion and a friend to you on the journey. Build meaningful relationships and create a sense of belonging to inspire and foster joy.

- **Enjoy, play, laugh, and experience flow.** Connect to the music of your soul with awe and wonder. Let playfulness be a guiding light on your journey. Surrender to the rhythm of life to bloom JOYBeing.

- **Always remember that joy is in us and is accessible.** Notice moments of joy and savor them. Joy can be found in the simplest of moments, even amid challenges.

- **Thrive and connect with your creative energy.** Let your imagination soar and allow your unique talents to shine in all you do. Nurture your creative spirit to transform your life and the lives of those around you.

- **Embrace all of your inner voices.** Your inner child, wise self, and inner critic are all essential parts that bring learning and possibility. Accept that you are whole, capable, and resourceful.

- **Trust the process.** Every step you take offers the opportunity for learning and growth. Have faith in the journey even when the path seems uncertain and challenging. Connect with your inner wisdom to make choices that foster harmony and joy.

- **Be curious.** Let your sense of wonder guide you to new discoveries. Embrace the unknown with an open mind. Look at the world with new eyes.

CHAPTER 9 The Ripple Effect: Impacting the World Through JOYBeing

- ✓ **Be grateful to life and its offerings.** Remember to cherish the little things and find joy in the simple moments. Appreciate the wonder of who you are and the miracle of all creation.

- ✓ **Be compassionate.** Be empathetic and share kindness. Give love to yourself and others. Love will grow each time you give it away. Foster deeper connections by contributing to a more caring and supportive community.

- ✓ **Spread joy.** JOYBeing is contagious and is amplified when you share it with others. Echo it throughout the universe so that you touch every soul you encounter and uplift their spirit.

- ✓ **Be present.** Pay attention and cherish the beauty of your inner and outer landscape. Find joy in the ordinary—the colors of the sky, the melody of birds, or the kindness in a stranger's smile. Dance to the rhythm of your heart.

- ✓ **Nourish yourself and others.** Care for your body, mind, and spirit to build a strong foundation of resilience. When you attend to your wellbeing, you are able to thrive amid challenges, inspire those around you, and restore the weary souls in the world.

- ✓ **Don't lose hope, no matter how dark the world may seem.** Even in the most challenging times, remember light is always waiting to break through. Hold onto your optimism and belief in brighter days because your hope can be a guiding force and a source of strength for both yourself and those around you.

JOYBeing

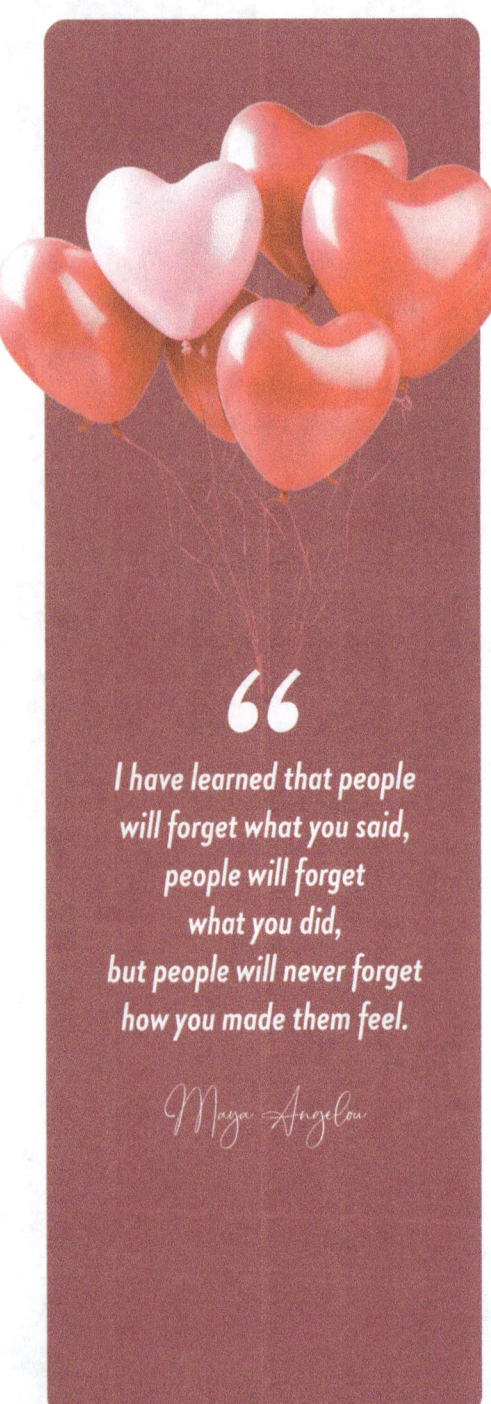

> I have learned that people will forget what you said, people will forget what you did, but people will never forget how you made them feel.
>
> *Maya Angelou*

Our wish for you is that you plant, tend, and nourish your inner seeds of JOYBeing. May you reap the bountiful fruits and savor the beauty as you connect and embrace a life of inner joy and vibrancy. May your radiant spirit inspire others, spreading the seeds of joy to heal our planet, expanding our sense of possibility, and making a difference for all. As each soul awakens to its own garden of joy, may the world bloom with the everlasting fragrance of aliveness and fulfillment.

As for Ann and Gila, we both see this not as an ending but as the beginning of a new chapter in our story. We are committed to sharing the value and power of JOYBeing as well as cherishing our friendship and living fully embodying JOYBeing.

*JOYBeing is the essence we bring to the rhythm of life,
rooted in love, blossoming in presence.
In darkness, it whispers of hope;
in light, it dances freely, inviting us
to make space for all that is.*

*Each step is a gift, each moment a choice,
to nurture, to share, to belong.*

*As we walk, we leave a trace,
a story of compassion, of courage, of light.*

*Step by step, let your essence shine,
for the path you walk shapes the world
and becomes your footprint.*

Notes

CHAPTER 1

Ben-Shahar, Tal. *Happier.* New York, NY: McGraw-Hill Books, 2007.

Seligman, Martin Seligman. *Authentic Happiness: Using the New Positive Psychology to Realize Your Potential for Lasting Fulfillment.* New York, NY: Free Press, 2004.

Greater Good Science Center. https://greatergood.berkeley.edu/.

Brown, Brené. *Atlas of the Heart: Mapping Meaningful Connection and the Language of Human Experience.* New York, NY: Random House, 2021.

Vaillant, George. Cited in "Joy: An Introduction to This Special Issue" by Robert Emmons. *Journal of Positive Psychology.* 15.1 (2019): 1-4.

Vaillant, George. *Spiritual Evolution: A Scientific Defense of Faith.* New York: Broadway Books. 2008. p.134.

Hanson, Rick. *Hardwiring Happiness: The Brain Science of Contentment, Calm and Confidence.* New York, NY: Harmony, 2013.

Dweck, Carol. *Mindset: The New Psychology of Success.* New York, NY: Random House, 2006.

Van Eron, Ann. *Open Stance: Thriving Amid Differences and Uncertainty.* Chicago, IL: Open View Press, 2021.

Snel, Eline. *Sitting Still Like a Frog: Mindfulness Exercises for Kids (and Their Parents).* Boston, MA: Shambhala Publications, 2013. Excerpt reprinted by arrangement with Shambhala Publications, Inc., Boulder, Colorado. www.shambhala.com.

Strozzi-Heckler, Richard. *The Leadership Dojo.* Berkeley, CA: Frog Ltd. Books, 2007.

CHAPTER 2

Tolle, Eckhart. *The Power of Now: A Guide to Spiritual Enlightenment.* New York, NY: New World Library, 2004.

Langer, Ellen. *The Mindful Body: Thinking Our Way to Chronic Health.* New York, NY: Ballantine Books, 2023.

Nhat Hanh, Thich. *The Miracle of Mindfulness: An Introduction to the Practice of Meditation.* Boston, MA: Beacon Press, 1999.

Boroson, Martin. *OOM—One Moment Meditation* app.

Strozzi-Heckler, Richard. *The Anatomy of Change: A Way to Move Through Life's Transitions.* Berkeley, CA: North Atlantic Books, 1984.

CHAPTER 3

Frederickson, Barbara. *Love 2.0: Creating Happiness and Health in Moments of Connection.* New York, NY: Penguin Books, 2013.

David, Susan. *Emotional Agility: Get Unstuck, Embrace Change, and Thrive in Work and Life.* New York, NY: Penguin Books, 2016.

Hawkins, David R. *Power Vs. Force: The Hidden Determinants of Human Behavior.* Carlsbad, CO: Hay House, 2014.

Frederickson, Barbara. *Positivity: Top-Notch Research Reveals the 3 to 1 Ratio That Will Change Your Life.* New York, NY: Harmony, 2009.

CHAPTER 4

Van Eron, Ann. *Open Stance: Thriving Amid Differences and Uncertainty.* Chicago, IL: Open View Press, 2022.

Neff, Kristin. *Self-Compassion: The Proven Power of Being Kind to Yourself.* New York: William Morrow, 2015.

Germer, Chris. "Psychologist: Asking Yourself: 'What Do I Need?' Is an Act of Kindness." *Full Circle with Anderson Cooper* (video). https://www.cnn.com/videos/us/2021/08/09/psychologist-chris-germer-self-compassion-acfc-full-episode-vpx.cnn.

CHAPTER 5

Schwartz, Richard. *Introduction to Internal Family Systems.* Boulder, CO: Sounds True, 2023.

Taylor, Jill Bolte. *My Stroke of Insight: A Brain Scientist's Personal Journey.* New York, NY: Penguin Books, 2009.

Brackett, Marc. *Permission to Feel: The Power of Emotional Intelligence to Achieve Wellbeing and Success.* New York, NY: Celadon Books, 2020.

Willcox, Gloria. *Feelings: Converting Negatives to Positives.* Kearney, NE: Morris Publishing, 2001.

McGonigal, Kelly. *The Upside of Stress: Why Stress Is Good for You, and How to Get Good at It.* New York, NY: Avery, 2016.

Friedman, Howard S. *The Self-Healing Personality: Why Some People Achieve Health and Others Succumb to Illness.* Bloomington, IN: iUniverse, 2000.

Siminovitch, Dorothy E. *The Gestalt Coaching Primer: The Path Toward Awareness Intelligence.* Cleveland, OH: Gestalt Coaching Works, 2017, 2022.

Hübl, Thomas. *Attuned: Practicing Interdependence to Heal Our Trauma—and Our World.* Boulder, CO: Sounds True, 2023.

CHAPTER 6

Aaker, Jennifer and Naomi Bagdonas. *Humor Seriously: Why Humor Is a Secret Weapon in Business and Life (and How Anyone Can Harness It. Even You.)* New York, NY: Random House, 2021.

Magsamen, Susan and Ivy Ross. *Your Brain on Art: How the Arts Transform Us.* New York, NY: Random House, 2023.

Schwartz, Richard. *No Bad Parts: Healing Trauma and Restoring Wholeness with the Internal Family Systems Model.* Boulder, CO: Sounds True, 2021.

Nhat Hanh, Thich. *Reconciliation: Healing the Inner Child.* Berkeley, CA: Parallax Press, 2010.

CHAPTER 7

Ben-Shahar, Tal. *Happier: Learn the Secrets to Daily Joy and Lasting Fulfillment.* New York: McGraw Hill, 2007.

Waldinger, Robert and Marc Schulz. *The Good Life: Lessons from the World's Longest Scientific Study of Happiness.* New York, NY: Simon & Schuster, 2023.

Murthy, Vivek. *Together: The Healing Power of Human Connection in a Sometimes Lonely World.* New York, NY: Harper, 2023.

Bethell, Christina. "Building Health and Healing Competencies of Leaders and Organizations." Presentation to the Trauma Informed Coach and Consulting Program. June 10, 2024.

Hobson, Katherine. "Feeling Lonely? Too Much Time on Social Media May Be Why." National Public Radio. https://www.npr.org/sections/health-shots/2017/03/06/518362255/feeling-lonely-too-much-time-on-social-media-may-be-why.

Oxford University Said Business School. "Happy Workers are 13% More Productive." October 24, 2019. https://www.ox.ac.uk/news/2019-10-24-happy-workers-are-13-more-productive.

Gallup Poll 2022. www.Gallup.com.

Killingsworth, Matthew A. and Daniel T. Gilbert, "A Wandering Mind Is an Unhappy Mind." *Science.* 330.6006 (2010): 932. doi: 10.1126/science.1192439.

Moss, Jennifer. "Creating a Happier Workplace Is Possible—and Worth It." *Harvard Business Review.* October 20, 2023. https://hbr.org/2023/10/creating-a-happier-workplace-is-possible-and-worth-it.

Gallup Poll 2022. www.Gallup.com.

Dhingra, Naina and Bill Schaninger. "The Search for Purpose at Work." Podcast. June 3, 2021. https://www.mckinsey.com/capabilities/people-and-organizational-performance/our-insights/the-search-for-purpose-at-work.

Van Eron, Ann. *OASIS Conversations: Leading with an Open Mindset to Maximize Potential.* Chicago, IL: Open View Press, 2016.

Porath, Christine. "Half of Employees Don't Feel Respected by their Bosses." *Harvard Business Review.* November 19, 2024.

Duhigg, Charles. "What Google Learned From Its Quest to Build the Perfect Team." *New York Times.* February 25, 2016.

Gallup Poll 2022. www.Gallup.com.

Sull, Donal, Charles Sull, and Ben Zweig. "Toxic Culture Is Driving the Great Resignation." *MIT Sloan Management Review.* January 11, 2022. https://sloanreview.mit.edu/article/toxic-culture-is-driving-the-great-resignation/.

Dutton, Jane E., Kristina M. Workman, and Ashley E. Hardin. "Compassion at Work." *Annual Review of Organizational Psychology and Organizational Behavior.* 1 (2014): 277-304. https://doi.org/10.1146/annurev-orgpsych-031413-091221.

Fineman, Stephen, ed. *Emotions in Organizations.* Thousand Oaks, CA: Sage Publications, June 19, 2012. https://sk.sagepub.com/books/emotion-in-organizations-2e.

Van Bommel, T. *The Power of Empathy in Times of Crisis and Beyond.* New York, NY: Catalyst, 2021.

Kabat-Zinn, Jon. https://themindfulbrain.net/jon-kabat-zinn-about-mindfulness/.

Deloitte Study 2023. https://www2.deloitte.com/us/en/insights/topics/talent/workplace-well-being-research.html.

Putnam, Robert D. *The Upswing: How America Came Together a Century Ago and How We Can Do It Again.* New York, NY: Simon & Schuster, 2021.

CHAPTER 8

Boyes, Alice. "6 Benefits of an Uncluttered Space." *Psychology Today.* February 12, 2018. https://www.psychologytoday.com/us/blog/in-practice/201802/6-benefits-uncluttered-space.

About the Authors

Gila Ancel Seritcioglu, MA, MCC and the founder of Gila Ancel Seritcioglu Coaching, brings more than thirty years of expertise in unlocking the potential of leaders worldwide. With a diverse background as a registered Expressive Arts Therapist, a Global Gestalt and Certified Somatic Coach, facilitator and trainer, she partners with top executives and teams to drive profound transformation. She orchestrates change as an advocate of awareness, empowering leaders to cultivate resilience and innovation, transforming challenges into opportunities. Gila's work is a catalyst for meaningful change in individuals, teams, and organizations. She collaborates with a broad spectrum of industries worldwide, including Fortune 500 companies, guiding visionary leaders and teams toward transformative impact and sustainable growth. She co-founded the *Gestalt Center for Coaching*, whose flagship offering is the ICF accredited *Gestalt Coaching Program*, of which she serves as co-chair and faculty. Gila is the founder of the *"Coming Back to Center"* workshop series, held in Tuscany, Italy, which aims to create awareness and a powerful leadership presence in individuals through a variety of experiential transformational practices like somatics, expressive arts, and horses, all in nature. Gila's dedication to the coaching field extends to her role as a visiting faculty member in the HEC Global Executive Coaching program in Paris since 2019. Married and the mother of two girls, she resides in Istanbul. Connect with Gila at gilaincrea@gmail.com and www.gilaseritcioglu.com.

Ann Van Eron, PhD, MCC is CEO and founder of Potentials, a global coaching and leadership development firm. With over thirty years of experience, Ann has dedicated her career to guiding leaders and teams toward creating positive environments where people engage in open-minded and productive conversations that lead to unparalleled relationships, positive results, and overall wellbeing. Potentials has been engaged in supporting organizational culture change, executive coaching, team coaching, and providing leadership mindset and skill development. Certified as a somatic Master Coach and organization development consultant, Ann works with leaders, teams, and organizations to create open-minded, collaborative, and engaged environments. Ann has a doctorate in Organizational Psychology from Columbia University. She is the author of *OASIS Conversations: Leading with an Open Mindset to Maximize Potential and Open Stance: Thriving Amid Differences and Uncertainty*. Ann focuses on creating awareness and meaningful connections, enhancing emotional and social intelligence, fostering engaging conversations, inspiring joy, supporting transformational change, and realizing potential. Signature leadership development programs include OASIS Conversations, Open Stance Leadership, Cultivating Team Culture, The Coach Approach for Leaders, Cultivating JOYBeing, and more. Ann trains facilitators to lead Open Stance Circles that create community and support people in being open-minded. She works with a diverse range of leaders and organizations, including Fortune 500 companies. Clients include CVS Health, the United Nations, The World Bank, New York-Presbyterian Hospital, and Ford Motor. Ann lives in Chicago. Connect with Ann at Avaneron@Potentials.com and www.Potentials.com.

www.ingramcontent.com/pod-product-compliance
Lightning Source LLC
Chambersburg PA
CBHW060458010526
44118CB00018B/2453